Cultura-Inspired

Intercultural Exchanges:

Focus on Asian and

Pacific Languages

 **NFLRC Monographs** is a refereed series sponsored by the National Foreign Language Resource Center at the University of Hawai'i, which presents the findings of recent work in applied linguistics that is of relevance to language teaching and learning, with a focus on the less commonly-taught languages of Asia and the Pacific.

Noticing and second language acquisition: Studies in honor of Richard Schmidt
Joara Martin Bergsleithner, Sylvia Nagem Frota, & Jim Kei Yoshioka, (Editors), 2013
ISBN 978-0-9835816-6-6

Practical assessment tools for college Japanese
Kimi Kondo-Brown, James Dean Brown, & Waka Tominaga (Editors), 2013
ISBN 978-0-9835816-5-9

New perspectives on Japanese language learning, linguistics, and culture
Kimi Kondo-Brown, Yoshiko Saito-Abbott, Shingo Satsutani, Michio Tsutsui, & Ann Wehmeyer (Editors), 2013
ISBN 978-0-9835816-3-5

Developing, using, and analyzing rubrics in language assessment with case studies in Asian and Pacific languages
James Dean Brown (Editor), 2012
ISBN 978-0-9835816-1-1

Research among learners of Chinese as a foreign language
Michael E. Everson & Helen H. Shen (Editors), 2010
ISBN 978-0-9800459-4-9

Toward useful program evaluation in college foreign language education
John M. Norris, John McE. Davis, Castle Sinicrope, & Yukiko Watanabe (Editors), 2009
ISBN 978-0-9800459-3-2

Second language teaching and learning in the Net Generation
Raquel Oxford & Jeffrey Oxford (Editors), 2009
ISBN 978-0-9800459-2-5

Case studies in foreign language placement: Practices and possibilities
Thom Hudson & Martyn Clark (Editors), 2008
ISBN 978-0-9800459-0-1

Chinese as a heritage language: Fostering rooted world citizenry
Agnes Weiyun He & Yun Xiao (Editors), 2008
ISBN 978-0-8248328-6-5

Perspectives on teaching connected speech to second language speakers
James Dean Brown & Kimi Kondo-Brown (Editors), 2006
ISBN 978-0-8248313-6-3

ordering information at nflrc.hawaii.edu

Cultura-Inspired

Intercultural Exchanges:

Focus on Asian and

Pacific Languages

edited by
Dorothy M. Chun

© 2014 Dorothy M. Chun

Some rights reserved. See: http://creativecommons.org/licenses/by/3.0/

Manufactured in the United States of America.

The contents of this publication were developed in part under a grant from the U.S. Department of Education (CFDA 84.229, P229A100001). However, the contents do not necessarily represent the policy of the Department of Education, and one should not assume endorsement by the Federal Government.

ISBN: 978-0-9835816-7-3

Library of Congress Control Number: 2014945326

book design by Deborah Masterson | cover photo ©2005 Bob Chinn

distributed by
National Foreign Language Resource Center
University of Hawai'i
1859 East-West Road #106
Honolulu HI 96822-2322
nflrc.hawaii.edu

*This book is dedicated to my parents,
Wallace and Theresa Chun,
who have taught and
inspired me in so many ways.*

About the
National Foreign Language Resource Center

The National Foreign Language Resource Center, located in the College of Languages, Linguistics, & Literature at the University of Hawai'i at Mānoa, has conducted research, developed materials, and trained language professionals since 1990 under a series of grants from the U.S. Department of Education (Language Resource Centers Program). A national advisory board sets the general direction of the resource center. With the goal of improving foreign language instruction in the United States, the center publishes research reports and teaching materials that focus primarily on the languages of Asia and the Pacific. The center also sponsors summer intensive teacher training institutes and other professional development opportunities. For additional information about center programs, contact us.

Julio C Rodriguez, Director
National Foreign Language Resource Center
University of Hawai'i at Mānoa
1859 East-West Road #106
Honolulu, HI 96822–2322

email: nflrc@hawaii.edu
website: nflrc.hawaii.edu

NFLRC Advisory Board 2010–2014

Robert Blake
University of California, Davis

Mary Hammond
East-West Center

Madeline Spring
Arizona State University

Carol Chapelle
Iowa State University

Contents

Editor's Introduction ix

Part I: **1**   *Cultura*: From Then to Now. Its Origins, Key Features,
Introduction   Methodology, and How It Has Evolved. Reflections on the
to the   Past and Musings on the Future
Cultura Model   *Gilberte Furstenberg & Sabine Levet* 1

                  2   A Meta-Synthesis of *Cultura*-Based Projects
                         Dorothy M. Chun 33

Part II: **3**   A Tale of Two Cultures
Research on   *Meei-Ling Liaw & Kathryn English* 73
Acquisition of
Intercultural   **4**   Developing Intercultural Communicative Competence
Communicative   Through Online Exchanges
Competence in   *Dorothy M. Chun* 97
Cultura-Based Models

Part III: **5**   Intercultural Learning on the Web: Reflections on Practice
Best Practices in   *Song Jiang, Haidan Wang, & Stephen Tschudi* 127
Implementing the
Cultura Model for   **6**   UH-UCLA Filipino Heritage Café and the Fil-Ams' Quest
Asian and Pacific   for Identity
Languages   *Nenita Pambid Domingo* 145

                  7   A High School Japanese and English Intercultural Exchange
                       Project: Design, Implementation, and Evaluation
                         Yukiko Watanabe, Yoichi Tsuji, & Cindy Wong 163

About the Contributors 181

Editor's Introduction

Although many online intercultural exchanges (OIE) have been conducted based on the groundbreaking *Cultura* model as described by Furstenberg, Levet, English, and Maillet (2001), most to date have been between and among European languages.[1] This volume presents a collection of chapters with a focus on exchanges involving Asian and Pacific languages, the culmination of what began as a Summer Workshop sponsored by the National Foreign Language Resource Center (NFLRC) at the University of Hawai'i at Mānoa in 2008.[2] Most of the projects that were begun at the workshop were carried out and reported on at two conferences at the University of Hawai'i in 2009: *Cultura*: Web-Based Intercultural Exchanges[3] and Language Learning in Computer Mediated Communities.[4] Many of the benefits and challenges of such exchanges are similar to those reported for European languages (Belz, 2003; Liaw & Bunn-Le Master, 2010; Müller-Hartmann, 2000; O'Dowd, 2003, 2007b; O'Dowd & Ritter, 2006; and Thorne, 2003, to name but a very few).[5] However, some of the difficulties reported in the Chinese and Japanese exchanges (Chapters 5 and 7) might be due to the significant linguistic differences between English and these two East Asian languages, suggesting that adaptations of the original model might be necessary. This volume adds to the body of emerging studies of Asian and Pacific languages (e.g., Jin & Erben, 2007; Wang, Berger, & Szilas, 2012; Wang-Szilas, Berger, & Zhang, 2013).

---

[1] http://cultura.mit.edu/archives-2/
[2] http://nflrc.hawaii.edu/onlinecafes/
[3] http://nflrc.hawaii.edu/llcmc/cultura.html
[4] http://nflrc.hawaii.edu/llcmc/index.html
[5] See also related publications at http://cultura.mit.edu/home/articles/ and sample projects listed at http://www.uni-collaboration.eu/sample_projects_all

Situating *Cultura* in the broader study of telecollaboration

Telecollaboration is an online educational activity, often used synonymously with the term online intercultural exchange (OIE). O'Dowd (2011) provides explanations of these terms:

> Traditionally, online intercultural exchange projects in foreign language education have involved the use of (text-based) online communication tools to bring together classes of language learners in different countries to learn the others' language and culture. Also referred to as telecollaboration (Belz, 2003; O'Dowd & Ritter, 2006) [and] Internet-mediated Intercultural Foreign Language Education (Belz & Thorne, 2006)…, online intercultural exchange has traditionally taken one of two forms or models during the first two decades of its existence— firstly, the e-tandem model and, secondly, what I usually refer to as the blended intercultural model. (p. 369)

This type of learning is becoming increasingly popular in foreign/second language education and is particularly widespread in higher education (see Dooly & O'Dowd, 2012; Guth & Helm, 2010; Warschauer, 1996). Almost 20 years ago, Warschauer compiled the proceedings of a Symposium on Local and Global Electronic Networking in Foreign Language Learning and Research, which was held at the University of Hawai'i, was sponsored by the NFLRC, and brought together educators concerned with these issues from university and K–12 institutions throughout the world. At that time, most of the telecollaborative projects used e-mail and other Web 1.0 capabilities, with the goal of facilitating learning environments "based on authentic communication, collaborative learning, and creative, goal-oriented activity" (p. ix). Guth and Helm (2010) edited the first volume in a series *Telecollaboration in Education*, focusing on the pedagogical processes and outcomes of engaging learners in different geographical locations in virtual collaboration together. Their volume updated the use of earlier Web 1.0 tools such as e-mail, synchronous chat, and threaded discussion, discussing the educational shift to Web 2.0 tools, such as wikis, blogs, social networking, and 3D virtual worlds. The second volume in the series, edited by Dooly and O'Dowd, synthesized the many methods and theoretical approaches that have been and are being used to investigate the different configurations of foreign language interaction and online intercultural exchange (OIE).

The 1st International Conference on Telecollaboration in University Foreign Language Education at the University of León in February, 2014, provided a broad overview of telecollaboration and how intercultural telecollaboration can contribute not only to second/foreign language learning and intercultural awareness, but also to general educational goals, internationalization of education, and electronic/digital literacies in higher education.[6] Of the 75 presentations at the conference, including three plenaries, one-third of them dealt with telecollaboration that was focused on goals and issues larger than language and culture learning, while two-thirds were concerned specifically with the teaching and learning of foreign/second language and culture.

Among the presentations that focused on or targeted language and culture learning, the enduring impact of *Cultura* was fully evident. One of the plenary speakers touted

---

[6] See the UNI-Collaboration project, sponsored by the European Commission, http://www.uni-collaboration.eu

the *Cultura* model as one of a select few that have impressive longevity and reach in terms of successful models of telecollaboration.

Strengths and limitations of *Cultura*-based exchanges

Cultura-inspired projects are often based on the premise that language and culture are inextricably connected and on a view of culture as a dynamic, ever evolving process of expressing both individual and collective identities, worldviews, ethics, morals, and values. As such, culture cannot be "taught" in the traditional sense of teachers imparting knowledge to students, but must be experienced by the learners as they co-construct cultural knowledge with others and develop what Byram (1997) termed Intercultural Communicative Competence (ICC). ICC involves five elements: attitudes (of curiosity and openness), knowledge (of social groups and their products and practices), skills of interpreting and relating, skills of discovery and interaction, and critical cultural awareness. This view is evident to varying degrees in all of the chapters of this volume and in most of the *Cultura*-based presentations at the 2014 Telecollaboration Conference.

The 2014 conference presentations not only reinforced previous studies and reports of the benefits of online intercultural exchange, but also reiterated some of the limitations of *Cultura*-based exchanges. *Cultura*-style online exchanges provide a student-centered collaborative approach to integrating online technologies into the classroom and actively engaging students in virtual intercultural communication with geographically distant peers. However, there are to be sure shortcomings of bilingual exchanges and limitations of telecollaboration between language learners. O'Dowd and Ritter (2006) reviewed the literature on telecollaborative exchanges up to that date and discovered many examples of "failed communication," when online intercultural exchanges did not result in successful communication or negotiation of meaning between the learners. They developed an inventory of factors that could lead to cases of so-called failed communication, divided into four levels: individual, classroom, socioinstitutional, and interaction. They also emphasized that points of tensions in intercultural exchanges should not categorically be avoided, but rather that such differences should be used as rich points to explain and discuss cultural contexts and practices that learners could analyze and make conscious efforts to understand. Lamy and Goodfellow (2010) summarized the various kinds of success in telecollaboration for language learning, as well as the many challenges that have been reported. They praise the field for its willingness "to review its own effectiveness regularly… and to move from the notion of 'conflict as accidental finding of research' to 'conflict as object of research'" (p. 109). Successes include personal and cultural benefits, linguistic and sociolinguistic improvements, development of communication skills, critical cultural awareness raising, and teacher professional development. On the other hand, difficulties, tensions, and failure can be ascribed to a wide variety of factors, for example, negative transfer, differences in negotiation or interactional "styles," professional misalignments, practical constraints, teacher workload, and conflicting worldviews.

O'Dowd (2011) discussed several additional criticisms of traditional approaches to telecollaboration, some of which were also found in the metasynthesis of *Cultura*-inspired projects in Chapter 2 of this volume. Firstly, there are organizational, institutional, and curricular difficulties with such exchanges, and teachers often find a lack of time to devote to such exchanges, particularly when they do not have institutional support or have different curricular goals and requirements than their partners. Secondly, short-term exchanges can actually have more negative than positive consequences on learners' intercultural awareness, as noted in a number of studies (e.g., Belz, 2003; Chun & Wade, 2004; Kramsch & Thorne, 2002; O'Dowd & Ritter, 2006; Ware & Kramsch, 2005). Thirdly, as Goodfellow and Lamy (2009) suggest, earlier proposals of a so-called "clash of genres" (Kramsch & Thorne) that result in dysfunctional intercultural exchanges may be questionable, as it is over-simplistic to compare one monolithic cultural communicative style (say, of the French) with another monolithic cultural style (say, of Americans). And finally, Hanna and de Nooy (2009) propose that class-to-class telecollaborations represent a limited level of "authenticity" in the sense that interactions are restricted to learners in classrooms and may not represent authentic communication beyond the classroom. They "found students often mired in a learner identity that is hard to shake off and that appears underpinned by certain classroom practices" (p. 187), but that participation in public Internet discussion forums offered opportunities for learners to develop an identity with a real audience.

Organization and individual chapters

The volume is divided into three parts. The first part introduces the *Cultura* model with a retrospective chapter by two of the creators of *Cultura* and a chapter presenting a meta-synthesis of *Cultura*-based projects based on an extensive survey of instructors who have implemented their own intercultural exchanges. The second part includes two research studies on the acquisition of ICC during *Cultura*-inspired exchanges: the first between classes of English as a Foreign Language in Taiwan and France, and the second between an EFL class in Germany and a German sociolinguistics class in the US. Although the latter does not involve either Asian or Pacific languages, it is included as a example of the type of research that can be conducted to assess the affordances, learning gains, and limitations of *Cultura*-type OIEs. The third part contains three chapters providing detailed descriptions of "best practices," that is, projects that were initiated at the NFLRC workshop in 2008 involving Asian (Chinese and Japanese) and Pacific (Filipino) languages, and how they were successful in realizing most of the goals that they had hoped the *Cultura* model would achieve.

In Part I, Chapter 1, Gilberte Furstenberg and Sabine Levet provide detailed insights into "*Cultura*: From Then to Now," including the key features and essential components of the model. They also reflect on possible reasons for the longevity of the model, and why it has been such a compelling and enduring prototype for OIEs. A wealth of captivating examples from the many exchanges that they have conducted over the years illustrates the discovery process that students go through in expanding and deepening their understanding of their own and the other culture. They also discuss the role of the teacher, which is primarily to provide opportunities for their students to share, reflect, discuss, and confront different points of view and to scaffold these explorations and analyses. They suggest ways in which intercultural understanding can be evaluated and how linguistic goals can be integrated into the exchanges. Finally, they discuss some of the new technologies that have been used in recent years, such as video conferencing, blogs, and wikis, emphasizing that such tools are not, per se, enough to make meaningful communication happen. The *Cultura* model is adaptable and has been adapted in a myriad ways, always keeping in mind the goals of intercultural learning and how technologies can best serve these goals.

In Chapter 2, "A Meta-Synthesis of *Cultura*-Based Projects," Dorothy Chun reports on an extensive survey of 18 instructors who have conducted *Cultura*-inspired intercultural exchanges. The purpose of the meta-synthesis is to find out about the goals of these instructors that led them to adopt the *Cultura* model, how they built toward these goals in the implementation of their projects, and whether they were able to achieve these goals. Survey respondents were asked about the learning outcomes that they desired for their students and how they were able to assess the outcomes. The chapter discusses the varied implementation processes and the common goals and challenges, ending with specific recommendations that might inform the design of future intercultural projects. Simply using the model by no means guarantees successful intercultural exchange. Meticulous planning and goal setting, mutual commitment to the project, curricular alignment, close communication, choice of appropriate tools and technologies, and flexibility in following students' suggestions and allowing their input are among the most important aspects to focus on.

Part II consists of two empirical studies of the acquisition of Intercultural Communicative Competence (ICC). Chapter 3 by Meei-Ling Liaw and Kathryn English, "A Tale of Two Cultures," uses the Lacanian concept of *extimacy* and Bakhtin's concept of *extopia* to analyze a variety of task-based written work by students in Paris and students in Taichung who were both learning English as a Foreign Language. Quantitative analyses of linguistic features reveal that French participants used lower percentages of "social process" words in their online forum postings, and the Taiwanese students used these types of words significantly more. This means that the Taiwanese wrote more about their family, friends, and other people than their French counterparts, suggesting a higher degree of interpersonal connectedness. Qualitative analyses within the framework of Lacan's *extimacy* explored students' perceptions of "self" and "other," in contrast to Bakhtin's *exotopia,* which involves more collective, culture-bound perceptions. As the online interactions intensified during the exchange, the participants developed interpersonal relationships with each other, and the levels of *extimacy* and *exotopia* deepened for both groups of students. Two of the Taiwanese students were able to extend their intercultural communication from the "lab" setting to the "real world" and actually visited Paris, experiencing firsthand what it means to be an "intercultural speaker" (Byram & Fleming, 1998).

In Chapter 4 by Dorothy Chun, "Developing Intercultural Communicative Competence Through Online Exchanges[7]," Byram's (1997) concept of ICC and Kramsch's models of discourse analysis (Kramsch & Thorne, 2002; Ware & Kramsch, 2005) form the basis of the analysis of data obtained from an intercultural exchange between university students learning German in the US and students studying English at a German university. The data reveal how culture is embedded in language and how the learners employed different discourse styles in their online postings, demonstrating their pragmatic ability to perform various types of speech acts, such as expressing curiosity or interest, negotiating meaning, seeking to understand the other, hedging, and reflecting on their own and the other culture.

---

[7] This article was originally published in the *CALICO Journal* 28(2), pp.392–419 and is reprinted here with permission of the journal's editors.

The students in the two groups interacted according to their own pragmatic norms, with the Americans asking more questions than the students in Germany, but not always possessing the pragmatic ability to realize that it is not only through questions that one can signal interest or curiosity. Both sides did demonstrate ICC in their synchronous chat session, employing an appropriate combination of knowledge, skills, and attitudes to interact with their interlocutors from a different culture. This type of analysis can serve as a model for future research on OIEs with Asian and Pacific languages.

Part III contains three chapters focusing on Asian and Pacific languages. Chapter 5, "Intercultural Learning on the Web: Reflections on Practice" by Song Jiang, Haidan Wang, and Stephen Tschudi, describes a project designed to teach culture to Chinese and American business students through a series of online interactive tasks based on the *Cultura* model. The web-based interactions helped to minimize cultural barriers and bridge the cultural gap, deepening mutual understanding between the two groups and also enhancing their interpretative and expressive abilities. The participants of both groups compared and discussed paired authentic cultural artifacts, worked through any points of differences in their understanding, and thus gained insights into cultural differences. For example, in comparing the results of their word associations, they came to realize that the "same" word in different cultures may represent a completely different concept with accompanying cultural implications. The students' observations and reflections indicated that they were able not only to notice key differences but also to hypothesize about these differences and thus reflect deeply on underlying cultural values. One difficulty encountered was that postings made in L1 by both sides contained authentic language about relatively complex ideas and consequently demanded a high level of L2 reading proficiency. Insufficient target language reading proficiency thus had a somewhat negative impact on the exchange.

In Chapter 6, Nenita Pambid Domingo discusses the "UH-UCLA Filipino Heritage Café and the Fil-Ams' Quest for Identity." Three exchanges among Filipino language classes in the US were conducted in 2008, 2009, and 2010, but the chapter focuses on the first exchange between the University of Hawai'i and the University of California, Los Angeles. Unlike most *Cultura* exchanges between students in different countries, the Filipino Heritage Café was adapted to two campuses that have large enrollments of Filipino Americans. Most were heritage learners who grew up in Filipino households and practiced Filipino customs and traditions. They had a range of proficiency in the language, from none to the ability to speak but with no formal training in the grammar, reading, or writing. The goals of the exchange were to improve linguistic and cultural competence, provide a virtual community of learners to examine Filipino identity, and allow the students to compare their experiences with Filipino culture with others in a different geographical location. Students felt that the exchange allowed them to dive deeper into the roots of the language as well as the culture that they are all a part of, in addition to improving their writing and grammar. Similarly, instructors noted increased participation from students in terms of quantity and quality in language production and writing. In addition, the built-in analytical tasks allowed students to compare and contrast the varying points of view expressed, forcing them to think critically and to see the world from the eyes of another, conceivably promoting mutual understanding.

The final chapter, Chapter 7 by Yukiko Watanabe, Yoichi Tsuji, and Cindy Wong, describes "A High School Japanese and English Intercultural Exchange Project: Design, Implementation, and Evaluation." Most *Cultura*-inspired projects have been conducted at the university level, so this exchange provides insights into how the *Cultura* model might be adapted for the high school level. The goals of the project were to provide opportunities for students to learn authentic language use from their peer counterparts and to learn about the diverse cultural perspectives of the value systems that underlie customs, opinions, and behaviors. Byram's (2008) Principles for Intercultural Citizenship Education were closely aligned with the *Cultura*-based tasks that the students undertook. Although there were a number of unanticipated challenges, the students enjoyed the online exchange: They were excited by seeing each other's developing second language, and their interest in learning the other's language was piqued. A striking result was that, compared to the text-based tasks, the audio-visual materials seemed to appeal more to the high school students, and they were able to identify behavioral characteristics of the other students, while also taking steps toward reflecting on their own behaviors.

Commonalities among the projects

Although the projects were by no means uniformly designed or implemented, they shared commonalities in many different ways. As might be expected, the projects differed in their initial goals, with some placing a greater emphasis on linguistic improvement and others on intercultural communicative competence (ICC). The proficiency levels of the students also varied, as did the specific *Cultura*-based tasks that students performed. Some projects allowed greater use of L1 than others, depending on the L2 proficiency of the participants. Some projects used both asynchronous and synchronous forms of computer-mediated communication, while others used primarily asynchronous postings to word association questionnaires and online discussion forums.

Despite these many differences, all of the projects report gains in both linguistic and cultural competence and awareness. Across all of the projects, the chapter authors recount that careful planning of program objectives and tasks plays a significant role in the success of the exchanges, both to ensure the active and enthusiastic participation of the students and to give the learners themselves the responsibility of being experts in their culture. This in turn assures that participants on both sides are given a kaleidoscopic and multi-layered view of the target culture. In addition, the role of the teacher changes. Although direct participation of the teachers may be reduced, they must be vigilant "behind the scenes" in planning tasks and following up in the classroom. One of the commonly stated pedagogical requirements is that instructors must create clear guidelines for the students in terms of what is required or expected in the students' postings. Many instructors express the advisability of seeking and heeding student input, so as to ensure the relevance of the exchange. Constant communication between project instructors is imperative, as is the need for adequate technical support. Both teachers and students must be given the technical training needed to navigate the websites and to appropriately use the technologies employed for the online tasks (see O'Dowd, 2007a, 2013).

The affordances of the Internet allow native speakers to play the role of expert cultural informant and participants often succeed not only in learning about the target culture, but in seeing their own culture through the eyes of others. Learners on both sides are exposed to authentic materials and language that have been created by their counterparts, making it more relevant than anonymously created cultural artifacts.

Common challenges reported by all of the projects involved organizational and infrastructure challenges (e.g., coordinating academic calendars, different time zones, technology policies, and technological difficulties). Differences in how the exchange was integrated into the respective curricula or syllabi affected the motivation of the participants. Except for the *Cultura* exchanges at MIT, all of the other projects incorporated *Cultura*-based activities into their normal curriculum, and many instructors found that there was insufficient time allotted to the *Cultura* activities to achieve all of the intended goals, particularly in-class time for follow-up of the online postings and discussion that were often done outside of class.

Specific findings for Asian and Pacific languages

The three chapters discussing exchanges with Asian and Pacific languages had unique circumstances that set them apart from the majority of previous *Cultura*-inspired projects. The Chinese-English exchange involved business students, unlike the great majority of exchanges that are between language (or culture) classes. The Japanese-English exchange took place between two high schools, whereas most exchanges that are reported in the literature deal with university level participants. And the Filipino exchange between classes at the University of Hawai'i and UCLA involved heritage learners in the United States and not native Filipino speakers.

Common to the Chinese and Japanese exchanges was the challenge of mixed levels of linguistic proficiency both within the individual classes and between the U.S. classes and their overseas counterparts. Since Chinese and Japanese are much more difficult linguistically for English native speakers than many Western European languages, reaching higher levels of proficiency requires much more time. In the cases of the two exchanges reported in this volume, the students in the US had much lower linguistic proficiency in Chinese and Japanese, than their respective partner classes' proficiency in English. This led the Chinese instructors at UH to suggest that exclusive use of L1 (which is a hallmark of the "traditional" *Cultura*) may not always be optimal. They found that their U.S. students learning Chinese were not able to take part in Chinese language-related activities with a uniform level of competence (e.g., some were not able to have in-depth discussions with their peers). Similarly, the Japanese instructors found that their beginning and low-intermediate language learners had great difficulties understanding academic prose and were not able to speak or write in L2 about cultural comparisons. One positive note, however, was that the high school students studying Japanese were able to watch video clips posted by the instructor in Japan and were able to identify cultural similarities and differences much more easily than in text-based online forum posts. This suggests that learners with lower linguistic proficiency, particularly in more difficult languages like Chinese and Japanese, might still benefit from online exchanges that use multimedia materials (in addition to text-based materials). Although the mixed levels of language proficiency was also mentioned by many survey respondents in the meta-synthesis chapter, the problem seems to be especially acute for more "difficult" languages like Chinese and Japanese, where a greater degree of language scaffolding and support is warranted.

Despite the additional challenges for the exchanges involving Asian languages, the overall consensus of the chapters in this volume is that designing appropriate tasks and materials for targeted sets of learners, as well as garnering the same level of commitment from partner classes, help ensure the success of *Cultura*-inspired intercultural exchanges. Ample time must be built into the syllabi and curricula for learners to explore and discover the nuances and intricacies of their own and other cultures, resulting in rewarding and memorable experiences, whether they be virtual or face-to-face.

Acknowledgments

I would first like to thank all of the chapter authors of this volume for their fine contributions. Special thanks go to an anonymous reviewer for very helpful and insightful suggestions. My colleagues and friends at NFLRC also contributed greatly to the entire endeavor, starting with the Summer Institute in 2008 up to the present: Dick Schmidt, David Hiple, Stephen Tschudi, Jim Yoshioka, Deborah Masterson, and Julio Rodriquez. Finally, I am especially grateful to my wonderful husband and sons for their abiding love and support, and to my parents, to whom this book is dedicated, for their unconditional love and inspiration.

References

Belz, J. A. (2003). Linguistic perspectives on the development of intercultural competence in telecollaboration. *Language Learning & Technology, 7*(2), 68–117.

Belz, J. A., & Thorne, S. L. (2006). Introduction: Internet-mediated intercultural foreign language education and the intercultural speaker. In J. A. Belz & S. L. Thorne (Eds.), *Internet-mediated intercultural foreign language education* (pp. iix-xxv). Annual Volume of the American Association of University Supervisors and Coordinators. Boston, MA: Heinle & Heinle.

Byram, M. (1997). *Teaching and assessing intercultural communicative competence.* Clevedon, England: Multilingual Matters.

Byram, M. (2008). *From foreign language education to education for intercultural citizenship: Essays and reflection.* Clevedon, UK: Multilingual Matters.

Byram, M., & Fleming, M. (Eds.). (1998). *Language learning in intercultural perspective.* Cambridge, England: Cambridge University Press.

Chun, D. M., & Wade, E. R. (2004). Collaborative cultural exchanges with CMC. In L. Lomicka & J. Cooke-Plagwitz (Eds.), *Teaching with technology* (pp. 220–247). Boston, MA: Heinle & Heinle.

Dooly, M., & O'Dowd, R., (Eds.) (2012). *Researching online foreign language interaction and exchange.* Bern: Peter Lang.

Furstenberg, G., Levet, S., English, K. & Maillet, K. (2001). Giving a virtual voice to the silent language of culture: The Cultura Project. *Language Learning & Technology, 5*(1), 55–102.

Goodfellow, R., & Lamy, M. N. (2009). Introduction: A frame for the discussion of learning cultures. In R. Goodfellow & M. N. Lamy (Eds.), *Learning cultures in online education* (pp. 1–14). London, England: Continuum.

Guth, S. and Helm, F. (Eds.) (2010). *Telecollaboration 2.0: Language, literacy and intercultural learning in the 21st century.* Bern: Peter Lang.

Hanna, B., & de Nooy, J. (2009). *Learning language and culture via public Internet discussion forums.* New York, NY: Palgrave Macmillan.

Jin, L., & Erben, T. (2007). Intercultural learning via instant messenger interaction. *CALICO Journal, 24*(2), 291–311.

Kramsch, C., & Thorne, S. (2002). Foreign language learning as global communicative practice. In D. Block & D. Cameron (Eds.), *Language learning and teaching in the age of globalization* (pp. 83–100). London, England: Routledge.

Lamy, M. N., & Goodfellow, R. (2010). Telecollaboration and Learning 2.0. In S. Guth & F. Helm (Eds.), *Telecollaboration 2.0* (pp. 107–138). Bern, Switzerland: Peter Lang.

Liaw, M., & Bunn-Le Master, S. (2010). Understanding telecollaboration through an analysis of intercultural discourse. *Computer Assisted Language Learning, 23*(1), 21–40.

Müller-Hartmann, A. (2000). The role of tasks in promoting intercultural learning in electronic learning networks. *Language Learning & Technology, 4*(2), 129–147.

O'Dowd, R. (2003). Understanding the "other side": Intercultural learning in a Spanish-English e-mail exchange. *Language Learning & Technology, 7*(2), 118–144.

O'Dowd, R. (2007a). Evaluating the outcomes of online intercultural exchange. *ELT Journal, 61*(2), 144–152.

O'Dowd, R. (Ed.). (2007b). *Online intercultural exchange: An introduction for foreign language teachers.* Clevedon, England: Multilingual Matters.

O'Dowd, R. (2011). Online foreign language interaction: Moving from the periphery to the core of foreign language education? *Language Teaching, 44*(3), 368–380.

O'Dowd, R. (2013). The competences of the telecollaborative teacher. *The Language Learning Journal,* 1–14. doi: 10.1080/09571736.2013.853374

O'Dowd, R., & Ritter, M. (2006). Understanding and working with "failed communication" in telecollaborative exchanges. *CALICO Journal, 23*(3), 623–642.

Thorne, S. L. (2003). Artifacts and cultures-of-use in intercultural communication. *Language Learning & Technology, 7*(2), 38–67.

Wang, J., Berger, C., & Szilas, N. (2012). Pedagogical design of an eTandem Chinese-French writing course. *Journal of Universal Computer Science, 18*(3), 393–409.

Wang-Szilas, J., Berger, C., & Zhang, L. (2013). eTandem language learning integrated in the curriculum: Reflection from students' perspectives. *Proceedings of the European Distance and E-Learning Network Annual Conference,* 12–15 June, 2013 (pp. 93–102).

Ware, P., & Kramsch, C. (2005). Toward an intercultural stance: Teaching German and English through telecollaboration. *Modern Language Journal, 89*(2), 190–205.

Warschauer, M. (Ed.) (1996). *Telecollaboration in foreign language learning.* Honolulu: Second Language Teaching & Curriculum Center, University of Hawai'i.

Part I:
Introduction to the *Cultura* Model

Cultura: From Then to Now. Its Origins, Key Features, Methodology, and How It Has Evolved. Reflections on the Past and Musings on the Future

Gilberte Furstenberg
Sabine Levet
Massachusetts Institute of Technology

This chapter first revisits the origins of Cultura, *a web-based pedagogical model designed to bring intercultural learning and discovery to the forefront of the language class. The basic components of the model and rationale for its development and evolution are presented in detail, along with extensive examples from actual online exchanges. The second part of the chapter discusses ways in which the teacher needs to scaffold the process of intercultural learning, and focuses on the importance of guidelines and tasks (both in the classroom and online) for ensuring the co-construction of knowledge, the integration of online and classroom activities, the assessment of students' learning, and the place of language study. The final section reflects on the ways in which* Cultura *has evolved and looks ahead to future directions and possibilities.*

Introduction

As the ensuing chapters in this book will show, *Cultura* (http://Cultura.mit.edu) is increasingly used as a web-based model for developing students' intercultural understanding, particularly within the context of foreign language classes.[1] Considering that it is also one of the earliest telecollaborative projects of its kind, this seems an opportune time not only to look back at the initial project and at what

---

[1] Levy (2007) aptly describes the features that help make *Cultura* a model.

Furstenberg, G., & . Levet, S. (2014). *Cultura:* From then to now. Its origins, key features, methodology, and how it has evolved. Reflections on the past and musings on the future. In D. M. Chun, (Ed.), Cultura-*inspired intercultural exchanges: Focus on Asian and Pacific languages* (pp. 1–31). Honolulu: University of Hawai'i, National Foreign Language Resource Center.

we[2] consider to be its essential features and components but also to reflect on the reasons why, we believe, this pioneering project has endured for so long.

In the first part, we explain the origins of *Cultura* and highlight its basic make-up (context, approach, goals, and content), emphasizing along the way the rationale for the decisions we made and thereby providing the reader with an insider's view. We then focus on the process that enables students to gradually expand, deepen, and refine their understanding of the foreign culture, providing many specific examples throughout, and highlighting the core features of the *Cultura* methodology—mainly its dynamic and constructivist approach—whose clear consonance with the goals of the project accounts, in our opinion, for its enduring appeal.

In the second part, we shift our focus to the teacher and the key role he/she plays in that endeavor, by concentrating on the design of appropriate pedagogical online tasks and classroom activities and the necessary seamless interplay between them. We also touch on assessment issues and the place of language study. The pedagogically sound base of *Cultura*, and its numerous tested practices (which we have refined along the way) are components that also greatly contribute, we believe, to the continued success and longevity of the project.

In the third part and last part, we look at how *Cultura* has evolved over the years and we share the most important lessons we have learned as well as the directions in which we see the project heading.

Our hope is that readers will be able to clearly see how the original *Cultura* functions, and thus better appreciate the many variations brought by the projects described in the ensuing chapters. The broad end goals are (a) to bring to light some of the fundamental choices to be made and issues to be considered when developing a telecollaborative intercultural project, and more broadly (b) to redefine what it means to "teach" culture in the digital age.

Original *Cultura* model

Cultura—created in 1997 by three French instructors in the Foreign Languages and Literatures Section at MIT, thanks to an initial grant from the Consortium for Language Teaching and Learning,[3] and a subsequent 3-year grant from the National Endowment for the Humanities—is an educational initiative born out of the desire to focus students in language classes on understanding a foreign culture. At that time, in most intermediate language classes, language development was the main focus of study, while culture tended to stay at the periphery. *Cultura* represents a deliberate attempt at reversing that traditional equation between language and culture. This aspiration was very much in accord with the overall necessity, starting to emerge at the time in many institutions of higher learning across the US and in Europe, to make culture and, in particular, intercultural communication an educational priority.[4]

---

[2] The authors of this chapter, Gilberte Furstenberg and Sabine Levet, are also the creators of *Cultura*, along with Shoggy Waryn, a Senior Lecturer who taught French at Brown University.

[3] The consortium was located at Yale University then and directed by Peter Patrikis.

[4] This goal has long been espoused by the Council of Europe's Common European Framework of Reference for Languages (http://www.coe.int/t/dg4/linguistic/Source/Framework_en.pdf). It has since been put forward as a national priority for Foreign Languages in Higher Education as seen in the MLA report (2007). See: http://www.mla.org/flreport/

The Internet and its communication tools provided a new impetus at the time, making it possible to connect classes and foster students' interaction across cultures,[5] thus greatly facilitating such an endeavor.

Origins of *Cultura*

Cultura is first and foremost a pedagogical project. It was not created out of specific theories on intercultural learning, although some very important ones were already emerging at the time, but was very much facilitated by the promises new communication technologies were opening up. Indeed, when *Cultura* first came into existence in 1997, we were aware of only one telecollaborative project,[6] and very little theory and research on telecollaboration and intercultural learning in the language class had yet been published. *Cultura* was started the very year Byram's (1997) seminal book was published, and most research papers in the field (with a few notable exceptions, such as Beauvois [1993], Godwin-Jones [1996], and Warschauer [1996]) were published after 2000. But what is clear is that *Cultura* dovetails very well with the research that has since been published and that highlights some key pedagogical principles, such as, the task-based approach, including the choice of tasks as well as its sequencing; the importance of scaffolding; the notion of process, and the creation of a dynamic and constructivist learning environment–core elements that are all present in *Cultura*. This led Levy (2007) to write,

> *Cultura* is exceptional for the ways in which its structure, content, tasks, strategies and techniques are designed...The authors of this framework have been able to transform an understanding of a facet of the culture concept, culture as contested, into an imaginative and workable pedagogy which fully utilises the options available with new technologies. (p. 119)

The idea behind the project started germinating after Gilberte Furstenberg had taught a successful French course based on the comparison of French movies and their American remakes. That course was particularly effective in sensitizing students to the cultural differences underlying the content and treatment of those films. After first identifying the differences, students were naturally led to speculate about the reasons behind the changes that had been made when moving from the original French version to its American remake: What did those changes say and illustrate about both cultures?

With the advent of online communication tools, it quickly became clear that this course would be greatly enriched if the two films were compared not just by our students within the confines of their French classroom at MIT, but also by students in France, with both sets of students exchanging their cultural perspectives on those films. This seemed a very promising avenue for bringing to light key aspects of the underlying cultures and a very auspicious approach for us, language teachers, for

---

[5] We partnered with different schools in France, ranging from Universities to Grandes Ecoles, such as Ecole Polytechnique.

[6] One of the earliest and most successful French telecollaborative courses on intercultural communication between American and French students had just been developed by Céleste Kinginger. See Kinginger and Gourves-Hayward (1997).

developing intercultural sensitivity while giving reality to what has always been our ultimate end goal: teaching both language and culture.[7]

This initial idea formed the basis for our proposal to the National Endowment for the Humanities. It suggested that students would start their intercultural exploration by comparing French films and their American remakes, and would then investigate a variety of other materials to see whether their initial findings about both cultures could be validated, altered, or refined. However, we quickly realized that starting with film comparisons was not necessarily an ideal way of embarking on an intercultural journey because the subject matter is far removed from the students' personal experiences. It seemed more logical to have students on both sides first answer a series of questionnaires that would engage them personally with the subject matter.

We had already started experimenting with such questionnaires earlier, thanks to the help of a high school colleague teaching French in Lenox, Massachusetts, who had agreed to test them with her partner school in France.[8] The questionnaires subsequently became one of our best-known features (we will detail the reasons why later in this chapter), even though they constitute only a starting point and are by no means the only material provided by *Cultura*.

Goals

The specific goal of *Cultura* is to bring students to understand the attitudes, values, and ways of thinking and interacting of those who live in the other culture–in other words, to help them access the "hidden dimension," the "silent language"[9] of culture. The approach we thought most germane is a *comparative* one that allows students to compare a variety of what Belz (2003) calls "parallel texts"[10]–similar types of documents/texts drawn (in our case) from French and American cultures. The juxtaposition process seemed most apt to allow similarities and differences to clearly emerge and thus become visible, an approach that had already borne fruit when we had compared French films and their American remakes.

To that end, we created a website accessible to both sets of students on which is juxtaposed a large variety of textual and visual materials derived from their respective cultures. They have been organized in a series of modules that can be explored in any order, but with the questionnaires always coming first.[11]

---

[7] Although we were not aware of it at the time, we were not the first ones to create a course based on French films and their remakes and to have French and American students discuss them via the Internet. Indeed, Céleste Kinginger had made the comparison of those very films the focus of her intercultural communication project.

[8] The experiment was conducted by Nicole Desrosiers, a French teacher at Lenox High School, and her French partner, an English teacher at the Lycée Marcelin Berthelot in Pantin.

[9] *The Hidden Dimension* (1966) and *The Silent Language* (1959) are two book titles by the famous American anthropologist Edward T. Hall.

[10] Belz (2003) wrote, "Parallel texts explore a phenomenon (e.g., racism or beauty) from different socio-cultural perspectives in different languages. The pedagogical rationale for their use is to provide opportunities for the exposure, juxtaposition, and exploration of cultural fault lines (Kramsch, 1993) with a view to the development of IC" (p. 75).

[11] See demo site at http://web.mit.edu/Cultura

Basic setup and level/partnership guidelines

The basic set-up is as follows: Two groups of students from two schools with similar background and interests,[12] sharing a common calendar and website, compare together the same sets of materials and discuss them online, under the guidance of their respective teachers.

From its beginning, *Cultura* has been designed to work within a blended environment and presupposes a mix of in-class and online interactions. Students on both sides of the Atlantic work in a series of stages. They first analyze and compare the materials individually at home and then collectively in class. They then discuss their findings on asynchronous online forums with their transatlantic peers. In the next stage, they share their new discoveries with their classmates and reflect upon them anew, in a continuous back and forth movement between class and online work.

Most of our partnerships through the years have been with students taking an English class at a French University or Grande Ecole. Experience has taught us that the more closely the interests and objectives of the two classes align and intersect, the more successful the exchange is likely to be. Interestingly enough, in our case, the students' respective levels of proficiency in L2 need not be similar. In fact, they have always been very different, with the French students always more proficient in English than the American students in French.[13] But the fact that both groups of students do not have the same level in L2 does not matter since everyone writes in L1 (see the rationale for this below). It is the students' reading proficiency level in L2 that will determine their ability to participate fruitfully in the exchange. Obviously, the students' reading proficiency in L2 is very different from language to language. For instance, whereas *Cultura* can be used in a third semester French class (this is the level at which we have always used the project), this will not necessarily be the case for a third semester Russian or Chinese class because of the intrinsic difficulty of those languages. All this means is that a *Cultura*-like project simply needs to take place in a more advanced Russian or Chinese class.

Materials

The materials presented on the *Cultura* website form the basis of the students' discussions. They are all selected by agreement of both teachers, with the exception of the Images module (see below).

None of our students (at MIT and in the French schools) being majors in either French or English, we opted for a broad spectrum of materials dealing with basic cultural concepts and notions. The first set of materials comprises a set of three online questionnaires. First is a word association questionnaire, where students spontaneously write associations with with words such as *individualism, success, freedom,* and *family.* The MIT students receive the list in English and answer in

---

[12] Primarily in terms of age, and secondarily in terms of the students' main fields of study. The exchange works better between two universities or two high schools for instance, so that the ages, the learning contexts, and interests overlap.

[13] Another inherent discrepancy is that French students usually know a lot more about American culture than our students know about French culture. This often gets offset, however, by the fact that students discuss a variety of topics they may never have encountered before.

English; the French students have the same list in French and answer in French. In the second questionnaire, students complete sentences such as "A good student is someone who...," "A good neighbor is someone who...," "A good boss...," "A well-behaved child...," and so forth. In the third, students are asked to react to hypothetical situations such as "You see a mother in a supermarket slap her child," "You see a student next to you cheating at an exam," "or You've been waiting in line for 10 minutes and someone cuts right in front of you."

Each item on the questionnaires has been carefully designed, both by the MIT and partner teacher, to access many different areas of life (e.g., family, work, public, private), different kinds of relationships (e.g., with family members, strangers, neighbors, colleagues), and different locations (e.g., in public, at home, in a professional environment). We purposely created questionnaires that would allow students to make observations across these different spheres, asking them for instance, to react to "a good neighbor" and also to "you meet your neighbor on the street and he/she does not say hello," so as to explore associations and reactions made both in the abstract and within specific contexts.

As will be seen in the following chapters, the questionnaires are part of every single *Cultura*-inspired intercultural project, and they seem to have become our staple. We believe the reasons they have been so successful are that (a) they engage the students personally from the very start (since they are asked to draw upon their own personal views and experiences); (b) they focus on commonplace words, daily encounters, and situations, making culture come alive in a very concrete way; (c) they instantly provide access to many of the underlying cultural core values and attitudes, making the cultural pay-off immediate; and (d) they are very easily replicated and/or changed by teachers according to the issues/topics they deem most relevant to the language or culture at hand.

Other materials

It is essential, however, that other kinds of materials be provided for the students to analyze–materials presented in other modules down the road–that will bring new angles of observation via different modes, such as photos, films, videos, and a variety of other types of texts. This allows students to put into a broader perspective their initial findings from the comparative analysis of the questionnaires, thus enabling them to develop an increasingly richer and more complex view.

Many different types of materials can be offered. The original *Cultura* allows students to access other materials[14] such as national French and American statistics and opinion polls on a variety of topics; films (in our case, French films and their American remakes); online media (e.g., for comparing the front pages of the *New York Times* and *Le Monde*); literary and historical texts (such as *The Bill of Rights* and *La Déclaration des Droits de l'Homme*); and finally images, a module that is different from all the others as it is the students themselves who upload photos and/or videos, based on topics they (and their French partners) have chosen to illustrate, whether it is their daily life (e.g., where we live, what we eat and where) or product advertising (e.g., about cars/beer/perfume), about which they then again exchange viewpoints.

---

[14] See http://web.mit.edu/Cultura

Key feature: Asynchronous online forums

We have somewhat diversified the modes of communication between students since the beginning of the project (see the final part of this chapter, "How *Cultura* has evolved over the years"), but the asynchronous online forums are still our main mode of communication as they seem the most appropriate and effective at allowing students to take a more deliberate and reflective stance on the issues and topics being debated. We feel that such forums are more apt than any other mode of communication at generating in-depth discussions, at giving students more time to think about the issues and/or problems before responding to them, and at allowing insights to gradually emerge. They also have two other intrinsic advantages: (a) Everyone can read what is written, which means that all the ideas and perspectives expressed can be shared; and (b) they can easily be archived and then analyzed by students and researchers alike any time, anywhere.

These online forums are at the heart of the process.[15] This is where the intercultural communication and reflection take place. This is where students share their discoveries and observations on the documents they have compared and ask questions. We very much insist on the latter feature, as questions and responses are, in our minds, essential in sustaining a conversation and keeping the ball rolling, so to speak, thus preventing the discussion forums from being a simple string of monologues between students. In these forums, students are also asked to make hypotheses, raise issues, answer their partners' questions in a constant and reciprocal process of inquiry, the ultimate goal being for students to try and understand the others' perspectives and to explain/reveal their own culture. We make these guidelines clear to the students from the outset and keep repeating them throughout the semester, so that students understand that they are to engage in a genuine dialogue.

The characteristics of the on-line forums are the following: They are multiple and concurrent (there is a forum attached to every word, phrase, and document), and individual students choose which items they want to participate in for each questionnaire; they are collective and are led entirely by students (they are in charge of the conversations, take them wherever they want, and the teacher never interferes); and they are written in L1.[16]

That last feature, the use of L1, is the least understood and most widely ignored feature of *Cultura*. It therefore warrants detailed explanation. As counter-intuitive as it may seem, the use of L1 in the online forums presents many advantages worth considering:

- It avoids any linguistic dominance by any group (the groups can be of very different levels) or any person within a group (everyone is on exactly the same footing since students use L1).
- Since students are not limited by their linguistic abilities, they can express their thoughts fully and are in a position to tackle complex subjects.
- In return for writing in their own language (in our case English), students read completely authentic French/Spanish/German/Japanese/Filipino and

---

[15] See http://web.mit.edu/Cultura

[16] The foreign students in both classes do not use their native language on the forums, of course, but the language of the country in which they are studying.

so forth and can thus also use and re-use the words of the native students (as they share with their classmates what they have discovered from reading their posts).[17] This often results in great improvement in their own reading skills, as they are very motivated to understand what their overseas partners are writing.

- The differences in written discourse can become a new cultural object that can in turn be analyzed, as the different writing styles reveal much about the underlying cultures.

The use of L1 online also seemed to us the best and only way to reach our initial stated goal, which is to enable our students to access the deep, complex layers of culture and thus avoid superficial questions and comments, something that would inevitably happen (at a third semester level) if our students were to write in the target language. Our choice of language was also clearly dictated by our goal. Congruence, again, was key.

It is important to emphasize that students use L1 online only. At MIT, students speak nothing but French in the classroom and express themselves exclusively in French in their papers and homework, just like in any other French class, with a big difference, however: Their language skills are enhanced and enriched by the completely authentic language used by their French peers, which our own students in turn incorporate in their discussions and writings.

These forums are key to the process of developing intercultural understanding, as they allow for in-depth discussions, constant queries, revisions, and clarifications that will gradually bring students to obtain a more refined and complex view of the other culture(s), compel them to move away from clichés, and prevent them from developing new ones and essentializing each others' cultures. The example below, taken from the Fall 2011 exchange between MIT students and students at the Université de Brest, is an example.

These excerpts—from a forum[18] where students examine their respective responses to the word *individualism/individualisme*[19]— offer a microcosm of how students help each other build an understanding of the other culture(s) as well as their own. As illustrated in this example from the Fall 2011, students simultaneously

- share their discoveries and observations, following them up with questions,

    I was surprised to see that you had such differing ideas from us about individualism. In general, we thought individualism was important and good, while you said it was selfish and not productive. Why do you think individualism is not productive? (D., MIT student)

- explain to their counterparts what individualism means to them personally (while revealing information about themselves and their background),

    America was the place that changed my concepts about individualism because it is not always that individualism is directly correlated to

---

[17] If their counterparts wrote in the target language, English in our case, our students would have to translate their partner's postings in order to share them with their classmates in French, which is not an optimal scenario in an intermediate foreign language classroom.

[18] See the entire forum at http://Cultura.mit.edu/2011-fall-mituniversite-de-brest-43/

[19] See the responses to the word associations *individualism/individualism*, at http://Cultura.mit.edu/2011-fall-mituniversite-de-brest-11/

> 'negative things'. It is more like respecting other people's privacy. (D., an MIT student)

- make hypotheses about their own culture as well as the other culture,

> I was surprised that the American responses were so varied but generally positive, and I think that comes from the nature of the US federalist system. There are 50 different states each with their own state flag, bird, flower, laws, etc. and when you add in the geographic diversity of the US it seems like a big push against individualism would surely fail," adding "I think that in a smaller, socialist country less individualism and more of a group mindset is essential. (K. an MIT student)

- occasionally address their questions to their classmates as well,

> K, you pointed out that France is a socialist country. What makes you say that? (I., MIT student)

- respond to their partners' queries, and

> C., a French student, explains why individualism is viewed as negative by the French *car cela empêche les gens de s'ouvrir aux autres,* adding,
>
> > il y a [eu] un sondage à la TV française, l'autre jour, qui disait que la cause principale du sentiment d'exclusion était dû à l'individualisme. (It prevents people from opening up to each other [...]. There was an opinion poll on TV the other day that said the main cause for the sense of exclusion felt by people was due to individualism.)

- engage in a real dialogue, thanks to students constantly asking questions, whether it is for clarification or wanting to know more. M. for example, writes,

> I don't understand the phrase *[cela empêche] les gens de s'ouvrir aux autres.* Can you explain what you mean?

Sometimes, the conversations can become a bit "hot," with the French sometimes reacting in very forceful ways. Thus C., responding directly to K's earlier comments about socialist countries, writes—in capital letters and with many exclamation points,

> La FRANCE N'EST PAS UN PAYS SOCIALISTE, loin de là!!!! En ce moment, le gouvernement est tout sauf socialiste!
> (FRANCE IS NOT A SOCIALIST COUNTRY, far from it!!! Right now the government is anything but socialist!)[20]

To which K. responds,

> Please don't shout, it's not necessary. I am certain that you know much more about French government than I do, but these comments reflect my current understanding of the situation.

Interestingly enough, students will sometimes come to each other's rescue. Thus, M. tries to explain K.'s view of "socialism,"

---

[20] This message was written in the Fall of 2011 when the French Government was led by the UMP, a political party from the French right. The political situation has since changed in France since as of May 13, 2012, France has had a Socialist President.

> I think that a lot of Americans see France as leaning more toward socialism *in comparison to* [her emphasis] America. I'm not saying it's good or bad, but I think we use our country's political views as sort of a political ruler, if you will.

In such forums, students often try to reconcile different viewpoints. This is particularly true of foreign students. This is the case of I., a Bulgarian student at MIT, who writes,

> By and large, [the word] *individualism*... shows a stark contrast between the two perspectives: the American's *benign self-expression* versus the French's *mauvais égocentrisme*, (bad self-centeredness). I am neither American nor French (in fact Bulgarian), but I partly subscribe to both views: individualism as necessary for preserving self-independence but also as possibly detrimental to being a worthy member of society.

Foreign students do play a very interesting and unique role in that regard. As both outsiders and insiders, they often spontaneously play the role of cultural mediators, addressing themselves both to the Americans and the French, explaining what their classmates may mean. They also provide other voices, who offer yet different perspectives which they share (they always identify themselves), greatly enriching the intercultural tapestry.

Students will also often try to spontaneously offer reasons and explanations (often based on the differences in both histories) for the different points of view, as seen in M.'s posting:

> Les Français ont tendance à voir l'individualisme comme un défaut, quelque chose de mal, car nous avons un système de sécurité sociale qui fait que nous valorisons plus la solidarité (en théorie). Aux Etats-Unis, la protection sociale est moins courante (assurance maladie pas obligatoire par exemple) et il y a beaucoup moins de partis de gauche, en tout cas pas comme en France. Le contexte historique est aussi différent: les Français et la révolution, les américains et leurs pionniers... bref, tout ça explique que nous n'avons pas le même point de vue.

> (The French tend to see individualism as a fault, something bad because we have a social security progam that values solidarty more [in theory]. In the US, social protection is less prevalent [health insurance, for instance, is not compulsory] and there are fewer leftist parties, at least not like in France. The historical context too is different: the French and the Revolution, the Americans and their pioneers... in short, all of this explains why we don't have the same point of view.)

More questions also spontaneously come up: Is the notion of individualism related only to the political sphere? How about the personal one? Some MIT students said they thought of it mostly in personal terms, saying what it means to them, as a person: "Be who you want to be" (P.). Spurred by references made by some students in their postings new questions arise: "What does Descartes have to do with individualism?" asks an MIT student. "Certains d'entre vous ont utilisé le mot 'pionnier' pour l'individualisme. Pourquoi?" asks a French student (Some of you used the word "pioneer" in reference to individualism. Why?).

The above examples reflect typical types of exchanges found in the online forum discussions. As students move on to other materials, the discussions at hand will suddenly stop, and some questions will inevitably stay unanswered. But what is important is that students on both sides be involved in a constant and reciprocal process of knowledge sharing and inquiry, and, of course, learn something of value along the way.

It also needs to be emphasized that students are totally in charge of those discussions. They are the ones leading them and they are free to take them in whatever direction they want. No forum on a same word, sentence, or situation is ever the same from one semester to the other. Students will also have a chance to encounter the same notions again (on "individualism," for instance) and expand on them, as they revisit them within other contexts further down the road, when looking at other materials, such as national opinion polls or newspaper articles or texts offering a cross-cultural perspective.

These forums are viewed as central to the process of intercultural learning not just by the authors of *Cultura* and the teachers, but by the students themselves. As one MIT student once wrote, in an end-of-semester evaluation of the project,

> The forums were an invaluable part of my French course experience. It was good to interact with peers in another country and gain insight into a different cultural perspective on common themes and motifs. Through the word associations forum I was able to get a glimpse of the thought processes of my French peers. It's interesting to see how ideas are connected within the minds of individuals in another culture, in comparison to my own, so to better understand the other culture.

For these forums to be successful, reciprocity is, of course, key. It is essential that teachers on both sides stress that all their students participate in the forums regularly and in a timely manner. Nothing can be more frustrating to students than writing comments and asking questions and not receiving anything in return or only days later.

Role of the teacher

In such an environment, new roles for both teachers and learners inevitably emerge. With *Cultura*, the teacher is no longer the sole source of information and the only authority, as multiple other voices are heard and integrated into the classroom. This drastically changes our role, which will shift from mainly imparting cultural knowledge to providing students with opportunities to share what they have learnt and discovered, reflect, discuss, and confront points of view, both with their classmates and their partners. This creates a new role for learners as well, as they are now fully engaged in constructing and co-constructing their own knowledge. The very nature of that knowledge changes as well: with *Cultura*, learning about another culture is not simply a matter for students to accumulate facts and knowledge: It entails a dynamic process of discovery, exploration, inquiry, and co-construction that favors a decidedly constructivist approach to learning, with students progressively building an increasingly complex and rich understanding of the foreign culture (see Brooks and Brooks, 1993).

Kern, Ware, and Warschauer (2004) aptly wrote,

> Through the interactive exchange of viewpoints and perspectives, students using *Cultura* are not "receiving culture" but are involved in a reciprocal construction of one another's cultures. The cultural literacy that *Cultura* aims to develop is therefore not transmitted (as in an E. D. Hirsch 'list'

variety), but rather created and *problematized* through juxtapositions of materials, interpretations, and responses to interpretations... This marks a key pedagogical change: The teacher shifts out of the "omniscient informant" role and focuses on structuring, juxtaposing, interpreting, and reflecting on intercultural experiences. Learners' understandings are confirmed, questioned, or contradicted in the light of new materials. (p. 249)

The teacher's role will then be to facilitate the process of intercultural learning.

Facilitating the process of intercultural learning

Our 17-year experience has taught us that the teacher's role is crucial in that endeavor. As Belz (2003) observed in the conclusion to her article,

The importance (but not necessarily the prominence) of the teacher and, ultimately, teacher education programs... increases rather than diminishes in Internet-mediated intercultural foreign language education precisely because of the electronic nature of the discourse (p. 13).

Besides initially setting up the calendar with the partner abroad, deciding which materials to use, making the goals of the project explicit to students from the start, and explaining the methodology, the teachers' overall and crucial task is to accompany/scaffold the students' explorations and analysis and facilitate the learning process.

Creating tasks/scaffolding the process

The overall task is one that will scaffold the process of intercultural learning and help along the students' process of co-construction. In our experience, this can be achieved only by providing them with specific tasks that build upon each other. As many researchers in the field have shown (e.g., Guth, Helm, & O'Dowd, 2012; Müller-Hartmann, 2000; and O'Dowd & Ware, 2009), tasks are absolutely essential.

Scaffolding needs to include such basics as providing very specific instructions to the reading of documents,[21] clarifying the function of the forums, providing appropriate prompts,[22] and adding new forums when/if the need arises (e.g., current events, coffee break).[23] Teachers will also need to create specific tasks that will help the process of intercultural learning unfold along a series of steps, as students work first with the questionnaires and then with the other documents.

---

[21] Precise instructions need to be given to students for comparing and analyzing the materials at hand. In terms of the answers to the questionnaires for instance, we believe it is important to provide students with analysis sheets that will guide their observations, instructing them, for example, "Print the responses selected and for each of them, write down the words and expressions that appear the most often in both languages; organize them into categories; note these categories." Further prompts are "Are the connotations negative, positive, or neutral? For each side, note the responses that only show on one side but not on the other. Write your observations, hypotheses, and questions." These comments will be used as a starting point for the classroom discussions and for the forums.

[22] Here is an example (in reference to the work on the comparison of national French and American polls): "Please post here any message related to polls or statistics you may have found that illustrates, illuminates, or seems to contradict an aspect of American or French culture that you have been investigating. When you make a reference to a particular document on the Internet, please make sure you provide the url."

[23] When an important political or social event takes place in one country or the other, we will automatically open a new forum entitled "Current Events," so that students can also share their perspectives on those. We feel it is important that *Cultura* not exist in a vacuum. Conversely, the Coffee Break forum is intended for students to share thoughts on topics not covered by the materials at hand.

These steps provide the scaffolding students will need in order to go beyond the surface and delve deeper and deeper into the materials. We will illustrate these steps, taking as an example the week when students analyze responses to the second questionnaire: "Finish the following sentences: A good neighbor..., A good boss..., The most important events in my life..., etc."

Step 1: As homework, students are asked to select three of the sentences proposed and compare their own responses to those of the French, based upon an analysis sheet that has been given to them by the teacher.[24]

Step 2: In class, students are asked to find two other students in the class who have analyzed one or two of the same sentences and share their findings with each other, thus expanding their own individual observations.

Step 3: Then each group, having selected a different sentence to analyse, summarizes their findings on the whiteboards (our classroom walls are covered with boards). Once they have finished, each team is asked to go from board to board and see whether cultural patterns emerge: Do they see same type of differences crop up in different contexts? In what form? They draw connecting lines as they move around.

Step 4: Students are then asked to say whether they see cultural patterns emerge.

This is where they may discover, for instance, the tendency[25] on the part of "the French" to be more abstract, more "socially oriented," as well as more direct and confrontational, and for "the Americans" to see situations through a more "individual" prism as well as view relationships (with teachers, friends, doctors, or bosses) through the prism of affect, putting the emphasis on the need to be "caring," "loving" and not hurting other people's feelings.

The above series of steps—(a) making personal observations, (b) sharing them with others (their classmates as well as their foreign peers) in order to expand their own vision, and (c) making connections through the use of the white boards, in order to see cultural patterns come to light—is all essential, in our view, for developing in-depth intercultural skills.

Facilitating the online discussions

As mentioned earlier, teachers never interfere in the forums, but they do have an important role to play beforehand. Experience has taught us how important it is for them to provide students with extremely clear guidelines. We will share here some strategies important for making those forums as successful as possible.

- Make sure students address their peers directly. Even though teachers do have access to those forums, it is incumbent upon us to tell/remind students that their interlocutors are the other students. Prompts are essential in that regard, as they guide (without being overbearing) the students' discussions. However, they need to be articulated in such a way that students will not direct their messages to the teacher (as would otherwise happen) but directly to their "peers."

---

[24] See note 21.

[25] We always stress having students articulate their findings in terms of "tendencies," saying such things as, "From this document, it looks as if the Americans/French—at least in this context—tend to..."

- Impart upon students the importance of making references to specific contexts and distinguishing between them (e.g., MIT versus other schools; New England versus the South or California; big city versus small town) or to pay attention to different social milieux (e.g., suburbs versus inner city). We also encourage them to disclose parts of their background (e.g., where they come from, even more so in the case of the foreign students) so that their partner students do not think they all come from the same mold and do not get a monolithic view of the other culture.

- Encourage all students to express their own views and not necessarily join the majority viewpoint. This is something we have strongly stressed from the very early years of the project. One semester,[26] for instance, when discussing the notion of individualism, even though the large majority of American students talked about it in an extremely positive way, one student wrote,

    > As has been said, we obviously have very different ideas of what the word means. MIT students in particular tend to be the people who were the outsiders in their high school, because they did better in classes and sometimes weren't so popular. I think that among some other groups in America, individualism is not seen so positively. There are many stories of people who have different opinions, different fashions, etc. being considered wrong or dangerous by their communities (schools, towns, and so on). So I don't think that every American would agree that individualism is a good characteristic, even though it is very important to me.

- It is extremely important to us that as many different points of view as possible be expressed. Cultures everywhere in the world are increasingly hybrid and heterogeneous, and the last thing we want is for our students to receive a monolithic view of "French" or "American" cultures and for "minority" perspectives to be drowned in a sea of consensus, with students concluding that French culture is this, while American culture is that. In response to a very valid remark made by Malinowski in a blog following a workshop held at Brown University in October 2013, it is worth emphasizing that even though *Cultura* starts with simple two-sided questionnaires, which may indeed seem to accentuate a simplistic French-American duality, the online discussions are exactly the place where the initial observations become more complex, where multiple voices gradually emerge, and where students get a much more nuanced and complex view of the cultures at hand. The questionnaires simply act as initial springboard that allow broad cultural differences to emerge, but the forums are where the "hidden," more complex and multi-faceted aspects of cultures then emerge.

- To that end, encourage students not to shy away from potentially difficult topics. Even though confrontation is often seen as the reason for "failed communication," at MIT we purposely do not stay away from topics that could possibly generate conflicts and we suggest to students that they NOT avoid confrontation at all cost (something they may not necessarily feel comfortable with), as the end goal of these on-line discussions is not

---

[26] Fall 1999 exchange: http://Cultura.mit.edu/1999-fall-mit-int-22/

to create a consensus among all students but rather to be a forum where issues are constantly raised and debated at every turn.

- If by any chance a student goes "overboard" in their criticism, we do not interfere either, and interestingly enough, more often than not, the other students themselves will write something in the forums, asking the "guilty" one to tamper his/her own judgements. As a case in point, recall the example given earlier (in the forum on individualism), where a French student wrote, "la FRANCE N'EST PAS UN PAYS SOCIALISTE, loin de là!!!!" and the American student's response, "Please don't shout, it's not necessary."

- Sometimes we talk about it in class and provide examples of French students being "overly" critical of each other, to show that this is not directed at them personally, but that "being critical" could be viewed as a cultural trait.

- Consider creating a forum dedicated to raising paradoxes and contradictions. In our experience, one of the most fruitful avenues for helping students debate issues that may be deemed too sensitive or difficult is to create such a forum.[27] We created this forum half way through the *Cultura* years, out of the realization that students in general tend to stay away from controversy (Is it simply the result of "netiquette" or a natural aversion to avoid difficult topics, which in itself may be cultural based?). However, for true intercultural communication, we felt it was crucial that students be encouraged not to shy away from controversy. In fact, we found out that, when encouraged, students are not afraid to challenge their peers, as is illustrated by the following two postings. An MIT student, discussing the French students' response to the situation "You see a student cheating at an exam,"[28] and their avowed reluctance to report on the cheater (an attitude which they traced to events that took place during World War II) once wrote,

    > I think there is a great difference between denouncing a Jew in WWII and denouncing a student who is cheating on an exam. Jews were innocent people and the treatment they received was immoral (to say the least). However, the punishment of a student who is copying is not immoral. I think it is unacceptable to tolerate cheating. If an exam is important, then people should take action when they see somebody attempting to cheat….

- In most discussions in the forums so far, you (the French students) have advocated for social justice, yet you inexplicably tolerate being cheated.

Another example from Regina, an MIT student is,

> To add to Irene's comment # 17. I'm surprised politeness is claimed to be the most important word in the French language. Is it really important to the French to be polite to strangers? The commonest complaint I've

---

[27] We introduced this forum in the following way: "This forum is (1) for raising what you see as paradoxes in the other culture (which you have discovered across several questionnaire answers and/or the comments on the forums) and (2) for offering possible hypotheses and interpretations to your transatlantic partners' queries."

[28] http://Cultura.mit.edu/2012-spring-mitenseirb-matmeca-56/

heard about French people is that they are sarcastic and rude. I've witnessed a lot of the sarcasm in the course of this forum and a little bit of the rudeness. I'm having a little trouble relating French politeness and their sharp sarcasm. Could someone help me out?.

- Such forums might be thought to be difficult, but they yield very interesting riches, as a student wrote in one end-of-semester survey,

    Paradoxes are hard to come up with, but once you stumble upon one, they are pretty easy to write about. These discussions are among the more interesting because in this topic, the students are synthesizing more new ideas.

- Finally, design activities that will ensure that the online discussion forums are integrated and brought back into the classroom so as to bring the voices of the French students alive. One simple way this can be done is by asking students to go into the forum and bring back to class one or two comments from the French students that they find either illuminating or intriguing or surprising, and be ready to share it with their classmates. This will not only bring the voices of the French students into the American classroom, but start new conversations on the topics.

Teacher's role in the classroom

What happens in the classroom is crucial. As seen earlier, this is where students take center stage, sharing their discoveries with each other about what they have observed from reading or viewing documents presented online or from reading the comments written by their counterparts on the forums. As we have seen, it is through discussions with their peers that they develop new insights, raise new questions and paradoxes, take a broader view, look for patterns and start synthesizing, arrive at new interpretations, and constantly refine their understanding of the other culture, both expanding their individual knowledge and trying to put the overall cultural puzzle together.

This does not mean that the teacher recedes in the background. It is important for her/him to also take center stage in order to, for instance, (a) clarify a particular misunderstanding (e.g., *éduquer*[29]); (b) bring students' attention to a particular document that he/she thinks is particularly culturally informative, such as to whom and how to say *bonjour*, or which he/she think provides a lot of information that may be opaque to the student or may bring particularly interesting cultural and/or linguistic information; and (c) bring outside documents that might illustrate or illuminate a conversation. For example, when examining the American and French responses to the situation where a mother is seen slapping her child in a supermarket, we often show in class a TV excerpt from the French news, where a French politician, a candidate for the presidential elections in 2002, is seen slapping a child on the street,[30] an incident that has not prevented that politician from being a candidate in presidential elections twice again. That video then sparks new conversations in the classroom.

---

[29] The different meanings of the word in French and in English can be a source of misunderstanding that often needs to be clarified; in French *éduquer* means to instill values, shape character, not to teach or instruct (a subject).

[30] http://youtu.be/qu5G0iBrj2Q

Finally, another essential task for the teacher, one that is central to the classroom process and that is again part of the scaffolding set-up, is to design activities that will ensure students do make connections when exploring new documents, and that they are subsequently able to reflect upon and synthesize what they have learnt along the way.

Here is the task given to the students when they are asked to explore the module "surveys and statistics" on the website prior to coming to class:

> You will now enlarge your horizon and explore French national polls about the attitudes of the French regarding a topic found in the questionnaires. Look at some of these polls and find a relevant topic that interests you (whether family, work, neighbors, etc.). Print those polls, then underline the parts that you find most interesting and bring them to class. Be ready to share this poll with your classmates and say whether (1) they validate or invalidate what you discovered through the analysis of the three questionnaires and (2) they reveal an attitude that surprises you.

Likewise, when students compare French and American films or images or commercials and present their findings in class, they are always encouraged to draw parallels to differences they may have discovered earlier with the analysis of other documents or their online discussions with their transatlantic partners.

What this changes, in terms of our role as teachers, is that we are no longer there to only make sure that the students have seen, understood what we want them to know and understand, but to have them tell us what they have seen, discovered, learnt. We are no longer "teaching" culture, in the traditional way, but putting students in a position where they themselves will gradually discover what that "other" culture is like, and like cultural anthropologists, will attempt to put that cultural puzzle together, through their readings, forum discussions, and in-class interactions.

Assessing

Assessing and evaluating has always been one of the teacher's main responsibilities, and it is no less crucial here. Yet, it poses a particularly difficult challenge, since one usually evaluates a finished product, such as an essay, a paper, or a project. In the context of *Cultura*, where the focus is clearly on the process of intercultural understanding, the question becomes: How do you assess a process? A second relevant question is What do you assess?

Byram's (2000) well-known categories of intercultural competence, which are very helpful in that respect, outline the following aspects:

Attitude is a factor that includes "curiosity and openness, readiness to suspend disbelief about other cultures and belief about one's own." (Byram, Gribkova, & Starkey, 2002, p. 12)

Knowledge of one's self and others equals knowledge of the rules for individual and social interaction both in one's one culture and in the other culture.

Skills of interpreting and relating describe an individual's ability to interpret, explain, and relate events and documents from another culture to one's own culture; skills of discovery and interaction that allow the individual to acquire "new knowledge of culture and cultural practices."

Critical cultural awareness

The question then becomes How do you measure those attitudes, the knowledge acquired, the skills developed, and the notion of cultural awareness?

First and foremost, appropriate tools need to be used. The tools of choice for assessing a process are clearly portfolios.

With *Cultura*, we have asked students to write weekly logbooks (*carnets de bord*) and answer the following questions: What items did you analyze this past week? What did you learn (from comparing the answers and the postings of the French students)? What questions did you ask? What comments did you make? What questions were answered? Did some answers surprise you (because they contradicted or reinforced a cliché)? This was followed by a personal journal outlining what they had reflected upon that week. Such logbooks are best at capturing what students have seen/observed, what connections they have made, and what they have learned, and lead toward a great deal of personal reflection, a crucial component.

At one point, we introduced discovery logbooks (*carnets de découverte*)[31] in which students were asked to write just two items: (a) what I discovered and (b) what surprises me and why. Below is an example of a student's *carnet de découverte* (written in L1).

> It surprised me also that the French students said that they would speak up in the theater more than we American students do. I would think it would surprise them too, as Americans are often seen as very individualistic, blunt (*francs*), and set on getting their way (including getting someone who is annoying them to be quiet immediately). Again, I wonder what the cause of this difference is and how we can extrapolate to other situations (i.e., when can we predict that the French will be more or less outspoken?). It could be that the French become more indignant about politeness than Americans.

Another useful tool for assessing intercultural understanding consists in having students periodically synthesize what they have learned. The following assignment, given to the students three weeks into the semester (after they have compared the answers to the three questionnaires) is an illustration:

> Basing yourself on the French responses to the three questionnaires (word associations, sentences to be completed, and situations) as well as the comments of the French students in the online discussion forums, choose a concept that seems to you central to French culture. State in what different contexts and under what forms, this concept emerges. Are there cases and examples that seem to contradict this view or that, on the contrary, reinforce it? Give specific examples and elaborate. Include a diagram based on all the materials you used to illustrate your point.

Here is a sample of essay topics about French culture and society, which the students themselves chose and wrote entirely in French, that show a wide range of interests: *la notion de respect dans la société française* (the notion of respect in

---

[31] These *carnets de découverte* were designed by Virginie Trémion, a doctoral student from the University of Lille, France, who spent a semester coming to every class and interviewing students. She herself had been inspired by *Le Journal d'Etonnement*, created by Christine Develotte (2006) http://lidil.revues.org/index25.html

French society); *l'importance de l'égalité dans la culture française* (the importance of equality in French culture); *le concept de "savoir" dans la culture française* (the concept of "savoir"); *le rapport à l'argent* (the French and their relationship to money); *l'importance de la vie privée* (the importance of private life in the French culture); *le rôle de l'individu* (the role of the individual); *l'importance des règles* (the importance of rules); *le conformisme et l'anti-conformisme* (conformism and anti-conformism); *la France si douce, mais si aigre* (France so sweet, yet so bitter); *la notion d'ordre* (the notion of order).

Finally, end of semester class presentations (in PowerPoint or other formats) also provide a good base for students to synthesize and make essential connections. For example, once when students were analyzing the images they had uploaded on the site in order to illustrate a topic (e.g., daily life on campus; what we eat, where and when; commercials on beer or cars, etc.) they had themselves selected, students ended up comparing and analyzing not only the content of the photos, but also the type of photos taken.

A group once remarked that the American students tended to take photos in which they themselves appeared (with them eating or studying, for example), whereas the French tended to take photos of either the dish itself or just a library or a café, devoid of the subject, namely themselves. They would then draw a parallel between that and the way in which the students expressed themselves in the forums, with the American students tending to put themselves in the middle of their discourse and the French staying outside of it, focusing on the "object" of analysis (the topic), not on the subject (themselves). What an extraordinarily astute remark this was, we felt, especially for a third semester student in a French language class—one that clearly illustrates, in our mind, what Byram calls the crucial intercultural skills of "interpreting" and "relating."

An interesting question arises, worth asking oneself in the context of evaluation within the *Cultura* methodology: Who does the evaluation? Usually and without any question, it is the teacher. Here, where teachers no longer are the only voice of authority, would it not make more sense to also have our students send their paper (with a copy to their teacher) to one of the French students involved in the exchange, as opposed to their teacher alone? The French students would then write remarks, not on the accuracy of grammar and syntax, but on the content of the paper, focusing on how well it reflected about French culture. We tried it once, with great success, and are definitely planning on doing it again. In recent semesters, as described below, we have also used Skype sessions for students to provide evaluative feedback to their papers.

Integrating the study of language

As mentioned earlier, *Cultura* was first developed in a third semester language class, which is part of a four level sequence of language classes at MIT. We owe it to our students to make sure that their language skills are adequate to move on to the next level. It is especially important since many of them will then go to France to intern at large companies or labs, so training them in both language and culture is part of their necessary preparation.

In many respects, our linguistic goals are the same as in many other language classes. We use a grammar book and schedule the systematic review and study of vocabulary and grammar into our daily activities throughout the semester. What is different from most language classes, though, is that the work on language is inscribed within the tasks aimed at understanding the other culture, and the postings on the forums become our textbook. With traditional textbooks, the accompanying grammar is, by necessity, organized sequentially. For instance, compound relative pronouns[32] come after simple relative pronouns; the study of the subjunctive mode comes after the indicative and the conditional, at the end of the book, and often at the end of the semester as well. It indirectly gives students the idea that this sequence reflects a progression, from simple to complex, and that the later topics can be tackled only once the earlier topics are mastered. It also hints that the later subjects need a higher level of sophistication, or even that the use of compound relative pronouns or subjunctive, for instance, might belong to a higher language register.

But the *Cultura* forums show our students that using compound relative pronouns or the subjunctive is not a question of register, but a question of necessity. When expressing doubts, their 20-year-old French peers will say, using the subjunctive,

> Je ne pense pas qu'il y ait une réelle compétition à l'ENSEIRB (C., forum "you see a student cheating at an exam," spring 2012)
> (I don't think there is a real competition at ENSEIRB).

They will also use compound relative pronouns liberally throughout the forums, such as in the following comment:

> Il y a 3 types de comportements vis à vis du travail: 1. Ceux qui ne cherchent pas forcement de reconnaissance au travail, pour qui c'est une obligation dont ils se passeraient bien, qui font leurs heures et pas plus. (J., forum "a good job," spring 2012)
> (There are three attitudes regarding work: 1. Those who are not necessarily trying to get recognition from work, for whom it is only an obligation that they would love to avoid, who only do their hours.)[33]

The forums, as demonstrated in many examples given earlier, are an extremely rich source of speech acts (ways to express an opinion, an agreement, a disagreement, a hypothesis, presenting arguments) and vocabulary in context. Our students discover colloquialisms and phrases they would not find in a third semester textbook. To their questions about vocabulary, their partners often answer with definitions which give a context to the words they are clarifying, going beyond a simple word for word explanation, such as in the following example in the forum about "Europe" (spring 2012).[34] An MIT student who asked what is "l'ex-URSS," received the following explanation from J.:

> L'URSS c'est l'union soviétique, union d'une quinzaine de pays socialistes/communistes, telle qu'elle existait jusqu'en 1991. Il s'agit en fait de la Russie et de ses voisins. Aujourd'hui, l'URSS n'existe plus, on parle donc d'ex-URSS.
> (The USSR is the Soviet Union, a union of about fifteen socialist/communist countries, which existed until 1991. It is in fact Russia and its neighbors. Today, the USSR does not exist anymore, therefore we talk about ex-USSR.)

---

[32] Note that the French term is *pronoms relatifs composés*, which has been translated as "compound relative pronouns," but the French *pronoms relatifs composés* differ from English compound relative pronouns.

[33] http://Cultura.mit.edu/2012-spring-mitenseirb-matmeca-50/

[34] http://Cultura.mit.edu/2012-spring-mitenseirb-matmeca-43/

The students have a large degree of autonomy: They decide what forums to participate in, what comments to react to, and what they want to say. They become active learners, take initiatives, and develop strategies to make sense of the comments posted by their peers and develop a reading literacy that goes beyond lexical and grammar usage. They actively reflect on the connection between language and culture through direct observation, discussing together for instance the use of different modes of address such as *tu* versus *vous,* or the use of the first name as opposed to *Monsieur* or *Madame.* For instance, in the forum for "you are cashing a personal check at the bank" (spring 2012),[35] they examine the interplay of multiple criteria such as context, age, and level of familiarity to determine a mode of address, and ponder statements from their partners such as student G.'s comment,

> En France, se faire appeler par son prénom par un étranger est assez infantilisant.
> (In France, being addressed by our first name by a stranger is rather infantilizing.)

Words and their meanings are at the heart of *Cultura*, so when students analyze the answers to the questionnaires and are asked to classify the answers into "positive," "negative," or "neutral" connotations, they learn to examine the words from different angles and they realize that reading a text means interpreting it. For instance, noticing that the word *puissant* (powerful) has shown up multiple times on the French side in the associations with "USA" (spring 2012),[36] an MIT student asks, "I noticed a couple responses about power and size—are these good things or bad things in your opinion?" (M.)

We do not give our students vocabulary lists, except at the beginning of the work on the questionnaires, where we create a reference sheet with vocabulary and expressions they will recycle multiple times during the semester, in class or on their daily worksheets, such as *Les Américains* (the Americans), *les Français* (the French), *les étudiants américains* (the American students), *les étudiants français* (the French students), *aux Etats-Unis* (in the United States), *en France* (in France), *du côté américain (*on the American side), *du côté français* (on the French side), *ils disent que* (they say that), and *ils parlent de* (they talk about). For the rest of the exchange, they create their own lists based on the postings they react to, the class conversations, and the written work they turn in every day. Their writing takes multiple forms: They prepare for class by noting their comments in a few sentences, summarize a posting they want to share with the entire group, and prepare a list of ideas regarding a question. There is a mutual reinforcement between reading, speaking, and writing as the students become more confident and expand their linguistic abilities at the same time as their cultural understanding.

How *Cultura* has evolved over the years

The original model of *Cultura* described above has been modified very little over the years in the French exchanges at MIT. The project is still taking place in a language class with a focus on intercultural understanding. Students still use L1 online and L2 in the classroom, with asynchronous forums attached to each specific topic or type of materials. They are asked to make hypotheses, ask questions to their partners, and answer partners' questions to make sense of the differences they observe between items taken from both cultures. So the basic process and the basic technology tools have remained the same, even though synchronous technology

---

[35] http://Cultura.mit.edu/2012-spring-mitenseirb-matmeca-58/
[36] http://Cultura.mit.edu/2012-spring-mitenseirb-matmeca-32/

such as text, audio, and video chat are now widely and cheaply available, and have been incorporated into our exchanges.

In the next sections, we will share our experiences using the different tools that we have integrated into our exchanges over the years.

Using asynchronous forums

Cultura was developed in the early days of web-based forums. Even today, forums are still particularly well adapted to the analytical tasks we ask students to perform, as the authentic, student-generated content is available to all, at all times. Contrary to synchronous modes of communication, there is no need to agree beforehand on a specific time when everybody would be available, which can be a challenge when working across time zones. Asynchronous forums enable students to access the L2 content at their own pace and develop strategies to make sense of it: reading multiple times, using a dictionary, using context clues to decode the meaning of a word or expression, making predictions based on what they already know, verifying their interpretation, and asking questions to the author of a specific posting, if they need clarification or want to react to it.

A typical exchange is organized by topics. Since many posts are attached to each topic, the sheer number of comments to read and respond to might seem overwhelming for the students. However, it is important to remember that all students are not expected to work on all topics, and that the exchange unfolds according to a specific calendar, which helps focus the discussions week after week. During week 1, the focus is on word associations. Students participate in 3 or 4 of the 12 topics, posting at least three comments for each. In week 2, the focus moves to sentence completions, and students participate in two or three topics. Week 3, the focus is on situations, and again students participate in two or three topics. Each student working alone sees only a small part of the overall postings but, during the class discussions, gets a larger view of the discussions going on at the same time on the other forums and can make connections that he or she could not have made alone. This renders the discussions in class all the more interesting. And as a student returns to the same topic many times and continues the conversation within this topic, he or she becomes more familiar with the context, which makes the discussion easier to follow and generates more in-depth discussions.

As each type of activity typically lasts only about a week, a subject is not necessarily exhausted by the time we move on. But later on, as they examine different materials, students might relate new discoveries and ideas they had encountered earlier and can return to earlier discussions to verify a point. This back-and-forth is an important part of the process we want our students to engage in.

Participation in the forums is required of our students, but we never know in advance what topics will generate the largest number of posts, as students are free to participate in any discussion. In fact, the most popular discussions (with the largest number of posts) vary from group to group and semester to semester. In the past, we occasionally opened a "Bonjour/Hello" forum at the very beginning of the exchange. In terms of participation it might have been deemed a success, since it generated lengthy discussions about food, travel, and pastimes. Even though it might have been popular, we found it disappointing, because the content was very repetitive and did not actually go very deep in terms of intercultural understanding.

We feel that our goal, as instructors, is to open our students' minds, to engage them and dare them to examine concepts they would not examine on their own and actively develop their critical skills. *Cultura* offers them this challenge and takes them beyond the mundane conversations happening on some popular forums that do not necessarily lead to intercultural understanding. Perhaps the main "secret" ingredient for ensuring a successful intercultural forum is having participants communicate, not just speak directly to teach other about each other (which often leads nowhere) but to congregate about a third object (i.e., the materials), through which they will reveal their culture and themselves.

Using online video conferencing and chat

The way people access information and communicate has changed tremendously since the early days of *Cultura* 17 years ago, and new technologies have enabled the project to evolve as well. The videoconferences of the past (for which we had to reserve a room weeks in advance) have been replaced by small group or one-on-one Skype sessions. Video calls, video chat, and videoconferencing complement the asynchronous forums very well.

These sessions need to be arranged around schedules and time zones and demand flexibility on the part of the partners. In our case, it can happen only thanks to our partners in France who move their class meeting later in the day two or three times during the semester to match our morning classes (which we would not be able to do at MIT). These necessary accommodations do limit the number of sessions we can organize during the semester. We try, whenever possible, to have a first session towards the beginning of the semester, to meet the other group, one at mid-semester, and one toward the end of the semester.

Interestingly, our students' feedback tells us that the awkwardness of having to talk online with a partner for a limited amount of time is reduced and the conversation flows more easily if we give them a specific task: for instance, getting their French partner's feedback on an essay, working on the statistics module, focusing their discussion on the specific data they collected before the session. We experimented with having students change partners at mid-session, so that they would hear more than one person. But then some of them felt that they had to go twice through introductions, and that the exercise was a bit repetitive and a waste of time (because of the time urgency during such synchronous sessions). Overall, they seemed to prefer groups of three, with two students on one side and one on the other, to one-on-one conversations.

We observed also that talking to only one partner could have some drawbacks, as the temptation is great to take what the other is saying at face value, taking one voice for the universal voice, and coming up with a distorted view of the issues. For instance, a student examining the different rules that govern society, based a large part of his analysis on an anecdote told by his French partner, who related that someone who had been caught cheating in college was punished not because of cheating but because he had used the familiar form of address (*tu*) when addressing the professor. Our student came to the conclusion that the French follow social rules more than the law, ending up with a simplistic view of reality. By contrast, as we saw earlier, the discussions on the asynchronous forums are public and open, which means that any individual student's statement can be tempered by others, leading to a more nuanced understanding of the notion being discussed. In the case just described above, it is a good idea to include time for classroom cross-examination after the Skype session, so as to correct the risk of giving more authority than necessary to one single voice.

Using wikis

We have used a wiki for collaborative work on the photo exchange part of the project. The "Images" module, where students from both sides upload their own images and analyze them in small groups, necessitates the highest level of collaboration and coordination between groups. While a wiki makes collaborative work possible, it is also a little bit difficult to manage, because everybody can modify the content at all times. Still, this very characteristic also enables students to manipulate the images, organize them in different ways, and interpret them.

We used a wiki during the two separate phases of working collaboratively with images. Phase one had to do with generating topics and organizing groups. During class discussions, a number of topics with too few or too many participants had to be discarded or modified, in order to make the project more manageable. Phase two had to do with actually working with the materials: Each group created its own page, posting images (giving each a title, saying where and when the photo was taken and what it illustrated), reacting to the others' images, and listing the cultural differences that seemed to be highlighted by their juxtaposition.

Based on our experience, a wiki was not the most appropriate tool for phase one, which might have been more easily managed in a regular forum. On the other hand, the second phase, the more creative and collaborative part of the work, benefited from the flexibility of a wiki.

Using a blog

Occasionally we have opened a class blog limited only to our MIT students (and stored within MIT's Course Management System) in parallel with the *Cultura* forums. Its purpose is to record what happens during class and make it possible to return to it at a later date. At each class meeting, a designated secretary is responsible for taking detailed notes for the entire session, and posting them to the blog before the next class. These posts (written in L2) are not addressed to anyone in particular, but they enable the entire group to have a collective memory of what happened during any given session. Most of these entries list the topics that were discussed and note briefly what main points were made. Interestingly, many entries reflect the analytical process that took place during class, with expressions such as such as *nous nous sommes demandé si...* (we wondered if...), *nous avons remarqué* (we noticed), *nous avons conclu que...* (we concluded that...), *on a fait l'hypothèse que...* (we hypothesized that...), and *on peut supposer que...* (one can suppose that...). It mirrors the process that we encourage our students to follow, with observations, hypotheses, and questioning.

It is also interesting to see that these postings give a large place to vocabulary. For instance, on one post, the following list of vocabulary was attached to the topic *banlieue* (suburb): *affrontement* (confrontation); *hlm* (housing project); *sweat à capuche* (hoodie); and *RER* (commuter rail). The secretary for that day indicated that the two words *dodo* and *karsher* were not elucidated during class, but a note was made to ask the French students. In the category *élite* (elite), the specific vocabulary that came up was *crâne d'oeuf* (egghead); *ENA Ecole Nationale d'Administration* (National School of Administration)[37]; *Polytechnique* (MIT, but in France); and *milieu social aisé* (euphemism for old money).

As a follow-up to the blog post, the secretary is also in charge the following session to provide an oral summary of what he or she has posted, to which other students contribute helped by notes they might have taken as well. The recap of what has been discussed during the previous session reinforces the retention of vocabulary, validates what has been said so far by bringing back the essential elements of the conversation, and helps students organize their ideas, which is important since classroom conversations touch so many topics. It is also a good way to start a class session because if focuses the students' attention on the task at hand and gives them a chance to get back to their own notes.

Adding to the materials we compare

More resources are available online for the instructors than in the early days of the web, and Word documents, images, and videos are easy to access. It has become easier to bring into our course film trailers, commercials, music clips, blogs, and discussion forums attached to news outlets, as well as archival documents from both cultures, which can be juxtaposed and compared. This has expanded what we do with *Cultura*. The work on commercials in particular, which were hard to come by in the past, is very rich now and enables students to recognize some cultural traits they have uncovered during their discussions. It is helped greatly by the existence of a French website (culturepub.fr) which focuses on advertising, and makes it easy to access a large number of clips and search them by country of origin, year, type of product, and theme.

We have had our students compare, for instance, commercials from American Airlines and Air France[38] as well as film trailers for a French film and its American version[39]–documents that have yielded particularly fertile intercultural gems.

An increasing number of online resources are also available for the students. As many of our students are active in online social networks, they have become fluent in the use of images and videos, in addition to text, to express themselves and communicate. Whereas in the past we, as instructors, were the ones to select materials we wanted to bring to our students' attention, now our students frequently link newspaper articles, video clips, images, statistics, and excerpts from blogs into the forums to support a point, engage their peers, and open up the discussions. For instance, in a forum about immigration (spring 2012), T., a French student, inserted a link to a Wikipedia article about *La Halde*, an institution that fights discrimination, as a quick way to explain to the MIT students what it is.

In a forum about Europe (fall 2010),[40] L., an MIT student, connected an article he had read with earlier discussions with the French students:

> I have come across an interesting article in the online journal *EU Observer* on the power of big countries (Germany, France) in determining common policies (even if only one or two countries profit, while other countries are at

---

[37] ENA is an elite school that trains future high-ranking civil servants.
[38] http://youtu.be/Rts3ezaXQBs and http://youtu.be/_w3OXa0QTJI
[39] http://www.dailymotion.com/video/x2o60f_la-marche-de-l-empereur-bande-annon_animals and http://youtu.be/L7tWNwhSocE
[40] http://Cultura.mit.edu/2010-fall-mituniversite-de-brest-44/

loss), the actions that the EU takes and, in contrast, the impotence of smaller countries. It illustrates what has cropped up in the discussion above: National interest still takes precedence over EU interest (e.g., farming subsidies from which certain countries and their farmers profit immensely, even though it would be better for Europeans—and many third world countries—if the market would be liberalized). Is there any chance that this will ever change? Why would any big country want this to change? What can small countries do? http://euobserver.com/9/30973.

Another student linked a video found on a major TV outlet website, directing her peers specifically to the 39th minute of the video. Another one quoted headlines from *Le Monde*, to prove that French newspapers report daily on what is going on in the US.

Working with partners

Even as technology has made it easier to access materials and communicate, the most important factor for the success of an exchange is our own ability to work with a partner across cultures. Our model involves two institutions anchored in two different cultures, with different educational systems, different roles for the teachers, and different expectations from the students. It is indeed a challenge to take all these elements into account as we try to set up an exchange. So when things do not go as planned, we have to recognize that working on a *Cultura* exchange is per se a practical exercise in cross-cultural collaboration and understanding.

It might take more than a semester for a partner to adapt and fully comprehend what is entailed in an exchange. Therefore we strongly recommend working multiple times with the same partner (even if the first try was challenging), being as flexible as possible, and trying to progressively develop a deeper working relationship. In our experience, once a partner has gone through the whole process at least once, he or she has a better sense of what happens during an exchange and what the particular demands are on the calendar, and can better communicate to his/her students what the purpose of the exchange is and what it entails on their part. Still it is interesting to note that, even though it is very important for the two groups to follow a similar calendar so that the students' participation is synchronized and will happen as planned during the agreed upon weeks, what happens in the partners' class does not have to be coordinated between the two groups. It is, however, very important that the partner students participate online according to the agreed upon calendar and meet our students in that shared online space.

What matters most, in our experience, is that teachers agree on the means to make that shared online space–where the French and the American students interact and which Kramsch (2009), borrowing from Homi Bhabha's (2004) concept, calls "the third space"–as reciprocal, rich, dynamic, and interactive as possible.

Over the years, institutional changes have also affected our exchanges. For instance, we have had to adapt to progressive changes in the French educational system, as it aligns itself with the European framework. It has influenced our individual partners' ability to make some pedagogical and curricular choices. Whereas in the past they would usually be able to make *Cultura* the central part of their course, it is now harder to find a partner with such freedom, who could be involved for 7 weeks or more. We now have to make choices regarding what materials we want to include, besides the intercultural questionnaires. Luckily the modularity of *Cultura* makes such variations possible.

Adaptations

Our model has been adapted in languages other than French and for different contexts, with changes in some of the parameters of the original model: the use of L1 or L2 in the forums; the type of documents used for comparison; the role of the teacher in the online forums; and classroom face-to-face discussions.

Besides all the projects described in the following chapters, which will show many different variations, other adaptations have been made: In a French business class,[41] for instance, the questionnaires included other relevant words and phrases such as "globalization," "recession," "a good product," and "a good commercial," and the students compared how different large companies presented themselves on their websites. One Russian exchange[42] focused on family and the role of men and women. In a US/Spain exchange,[43] besides the traditional L1/L2 model (where L1 is used online and only L2 in the classroom), the instructors opened some forums where both groups used the same language (either everybody used English or everybody used Spanish). In one model, English and Arabic speaking students (from Canada and Morocco[44]) enrolled in French immersion programs communicated on the forums entirely in French.

Finally, as can be seen in the following chapters of this book, several faculty members at the University of Hawai'i at Mānoa developed *Cultura*-inspired telecollaborative projects in Chinese, Filipino, Japanese, and Samoan after taking summer workshops at the National Foreign Language Resource Center there in 2008[45] and 2011.[46] They have adapted the original *Cultura* model in very interesting ways: The goal of the Filipino and Samoan projects was to bring together students of a same culture, who live in different places in the world, focusing on issues of identity and how they relate to their different geographical contexts; the Chinese online project was focused on issues of interest to business students in Hawai'i and the United States.

As discussed earlier, when the exchanges have a classroom component, both groups of students have opportunities to discuss the questionnaires and the forums with their own peers and their instructors in their own classrooms. In the original hybrid model, we consider the work done in the classroom essential, because it reinforces the process described earlier and gives students a chance to work within their own group, with their peers. It helps them deal with the online materials, also validating each one's participation and comments. The instructor

---

[41] This exchange was created by Anne Poncet-Montange of Bentley College. http://atc.bentley.edu/courses/resources/clic/jukebox/specialprograms/culturabiz/index.htm

[42] This exchange was created by Lynne deBenedette of Brown University. See http://Cultura.mit.edu/2010-fall-brown-mordovia-state-russia-university-family-men-and-women/

[43] This exchange was created by James Crapotta and Jesus Suarez-Garcia of Barnard College.

[44] This exchange was created by Bette-Joan Traverse of Simon Fraser University, Canada. See http://Cultura.mit.edu/1009-spring-university-of-the-fraser-valleyuniversite-chouaib-doukkali/ and http://Cultura.mit.edu/2010-summer-frasier-valley-canada-chouaib-doukkali-morrocco/

[45] http://nflrc.hawaii.edu/prodev/si08oc/

[46] http://nflrc.hawaii.edu/prodev/si11olc/
See also on YouTube, *Online Cafes: Intercultural Learning Communities*.

does not participate at all in the online discussions, but the online discussions are brought back to the classroom, which allows for further examination of the concepts and feedback. When there is no classroom component, as is the case in some adaptations, the role of the instructor has to be much more visible online, to give feedback on language and provide a model, facilitate the discussion, and give feedback on content.

The "online only" model might become more and more frequent and poses a number of interesting pedagogical challenges. In such an environment, it might be worth exploring ways of creating an online "classroom space," where members of the same cohort could meet and work together. Since an important element of *Cultura* is how one person defines himself or herself in relation to his or her own group, such a space could replace the classroom and give students a sense of their own group by enabling them to recognize what they share with their cohort.

Summary

Online communication tools are not, per se, enough to make meaningful communication happen. They make it possible, but have to be used in a purposeful way to serve well-defined pedagogical goals. They present the instructor with two sets of parallel challenges, which both have to be considered: On the one hand, how to stimulate communication and meaningful exchanges? On the other hand, how to deal with the multiplicity of voices brought back to the classroom? With *Cultura*, we found that the role of the teacher has to change, but is no less central than in the past.

The original *Cultura* model is highly adaptable to different contexts: New modules can be created, new content incorporated. In the future, the project will very likely make use of more and more Web 2.0 tools which will make it even easier to communicate, collaborate, and deal with information (with the ability, in particular, to read, annotate, and organize large amounts of text–written or audio-collaboratively).

Regarding the preferred mode of communication between groups, there are many practical advantages to the written text. It can be processed much faster than audio, because the eye can quickly scan the document, understand how it is organized, and find information. Images can be also annotated and tagged. But one could imagine in the near future being able to easily tag audio documents, which might then be combined into a common pool, and would be easily searchable. It would enable a student to quickly explore audio/video documents posted by others, and respond with their own annotations.

We can also imagine that text clouds, which are already changing the way people read text, might change the way students work with *Cultura*. Since the beginning, we have asked our students to count, circle, organize, and group words by semantic networks. Now automatically generated text clouds might offer an additional way to represent and visualize the answers to the questionnaires. However, even if a cloud makes the relative frequency of use for each term more visible, it does not diminish the need to analyze and try to interpret the data, which is an essential skill we want our students to develop.

But as it becomes easier to access, organize, and exchange information available online, we (the instructors) still have a very important role to play: Help our students deal with and approach the materials. This is why the methodology we developed with *Cultura* is more relevant than ever, for the goal of better intercultural understanding. New technology features will become available, new options will open. It is up to us to keep our goal of intercultural learning in sight, and see how new technologies serve it best.

Conclusion

As mentioned at the beginning of this chapter, *Cultura* is not the only telecollaborative project dedicated to the development of intercultural learning within a language class, but it remains one of the more influential ones that has endured for the many reasons cited above.

Many of those very same reasons are also brought up in the responses to the questionnaires sent out by Dorothy Chun to the users and adapters of *Cultura* (see Chapter 2 of this volume), which highlight in particular *Cultura*'s approach and innovative design ("A great and innovative idea that grips the learners when designed thoughtfully and implemented," writes one. "I have never seen such a good way to make students discover another culture," writes another. "A real eye opener," writes yet another). Respondents also often emphasize the impact of such a project in terms of the students' learning: the high level of motivation it creates; the improvement in terms of students' abilities to observe, abstract, and summarize; the opportunities afforded them for reflecting on both their own and the other culture and for allowing language learners' cultural, regional, and societal backgrounds be part of their learning experience; the ensuing lively class discussions; the focus on content; and the authenticity of exchanges.

Although *Cultura* may have been a pioneering project and may still be looked at as a model, it is clear that we must continue to innovate, to incorporate new tools and ideas so that its appeal will continue to be based upon an increasing array of reasons.

Finally, as indicated in this chapter and confirmed by all of the responses to the questionnaires discussed in Chapter 2, the ultimate success of *Cultura* and similar projects hinges in great part on one crucial factor: finding appropriate partners,[47] namely partners who are completely on board and fully committed to the project and who adhere to the same pedagogical principles, partnerships where the level of participation is equal in both institutions involved and where the place of *Cultura* within both curricula is also similar, that is, where it is not an add-on in one and a full-fledged course in the other.

We are very aware that finding the "ideal"[48] partner is difficult and that many curricular and institutional constraints exist that have a very large impact on the ultimate success or failure of the exchanges. The obstacles are high, indeed, and

---

[47] One of the best sources for finding partners is http://uni-collaboration.eu (based at the University of Leon, Spain).

[48] For us, the ideal partner has been Kathryn English, with whom we worked from 1998 through 2007. An English teacher at the University level in France, she had always been interested and involved in the field of intercultural communication, and we were extremely fortunate to have her as one of our first partners. As she changed institutions, we followed her. Our last partnership (with Ecole Polytechnique in 2006 and 2007) was also "made in heaven" as that Institution is so akin to MIT. In 2008, she partnered with a school in Taiwan and discusses the exchange in Chapter 3 of this volume. We have also worked closely, over many semesters, with Annick Rivens of Université de Lille 3, Marine Ledrast of Université de Brest, and LeAnn Stevens-Larré of ENSEIRB-MATMECA in Bordeaux.

we have faced many ourselves throughout the years.[49] Our task is therefore not an easy one. But, as we face the future, we need to resolve those differences and find a common ground, so that the common space students create online via their exchanges–whether they are written or take the form of photo exchanges or conversations via Skype or other means–suits their goals equally. Indeed, if we want our students to understand and bridge their cultural differences, we have no choice as teachers, but to try and bridge those institutional ones as well. The future of virtual telecollaborative projects such as *Cultura* depends on it.

References

Beauvois, M. H. (1993). E-Talk: Empowering students through electronic discussion in the foreign language classroom. *The Ram's Horn, 7,* 41–47.

Belz, J. (2003). Linguistic perspectives on the development of intercultural competence in telecollaboration. *Language Learning & Technology, 7*(2), 68–117. Retrieved from http://llt.msu.edu/vol7num2/belz/default.html

Bhabha, Homi K. (2004). *The location of culture.* Abingdon, England: Routledge.

Brooks, J., & Brooks, M. (1993). *In search of understanding: The case for constructivist classrooms.* Alexandria, VA: Association for Supervision and Curriculum Development.

Byram, M. (1997). *Teaching and assessing intercultural communicative competence.* Clevedon, England: Multilingual Matters.

Byram, M. (2000). Assessing intercultural competence in language teaching. *Sprogforum, 18,* 8–13. Retrieved from http://inet.dpb.dpu.dk/infodok/sprogforum/Espr18/byram.html

Byram, M., Gribkova, B,. & Starkey, H. (2002). *Developing the intercultural dimension in language teaching—A practical introduction for teachers.* Retrieved from: http://www.coe.int/t/dg4/linguistic/source/guide_dimintercult_en.pdf

Develotte, C. (2006). Journal d'étonnement. Lidil—*Revue de Linguistique et de Didactique des Langues, 34,* 1–12. Retrieved from http://lidil.revues.org/index25.html

Godwin-Jones, R. (1996). Creating language learning materials for the World Wide Web. In M. Warschauer (Ed.), *Telecollaboration in Foreign Language Learning. Proceedings of the Hawai'i Symposium* (pp. 69–82). Honolulu: University of Hawai'i Second Language Teaching and Curriculum Center.

Guth, S., Helm, F., & O'Dowd, R. (2012). *University language classes collaborating online. Report on the integration of telecollaborative networks in European universities.* Retrieved from http://intent-project.eu/sites/default/files/Telecollaboration_report_Final_Oct2012.0.pdf

Hall, E. T. (1959). *The silent language.* New York, NY: Doubleday.

Hall, E. T. (1966). *The hidden dimension.* New York, NY: Doubleday.

---

[49] Sometimes, markedly different calendars forced us to greatly reduce the amount of time we wanted to devote to the project, thus preventing us from going beyond the questionnaires; quite often, *Cultura* was only a portion of the course in the French University, which meant that teachers and students there did not put the same amount of energy or time into the exchange, forcing us again to greatly reduce the amount of time we could devote to the project.

Kern, R. G., Ware, P., & Warschauer, M. (2004). Crossing frontiers: New directions in online pedagogy and research. *Annual Review of Applied Linguistics, 24,* 243–260.

Kinginger, C., & Gourves-Hayward, A. (1997). Cultural awareness: A pilot exchange program of the Ecole Nationale Supérieure de Télécommunications de Bretagne and the University of Maryland School of Business. In A. Howley (Ed.), *Developing cultural competence for tomorrow's global leaders* (pp. 88–98). Huntington, WV: Marshall University.

Kramsch, C. (1993). *Context and culture in language teaching.* Oxford, England: Oxford University Press.

Kramsch, C. (2009). Third culture and language education. In V. Cook (Ed.), *Contemporary applied linguistics* (pp. 233-254). London, England: Continuum. Retrieved from http://lrc.cornell.edu/events/past/2008-2009/papers08/third.pdf

Levy, M. (2007). Culture, culture learning and new technologies: Towards a pedagogical framework. *Language Learning & Technology, 11*(2), 104–127. Retrieved from http://llt.msu.edu/vol11num2/levy/default.html

MLA report (2007): Foreign languages and higher education: New structures for a changed world. Retrieved from http://www.mla.org/flreport/

Müller-Hartmann, A. (2000). The role of tasks in promoting intercultural learning in electronic learning networks. *Language Learning and Technology, 4*(2), 129–147. Retrieved from http://llt.msu.edu/vol4num2/muller/default.html

O'Dowd, R., & Ware, P. (2009). Critical issues in telecollaborative task design. *Computer Assisted Language Learning, 22*(2), 173–188.

Warschauer, M. (1996). Motivational aspects of using computers for writing and communication. In M. Warschauer (Ed.), *Telecollaboration in foreign language learning. Proceedings of the Hawai'i Symposium* (pp. 29–46). Honolulu: University of Hawai'i Second Language Teaching and Curriculum Center.

A Meta-Synthesis of *Cultura*-Based Projects

Dorothy M. Chun
University of California, Santa Barbara

The purpose of this chapter is to present the results of a survey that was sent to 30 instructors who had previously conducted Cultura-inspired online intercultural exchanges. The responses of the 18 respondents (60% return rate) help to answer the following research questions: (1) What were the goals that led to the adoption of the Cultura model and what were the outcomes that the Cultura model might achieve? (2) What were the processes in the implementation of the project that built toward the goals? and (3) What kind of data was gathered in order to determine whether the goals were achieved, and how do the data reflect the types of learning outcomes that were addressed and assessed in the Cultura project? Although the goals and implementation processes varied from project to project, common learning outcomes were increased linguistic and cultural gains, in both skills and attitudes. Respondents also cited the necessity of careful planning and alignment of curricular requirements and commitments. These results can inform the design of future intercultural projects.

Introduction and background

As discussed in the first chapter of this volume, the *Cultura* project was created in 1997 initially as an intercultural exchange between American and French students (see also Furstenberg, Levet, English, & Maillet, 2001; Suárez García & Crapotta, 2006). In the years since, many related projects have been inspired by this compelling model (Bauer, deBenedette, Furstenberg, Levet, & Waryn, 2006; Chun, 2011; Chun & Wade, 2004; Liaw, 2006; Liaw & Bunn-LeMaster, 2010; O'Dowd, 2003, to name but a few). During the summer of 2008, the National Foreign Language Resource Center (NFLRC) at the University of Hawai'i at Mānoa convened a Summer Institute "Online Cafes for Heritage Learners of Filipino, Japanese, Samoan, and Chinese," led by one of the creators of the *Cultura* model. The Institute brought together teams that would be participating in online intercultural exchanges for the four languages. Institute participants collaborated to design their projects, each group with different needs and goals.

In the year that followed, each group implemented its iteration of the exchange, and in October 2009, the NFLRC hosted back-to-back conferences in which the groups reported on their projects. The first conference, "*Cultura*: Web-based Intercultural Exchanges," served as a pre-conference to the larger, second conference, and brought together teachers who had implemented a *Cultura*-like exchange and those who were interested to learn more about the project itself. It was a venue for sharing goals, materials, methodologies, tools, and classroom practices.[1] The second conference, "Language Learning in Computer Mediated Communities (LLCMC)," explored more generally the use of computers as a medium of communication in language learning communities).[2]

Both conferences demonstrated that *Cultura*-based projects were proliferating around the world, suggesting that a meta-synthesis of these projects could be useful both for documenting the variety of adaptations of the model and for helping those interested in developing similar exchanges. We therefore designed an extensive survey, which was sent to everyone who to our knowledge had conducted such a project. This chapter reports on the results of the survey and presents the research questions we sought to answer, the survey questions that were created to answer the questions, analyses of the results (both quantitative and qualitative), and recommendations for future such projects. It is hoped that this survey will help readers to address the pressing issues of how they could adapt the *Cultura* model to their own educational context, what would be possible, which aspects could be modified to meet their needs, and how they could assess student learning outcomes.

Research questions

Based on the underlying realization that in addition to linguistic and communicative competence, L2 learners must develop intercultural competence as well (Byram, 1997), the following research questions were formulated for this survey study and informed the constructs of the survey:

- **Research Question 1:** What were the goals that led to the adoption of the *Cultura* model and what were the outcomes that the *Cultura* model might achieve? In order to answer this question, we desired information about the constructs of learning related goals and outcomes, in particular, goals and outcomes regarding language proficiency, cultural knowledge, and intercultural understanding. *Cultura*-based projects were hypothesized to expand the instructional environment beyond the classroom.

- **Research Question 2:** What were the processes in the implementation of the project that built toward the goals? The sub-questions here are (a) How was the *Cultura* model adapted to local program contexts, and specifically, what types of adaptations or modifications were made in the (1) tasks, (2) modes of exchange, (3) language used, (4) role of the

---

[1] http://nflrc.hawaii.edu/llcmc/Cultura.html
[2] http://nflrc.hawaii.edu/llcmc/index.html

instructor, and (5) integration into the curriculum; and (b) What were the factors that were considered when adopting and implementing the *Cultura* model, in particular, (1) contextual or program factors, including time frame, available technology, instructor background, number of times implemented, and (2) learner factors, including linguistic ability and cultural knowledge or familiarity.

- **Research Question 3:** What kind of data was gathered in order to determine whether the goals were achieved, and how do the data reflect the types of learning outcomes that were addressed and assessed in the *Cultura* project?

Methods of survey study

Conducted during the summer of 2011, the purpose of the survey study was to solicit information on a variety of *Cultura*-based projects around the world. We sought to learn what the goals of the different projects were, how the *Cultura* model was adapted to each context to meet their students' needs, and what types of learning outcomes were found in these projects.

Participants

Participants were identified based on publications stating that the *Cultura* model was used and on the knowledge of the creators of *Cultura*, who kept records and emails of all who had inquired about *Cultura* or had availed themselves of the *Cultura* website and had created their own exchanges. Emails were sent to 29 individuals in the hopes of recruiting them to fill out the study survey. An initial email was sent in July 2011, and follow-up reminder emails were sent again in August and September 2011. The last question of the survey (#30) was "Do you know of any individuals who have implemented a *Cultura*-based/inspired project, so we can contact them for further insights?" Based on these replies, we then sent the survey to one additional individual. Of the total of 30 individuals we contacted, 18 completed the survey (60% return rate). See Table 1 for a list of the respondents.

Table 1. Participant information

ID	program setting	country	L2 taught
1	4-year university	US	Chinese
2	4-year university	Germany	English
3	4-year university	US	Spanish
4	4-year university	France	English
5	4-year university	US	German
6	4-year university (3+2)	Italy	English
7	4-year university	Germany	French
8	4-year university	Taiwan	English
9	high school	US	Samoan
10	2-year community college	American Samoa	Samoan
11	4-year university	US	Spanish

continued...

Table 1. Participant information *(cont.)*

ID	program setting	country	L2 taught
12	4-year university	US	English
13	high school	US	Japanese
14	4-year university	US	French
15	4-year university	Spain	English
16	4-year university	US	English
17	4-year university	Italy	English
18	4-year university	US	Filipino

Survey instrument

Based on the research questions and in consultation with the creators of *Cultura*, a survey instrument was developed to elicit answers to the constructs we had identified. The original survey was pilot tested with several colleagues who had conducted *Cultura*-based projects and was subsequently refined. Table 2 contains lists of the constructs, research questions, and survey questions. See Appendix A for the detailed version of the survey instrument.

Table 2. Research questions and corresponding constructs and survey questions

construct	research question	survey question
consent	--	1. Please indicate whether or not you consent to participate.
context/background	RQ 1	
instructional setting	RQ 1	2. What is your primary work setting?
instructor's background	RQ 1	3. What is your language background?
number of times model used	RQ 1	5. How many times have you implemented a *Cultura*-based project into your course?
course context	RQ 1	6. Please provide your and your partner's institution name as well as the most recent project starting date. 7. In which course did you adapt the *Cultura* model? Please specify the language and the level of the course. 8. Did you implement the *Cultura* project in multiple sections of the course?
students' background	RQ 1	9. What was the students' target-language proficiency in your course? ACTFL or CEFR scale 10. If English was the target language, standardized test used and approximate average score of your students 11. What were your students' cultural experience and exposure?
students' language proficiency	RQ 1	12. Did you feel there was a large gap in L2 proficiency between your students and your partner's students?

motivational factors	RQ 1	4. Why did you choose *Cultura* as a model?
goals and projected outcomes	RQ 1	14. What did you want your students to gain through the *Cultura* project (e.g., language proficiency, cultural awareness, sense of learning community)? 15. What was the relative importance of language learning versus cultural learning in the *Cultura* project?
implementation	RQ 2	
tasks	RQ 2	13. Which features/activities in *Cultura* did you use in your project?
modes of instruction	RQ 2	18. How was the *Cultura* project integrated into existing courses? Please provide information about your and your partner's courses. 19. What modes of interaction were used for the online exchange? 20. What was the language(s) of the online exchange? 21. What types of activities took place face-to-face in class?
timetable	RQ 2	22. How many weeks in total did the exchange last?
teacher involvement	RQ 2	23. To what extent was the teacher (you) present in the online exchange? 24. What role did the teacher (you) take online?
course materials	RQ 2	25. Were there any non-text based materials used in the exchange?
student learning outcomes	RQ 3	16. What were some of the greatest student learning gains you observed through the *Cultura* project? 17. For the learning outcomes described above, what kind of information did you gather to determine the degree to which students were able to perform the outcomes?
evaluation of the project	RQ 3	26. What were your overall impressions of the exchange?
student reactions	RQ 3	27. What were the overall reactions from the students?
challenges and recommendations	RQ 3	28. What were some of the challenges you encountered implementing the *Cultura*-inspired project in your course? 29. Any other comments you wish to share about your *Cultura* project experience?

The survey was comprised of seven main sections. Section 1, "Your background," asked questions about each of the participants, including whether they taught at the high school, community or junior college, or university level, and what their native and second languages were (Questions 2, 3). Section 2, "*Cultura*-inspired projects," inquired about why they had chosen *Cultura* as a model and how many times they had implemented a *Cultura*-inspired project into their course (Questions 4, 5). For the open-ended Question 4 about why *Cultura* was chosen, respondents were able to enter paragraph-length answers. Question 6 asked for their and their partner's institutions names, the most recent starting date, and the number of times in the past they had implemented a *Cultura*-based project.

The third section dealt with the "Program context" and asked for specific information about the course in which the *Cultura* model was adapted (language and level of the course) and whether it was implemented in multiple sections of the course (Questions 8, 9). The students' target language proficiency was then requested, either in terms of the ACTFL or the CEFR scale, or if English was the target language, in terms of the approximate average score on one of the standardized tests for English as a Second/Foreign Language (Questions 9, 10). Further information about the students was solicited, including their cultural experience and exposure, namely what percentage had visited a country in which the target language is spoken and what percentage were heritage language learners (Question 11). In addition, Question 12 asked whether there was a large gap in L2 proficiency between the two partner groups, and respondents could also add a longer explanation of their answer. Finally, Question 13 inquired about which features of *Cultura* were used in the project (e.g., questionnaires, forums, films, newsstand, data, images), and whether other online activities were incorporated into the exchange.

Section 4 of the survey concerned "Student learning outcomes," including expected learning gains, the relative importance of language learning versus cultural learning, and the actual gains observed (Questions 14, 15, 16). Question 17 asked what kind of information was gathered in order to determine the degree to which students were able to perform the outcomes. Questions 14, 16, and 17 were open-ended questions, and there was no limit to the length of the responses.

The fifth section of the survey sought to document the "Implementation of the *Cultura* model." Question 18 asked how the *Cultura* project was integrated into existing courses (online only, face-to-face only, online+face-to-face). Question 19 inquired about what modes of interaction were used for the online exchange (audio-only chat, text-based chat, voice recordings, text-based forums, video conferencing, other). Question 20 concerned what the language(s) of the online exchange were, specifically, whether (a) students sent posts in L1 and received replies in L2; (b) sent and received posts in L2; (c) sent and received posts in L1; or (d) a combination of sending and receiving posts in both L1 and L2. Question 21 asked about what types of activities took place face-to-face in the classroom (discussion of online questionnaires; discussion of online forums; discussion of films, newsstand, images, data; student presentations). Question 22 asked how many weeks the exchange lasted, and Question 25 whether any non-text based materials were used in the exchange. Furthermore, the extent to which the teacher participated in the exchange (on a scale from "not at all" to "a lot") and the role that the teacher took online, for example, discussion facilitator, model provider, provider of language feedback or content feedback, were questioned (Questions 23, 24).

Section 6 dealt with the "Evaluation of the *Cultura*-inspired project," asking participants for their overall impressions of the exchange, the overall reactions from the students, and for an account of the challenges encountered in implementing the *Cultura*-inspired project (Questions 26, 27, 28). For each of these questions, participants were given a textbox in which to write their comments and narratives.

The final section (7) inquired about further comments that participants wished to share about their experience (Question 29), also providing the opportunity for paragraph-length responses.

Procedures: Tallying of answers to questions and coding of open-ended responses

The number of answers to each factual question was tallied; they are shown in tables and graphs in the following Results section. The answers to the open-ended questions were compiled and analyzed by the author and a second rater for major themes and categories. A coding sheet was devised, listing and categorizing the types of answers that were given (see Appendix B). The two coders independently coded a quarter of the answers to each of the open-ended questions, compared their results, which showed an inter-rater agreement of 80%, discussed and resolved the differences, then agreed that the rest of the answers would be coded by only one coder.

Results

Research Question 1

Instructional setting and students' background

The majority (14) of the 18 respondents taught at 4-year universities; 3 of the 18 taught in high school; and 1 of the 18 taught in a 2-year community college. The L2s being taught were English (7 of 18), French (2), Spanish (2), Japanese (2), Samoan (2), Chinese (1), Filipino (1), and German (1).

Table 3. Program setting and L2 taught

program setting	no. (%)	L2 taught	no. (%)
4-year university	14 (77.8%)	English	7 (39%)
		French	2 (11%)
		Spanish	2 (11%)
		Chinese	1 (5.6%)
		Filipino	1 (5.6%)
		German	1 (5.6%)
high school	3 (16.6%)	Japanese	2 (11%)
		Samoan	1 (5.6%)
2-year community college	1 (5.6%)	Samoan	1 (5.6%)

Most of the respondents had implemented a *Cultura*-inspired project multiple times (see Figure 1).

The students' background varied from novice low to advanced mid on the ACTFL scale, and from A2 to C1 on the CEFR scale. For English learners, their proficiency was estimated based on six different tests (e.g., Cambridge, STEP, TOEFL, TOEIC) and ranged from B1-C1 on the CEFR scale. According to the instructors, six groups of students were in "intermediate" (second-year university level) and nine groups were in "advanced" (third- and fourth-year university level) courses. As the graphs in Figures 2 and 3 show, there were very few "novice" or A2 learners.

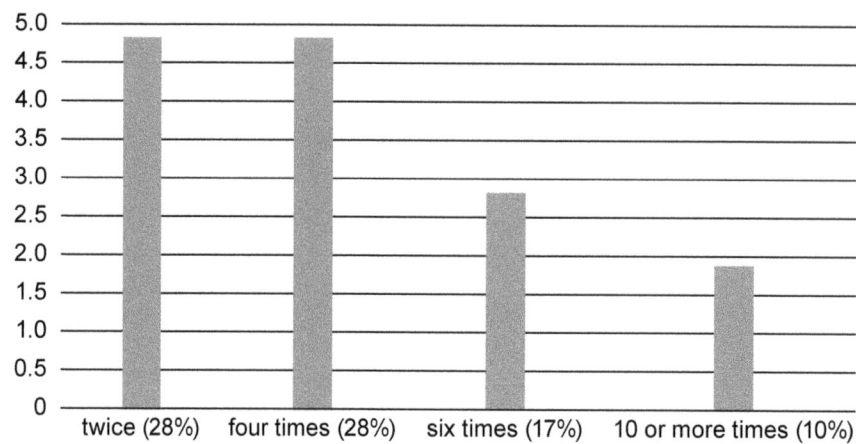

Figure 1. Number of iterations of *Cultura*-inspired projects

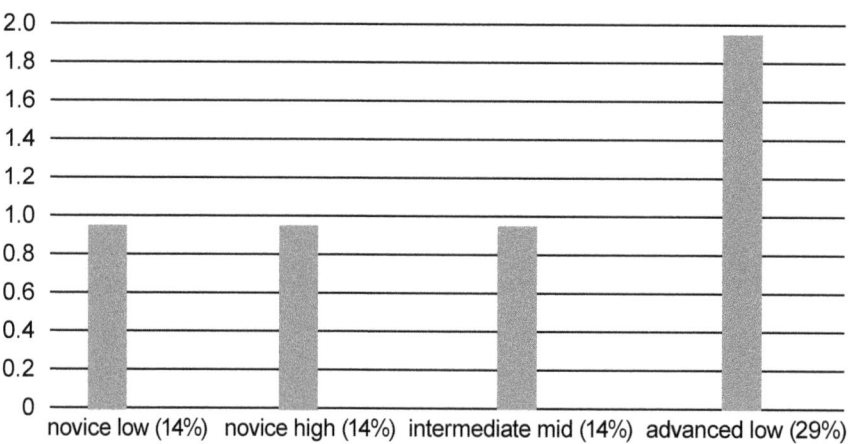

Figure 2. Students' proficiency levels based on ACTFL scales

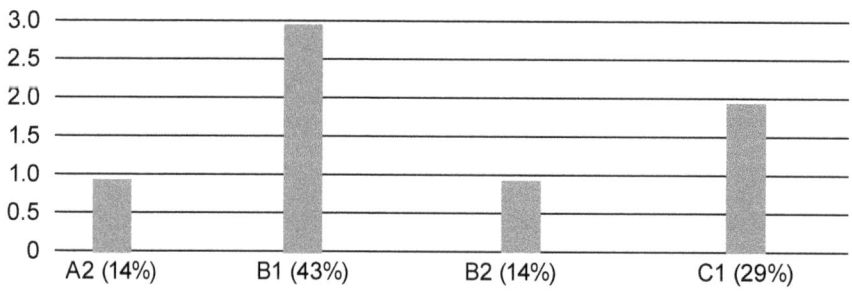

Figure 3. Students' proficiency levels based on CEFR scales

In terms of the students' prior cultural experiences and exposure to the L2 and C2, respondents were asked to indicate the percentage of their students who had visited a country where the L2 is spoken (see Figure 4) and for the percentage of their students who had a heritage background in the L2 (see Figure 5).

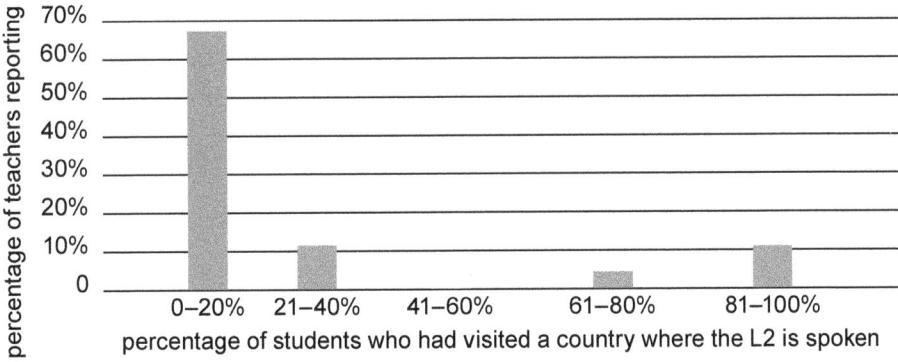

Figure 4. Students' background information: Visit to a country where L2 is spoken

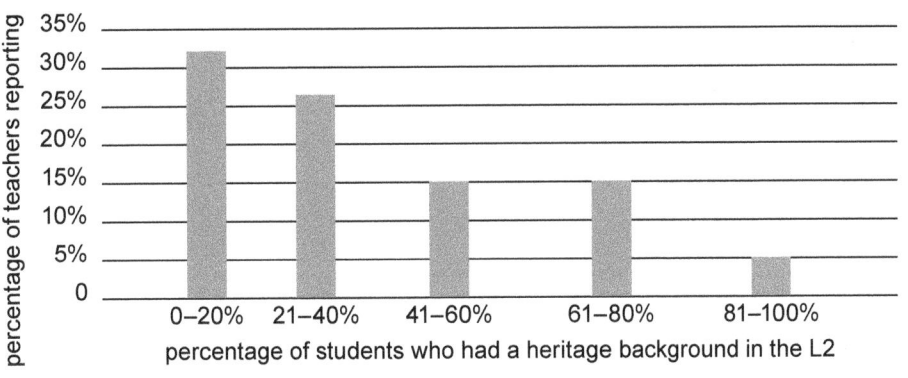

Figure 5. Students' background information: Heritage background

When asked whether they felt there was a large gap in L2 proficiency between their students and their partner's students, half of the respondents (9 of 18) said "yes" and the other half said "no" (8 of 18) or "not sure" (1 of 18). Of the 9 who believed there was a gap in L2 proficiency between the partner classes, 5 of them felt that the Americans' command of the L2 (German, Italian, Japanese, Samoan, Spanish) was weaker than their counterparts' command of the L2 (which was English). Other respondents mentioned the wide range of students' proficiencies, that heritage students can differ from typical foreign language students, and that their partner class was not a language class but a course on intercultural competence for business.

Reasons for choosing *Cultura* as a model

In conjunction with the course context and students' background, respondents were asked why they chose *Cultura* as a model (Question 4) and what they wanted their students to gain through the *Cultura* project, for example, language proficiency, cultural awareness, sense of learning community (Question 14). They were also asked what the relative importance of language learning versus cultural learning was in their *Cultura* project (Question 15).

Responses to these open-ended questions were coded based on the categories that emerged (see Appendix C) and revealed two types of motivation, "external" and "internal," for choosing the *Cultura* model as an instructional approach. For "external" motivation, the most common answer was the opportunity to learn and participate in a project, either by virtue of having attended a workshop or having been invited by a colleague to participate. With regard to "internal" motivation, the most common answers were (a) having the belief or interest in such a project, (b) bringing innovation to their existing language program, and (c) providing their students with additional intercultural learning opportunities. Many respondents' answers included both types of motivation, hence the arrows in Figure 6 suggesting that the different types influenced each other.

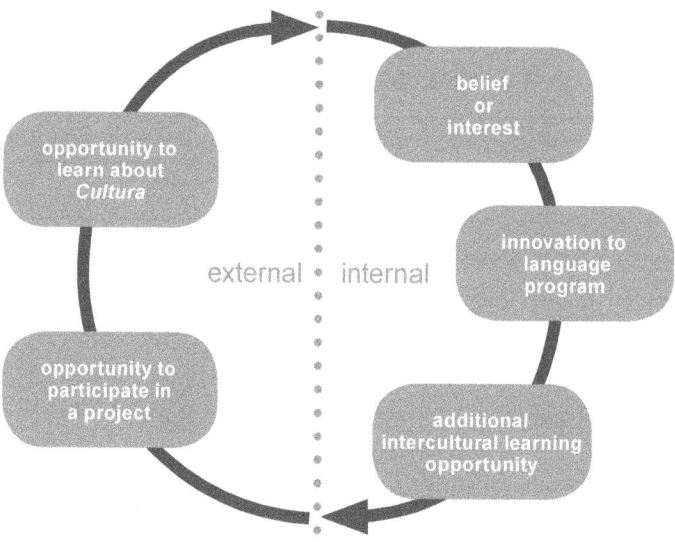

Figure 6. Motivation for choosing *Cultura* as an instructional model

Expected learning outcomes

With regard to the expected learning outcomes (what the respondents wanted their students to gain from the experience), answers fell into three categories: (a) language-related outcomes, (b) culture-related outcomes, and (c) miscellaneous outcomes. See Appendix C for the themes that emerged from the open-ended answers and Table 4 for the coding counts. Some respondents provided multiple answers as depicted in Figure 7.

Table 4. Expected learning outcomes

type of outcome	sub-type	coding count
	skill	15
language	knowledge	0
	attitudes	2

culture	skill	7
	knowledge	6
	attitudes	13
other	sense of learning community	3

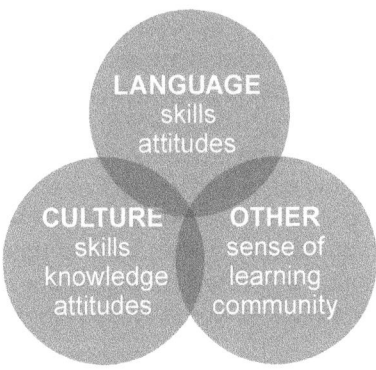

Figure 7. Expected learning outcomes

In response to the question of the relative importance of language learning versus cultural learning in the *Cultura* project, 5.6% felt that language learning was more important than cultural learning; 61.1% believed that cultural learning was more important than language learning; and 33.3% felt that language and cultural learning were equally important (see Figure 8).

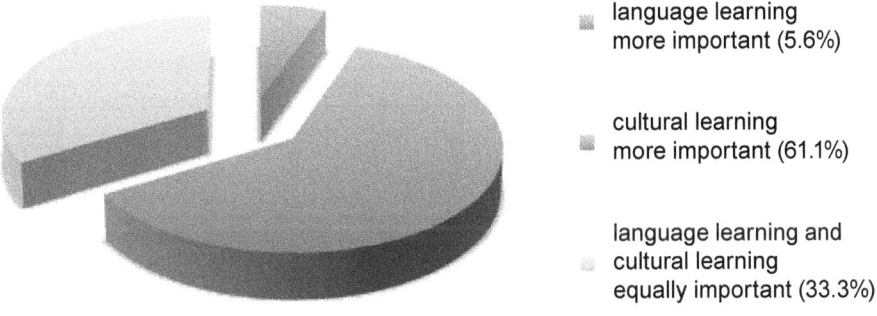

Figure 8. Relative importance of language vs. cultural learning in *Cultura* project

Summary of results for Research Question 1

Research Question 1 was "What were the goals that led to the adoption of the *Cultura* model and what were the outcomes that the *Cultura* model might achieve?" In terms of the participants, most of the survey respondents taught in 4-year universities, almost half of them taught English, and most of the students were intermediate or advanced L2 learners. About half of the respondents felt that there was a big gap in the proficiencies of their and their partners' students.

In answering open-ended questions about the goals and outcomes, respondents revealed both external and internal motivations for choosing *Cultura* as an instructional model. The most common external motivation was that they had an opportunity to participate in a *Cultura*-inspired project, and the most common internal motivations were that they believed in and were interested in such a model, stating that it provided an additional intercultural learning opportunity for their students. Specifically, they expected that their students' language skills of reading, writing, communicating, and discussing would improve, as would their confidence and motivation for communicating in the L2. Furthermore, they expected that their students' cultural knowledge and skills of analysis, abstraction, reflection, exploration, sharing, and critical identification of cultural similarities and differences would improve. The great majority of respondents hoped for or expected an improvement in their students' awareness and openness to another culture and their willingness to express themselves about these issues.

Research Question 2

Implementation of the *Cultura*-inspired project: Activities, modes of interaction, and language used

Unlike the original use of *Cultura* at MIT as the sole basis for an intermediate French course, most *Cultura*-inspired projects incorporate online exchanges as one of the activities of the course and sometimes as an extracurricular or optional activity (see Table 5 and Figure 9).

Table 5. Role of *Cultura* in respondents' courses

	main course activity	one of course activities	extracurricular or optional activity
your course	5 (27.8%)	9 (50.0%)	4 (22.2%)
partner 1's course	0 (0.0%)	10 (58.8%)	7 (41.2%)
partner 2's course	1 (16.7%)	3 (50.0%)	2 (33.3%)

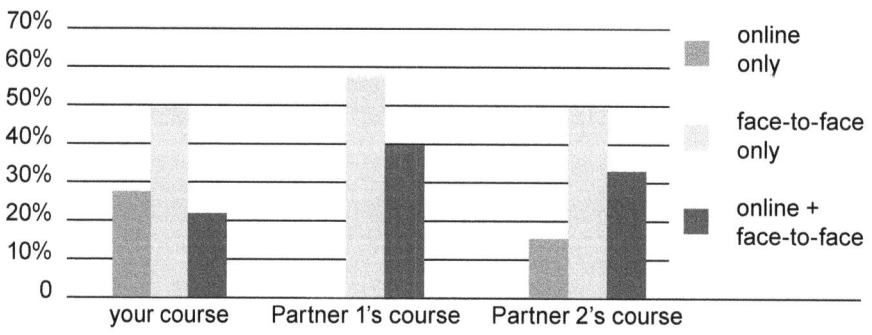

Figure 9. Respondents' answers regarding role of *Cultura* in their course

As seen in the graph in Figure 10, the most commonly used online activities were questionnaires (94.4%) and forums (88.9%). In addition, images were included in the activities in 55.6% of the projects; and in 22.2% of the projects, films, newsstand, data, and videoconferences were used.

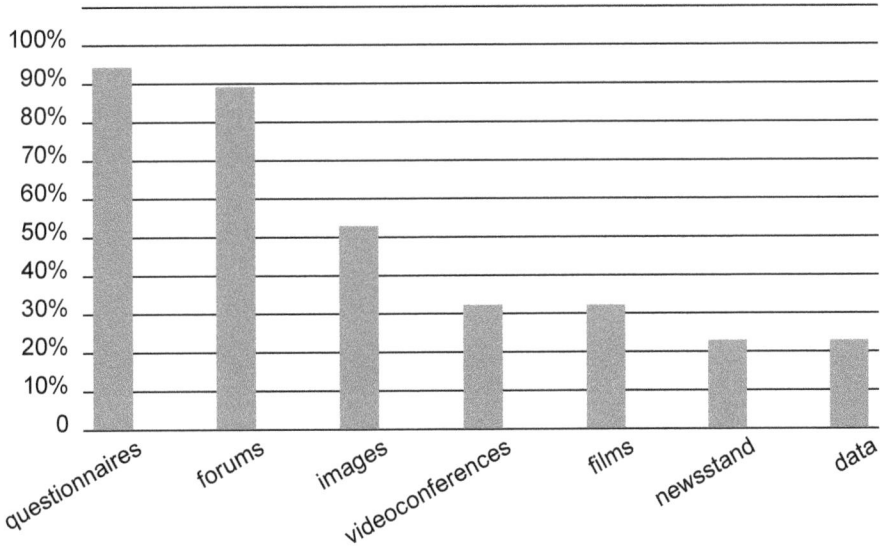

Figure 10. Features/activities used in *Cultura*-inspired projects

In the online exchanges, text-based forums (88.9%) and video-chats (55.6%) were the most commonly used modes of interaction (see Figure 11).

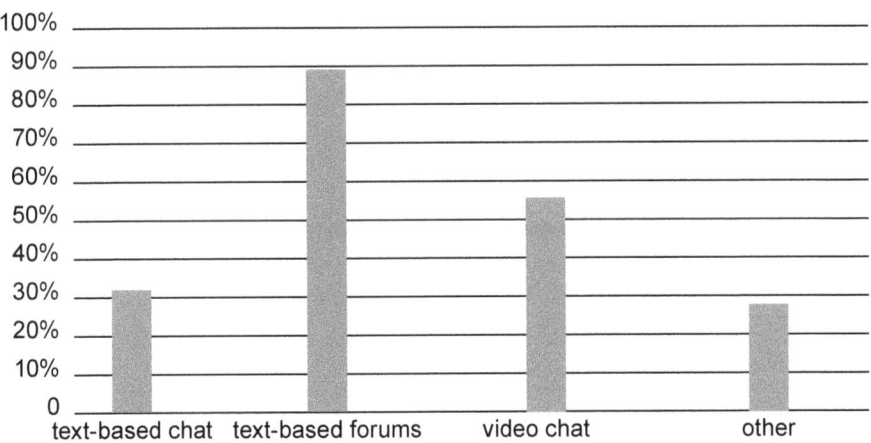

Figure 11. Modes of interaction

As for the language used in the online exchanges, in over half of the projects, a combination of L1 and L2 was used. Students sent and received postings and spoke in both L1 and L2 (see Figure 12).

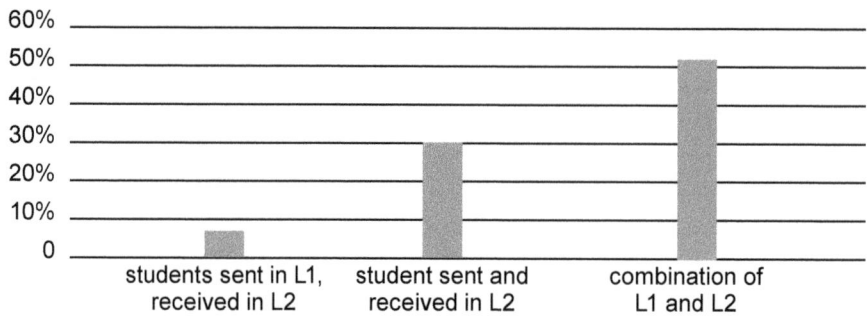

Figure 12. Language used in interactions

Implementation: Modes of instruction

Cultura can be implemented in a variety of ways, depending on the needs and levels of the students and the goals of the project. Table 6 and Figure 13 show the breakdown of the projects reported on in this chapter, with nearly half of the projects employing both online and face-to-face interactions among the participants.

Table 6. Modes of instruction of respondents' courses

	online only	face-to-face only	online+face-to-face
your course	22.2% (4)	33.3% (6)	44.4% (8)
partner 1's course	17.6% (3)	47.1% (8)	35.3% (6)
partner 2's course	33.3% (2)	00.0% (0)	66.7% (4)

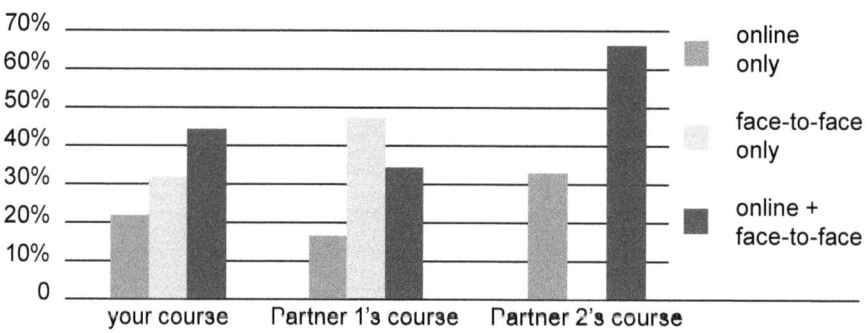

Figure 13. Modes of instruction of respondents' courses

During the face-to-face class meetings, a variety of *Cultura*-related activities took place, as shown in Figure 14.

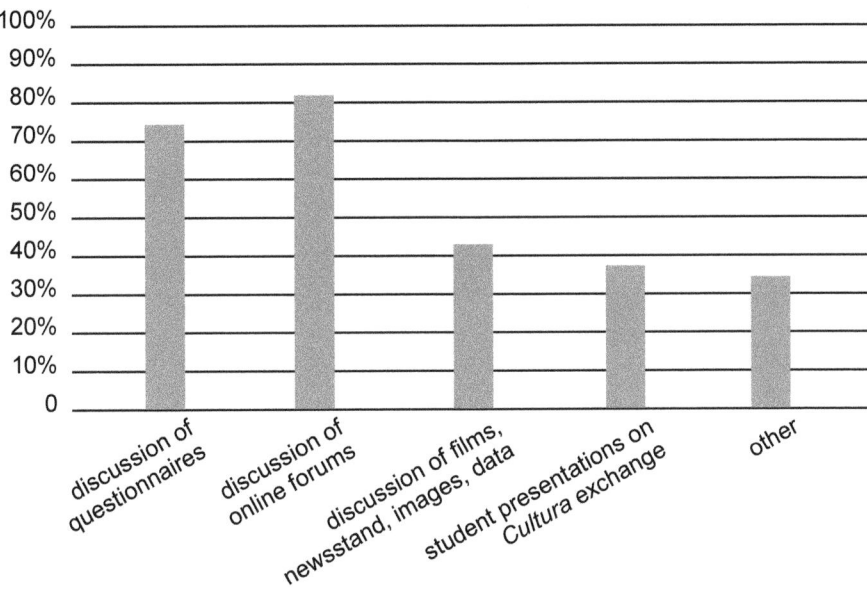

Figure 14. Types of activities in the face-to-face classrooms

Implementation: Teacher involvement

Two questions asked about the role of the teacher in the online exchanges. Figure 15 shows to what extent the teacher was present in the discussion forums and other online activities.

- not at all (44.4%)
- a little (16.7%)
- somewhat (33.3%)
- a lot (5.6%)

Figure 15. Extent of teacher involvement in online activities

Respondents were also asked to indicate which role they played online, and this is presented in Figure 16.

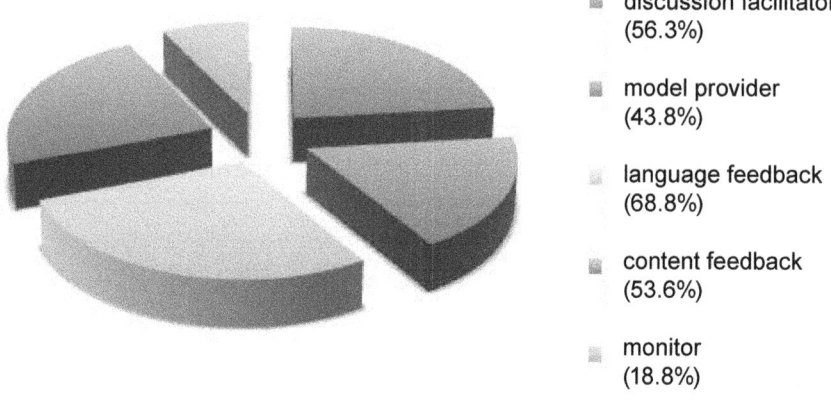

Figure 16. Percentages of different roles of the teacher in online activities

Implementation: Timetable and course materials

The 18 exchanges that are reported on in this chapter ranged in length from 3 to 24 weeks. Projects that were conducted for 3–7 weeks are classified as "short," those that lasted 8–12 weeks are "medium" and anything over 12 weeks is considered "long" (see Figure 17).

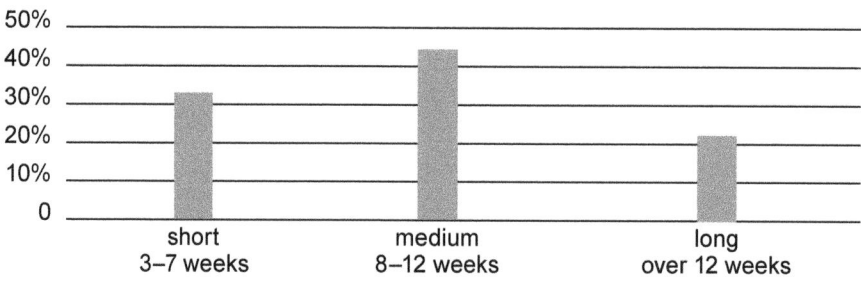

Figure 17. Length of the exchange of the *Cultura*-inspired projects

Respondents were also asked whether any non-text based materials were used in the exchange, and 77.8% replied "yes" while the remaining 22.2% replied "no." In Table 7 is a list of the different media that were used.

Table 7. Different media used in *Cultura* exchanges

media used	reason why	number of responses
images	provide clearer picture, interesting	3
photos	more personal connection, introduce students and environs to each other	3
game	body language	1
student PPT files		1
videos	cultivate interest, show local towns, on-campus activities, subliminal message	6

art, creative projects	stimulate conversations	1

Summary of findings for Research Question 2

The second research question sought to document how the *Cultura* model was implemented across the different projects. The results indicated that there was great variability, but that most of the *Cultura*-inspired projects were only part of the language curriculum and in some cases, they were extracurricular or optional activities. Questionnaires and forums were the two most popular activities in the exchanges, and text-based chat, text-based forums, and video chats were the most widely used modes of interaction. The great majority of projects used a combination of online activities with partners and face-to-face discussions in the classroom. Most projects also used a combination of sending and receiving texts or chats in both L1 and L2. For the most part, teachers' participation in the online activities was minimal, but when they did participate, they played the role of discussion facilitator, model provider, feedback provider with regard to both language and content, and monitor of both participation and content (in order to identify issues or topics to be discussed in the face-to-face classroom sessions). The projects varied greatly in terms of length of the exchange, ranging from 3 to 24 weeks, and many of the projects incorporated images, photos and videos into their online activities, primarily to cultivate interest and provide more personalized input.

Research Question 3

The third research question sought to determine what kind of data was gathered by the respondents in order to assess whether the original goals were achieved. One survey question asked whether the data that were collected reflected the types of learning outcomes that were addressed in the *Cultura*-inspired projects.

At the end of the survey, four open-ended questions were asked about instructors' overall impressions, general student reactions, challenges encountered, and additional comments.

Student learning gains

Survey question 16 asked about the "greatest student learning gains" that were observed during the *Cultura*-inspired project. Answers to this open-ended question were coded using the same codes developed for the sub-question 14 for RQ1 ("What did you want your students to gain through the *Cultura* project?"). Tabulations of the stated student learning gains are seen in Table 8.

Table 8. Learning gains reported

type of learning gains	sub-type	no. of responses
language	skill	5
	knowledge	1
	attitudes	7
culture	skill	5
	knowledge	5
	attitudes	6
other	sense of learning community	2

In contrast to the answers to Question 14 about the desired learning outcomes, which focused more on cultural rather than linguistic gains, answers to Question 16 about actual learning outcomes revealed that there were almost as many responses citing linguistic gains as cultural gains. In addition, teachers mentioned the affective gains, that is, students' attitudes, both linguistic and cultural, as often as the gains in skills.

Data gathered in order to determine learning outcomes

Question 17 was "For the learning outcomes described above, what kind of information did you gather to determine the degree to which students were able to perform the outcomes?" Table 9 reflects a variety of data types that were collected in the online exchanges and in the classroom and used to assess learning.

Table 9. Types of data gathered to assess learning outcomes

tools/data types	number of responses
online postings in questionnaires	3
online postings in forums	6
online chats	1
video recording of online communication	2
videoconferences	1
wikis, peer correction	1
blog exchanges	1
learner diaries, worksheets, essays	6
class presentations, discussions	4
reflective reports, self-assessment	4
post-project survey, interviews	5

Evaluation of the project by teachers and students

Question 26 was open-ended, asking about the teachers' "overall impressions of the exchange." Similarly, Question 27 asked about the "overall reactions from the students." For both questions, a coding system was developed to analyze these open-ended responses (see Appendix D). We first coded for whether the judgments made by the teachers and students were positive (O) or negative (X). We then placed them into categories with regard to different aspects of the exchanges that respondents addressed (see Appendix E).

In general, with regard to the teachers' impressions, there were more positive (10) than negative (2) comments, with several (3) of mixed comments and several (4) comments that were neutral. Positive comments included,

> Good and enjoyable to students and me as an instructor.
>
> It was very successful.
>
> It was positive and motivating for most of the students.
>
> Very useful – fun – stimulating.

One respondent expressed mixed impressions: "In principle it was a good idea, but in practice, the exchange faltered because of minimal participation by the [partner] students." Another respondent made a neutral comment: "It's a new way of teaching/learning; an extension to intercultural exchange."

In addition to general, overall impressions, teachers made specific evaluative comments, summarized in Table 10.

Table 10. Narrative comments about overall impressions of project

code #	category	success	no. of responses
a	instructional alignment and integration	O	2
		X	3
b	language learning	O	1
		X	2
c	culture learning	O	5
		X	0
e	management/logistics	O	0
		X	1
f	technology	O	0
		X	1
g	student motivation/interest/needs	O	0
		X	3
h	student participation/responsiveness	O	0
		X	1
I	activities	O	0
		X	1

note: O=positive; X=negative

Category #a, instructional alignment, and integration and category #c, culture learning, received the most specific comments (each had 5). There were 2 positive and 3 negative comments about instructional alignment and integration and 5 positive comments about culture learning.

Comments about category #a included,

> The students didn't take the course very seriously because it was optional...

On the positive side, for category #c, culture learning, the following comments were made:

> It worked well for my goals and served as the focus for content of my course, an advanced level culture course.

> I have never seen such a good way to make students discover another culture and to encourage them to learn more vocabulary.

Respondents' noted about category #e, management and logistics, the importance of planning, organization, communication and coordination,

> The organization and coordination is really the biggest issue.

> Exchanges usually go well, however careful planning and close communications between/among instructors are important factors to the success of the project.

Comments in category #g about student motivation included a positive result and a recommendation about the need to demonstrate the relevance of these cultural exchanges:

> …the enthusiasm encountered during these exchanges and the fact that each year more students want to be involved in them are evidence enough for us that the exchanges are generally positive for the students.

> …very worthwhile but students need convincing that this is all relevant for "language learning."

Note that these are suggestions of the instructors within the *Cultura*-based exchanges. One of the instructors who had conducted multiple projects had this to say about category #l, activities, in the iteration of the exchange that her questionnaire answers were based on:

> Having experimented with several different models over the years and with many different exchanges, I feel that several aspects of the *Cultura* model benefitted this iteration. First and foremost are the questionnaires which are so easy to complete and yet provide such hard-core evidence of similarities and differences and opportunities for interesting discussions. The questionnaires also help students understand that they are learning language even if they are writing in their own language, i.e., by reading what their peers write in L2 and say in L2 in Skype. Finally, we have used the questionnaires in numerous exchanges and created archives of the results which provide additional opportunities for reflection, particularly when the number of students is limited.

Question 27 asked for overall reactions from/of the students, and in general, students were thought to have had positive impressions of the exchanges (11), with only 3 mentions of mixed reactions, and 2 neutral reactions. The only negative comment was "[Students] were surprised at some of the very dogmatic and intolerant remarks of some of their partner students."

Positive comments about students' overall reactions included the following:

> They really enjoyed this kind of learning through virtual communities.

> The students loved connecting with their peers. They were more interested in just learning about each other and talking about random subjects.

> Most of them were enthusiastic about the project and wanted to keep in touch with the students abroad.

> Overwhelmingly positive on all aspects…

> They were very happy and enthusiastic.

> Students welcome the project and since the project has become an integral part of the course, in-coming students would anticipate their involvement in the intercultural exchanges and even start their preparation before the semester starts.

Table 11 summarizes the teachers' specific reports of their students' reactions.

Table 11. Respondents' reports of students' reactions

code #	category	success	no. of responses
a	instructional alignment and integration	O	1
a	instructional alignment and integration	X	1
b	language learning	O	3
b	language learning	X	0
c	culture learning	O	1
c	culture learning	X	0
d	learning community	O	3
d	learning community	X	0
f	technology	O	0
f	technology	X	1
g	student motivation/interest/needs	O	10
g	student motivation/interest/needs	X	1
h	student participation/responsiveness	O	0
h	student participation/responsiveness	X	2
m	attitudes toward the model	O	1
m	attitudes toward the model	X	1

note: O=positive; X=negative

Challenges, recommendations and other comments

The final two open-ended questions asked about the challenges that were encountered during implementation of the *Cultura*-inspired projects (Question 28) and for any additional comments respondents wished to share about their *Cultura* project experience (Question 29). The same coding system developed for Questions 26 and 27 was used for these last two questions. Responses to Question 28 regarding challenges encountered listed a number of different negative, unsuccessful or less than successful experiences.

Table 12 shows a tabulation of the number of times negative comments were made.

Table 12. Challenges encountered during implementation of projects

code #	category	no. of success=X responses
a	instructional alignment and integration	14
b	language learning	1
c	culture learning	1
e	management/logistics	22
f	technology	4
g	student motivation/interest/needs	5
h	student participation/responsiveness	3
k	partnering	1
l	activities	1
m	attitudes towards the model	1

Typical comments about category #a, instructional alignment and integration, included,

> [Challenges included] integrating the activity in the existing curriculum.

> The German students were not required to participate in the exchange. The two university cultures also differed in that in the U.S. students have many more assignments and exams; in Germany, assignments are not always mandatory.

> Commitment from both programs to be on task/time was difficult…

> The aims of my partner were different and he has a different pedagogical approach;… he actually uses the exchange as a extra-activity while it is the main part of my course.

> The other issue which is hard to overcome on an institutional level in both countries is convincing colleagues and 'bosses' that even if students are using L1 to a large degree, they are still learning L2 and, more importantly, learning about L2 and how it is used in context.

Many difficulties were described in category #e, management/logistics, including the following representative comments:

> [Challenges were] timeframe—mostly the different starting and ending time of semesters between China and U.S. Besides, there is 6 hour difference.

> It's easier to just manage a partnership between two sites, then to have 3 cohort sites meet up in an online environment.

> My biggest concern was my inability to spend the amount of time needed to make it work well.

In terms of challenges with categories #g, student motivation, and #h, student participation/responsiveness, the following comments are indicative of why student motivation and responsiveness waned:

> …one site was not as active as the other two, hence the uneven exchange. I believe that was one reason why some members of the other 2 cohort sites start to lose interest.

> The level of student participation depended on the level of curriculum integration the project had.

In contrast to the answers to Question 28, the responses to Question 29 requesting any other comments about the *Cultura* project experience were predominantly positive comments (10) and recommendations for future projects (11). There were only 3 negative comments, which expressed concerns about

- the difficulty in finding partner classes
- the binary nature of Cultura type exchanges and privileging the 'native speaker' as optimal interlocutor"
- the observation that although higher education in Italy is inexpensive and more or less accessible to all, the Italian students in the exchange "are being exposed to only a small portion of the U.S. population, i.e., those lucky or wealthy enough to attend college/university"

Table 13 shows a tabulation of the number of times suggestions and recommendations were made as to how *Cultura*-inspired projects might be improved.

Table 13. Recommendations by respondents for improving projects

code #	categories	no. of recommendation responses
a	instructional alignment and integration	3
b	language learning	1
e	management/logistics	1
f	technology	1
g	student motivation/interest/needs	1
k	partnering	1
l	activities	2
o	financial help to meet partner	1

Examples of positive comments included,

> It has provided an inspiration for many of my activities, and I have often used the questionnaire results and materials with students who are not doing the exchange.

> I wish all teachers could experience such a programme!

> It was great to work with such a supportive partner.

> I think *Cultura* is an excellent model that should be implemented all across higher education (and not only!)

In terms of the management/logistics of such exchanges, one of the respondents commented,

> [Next time we will] implement a 2-site project. I think this would be a more manageable partnership [than the 3 cohort sites this time]

Summary of findings for Research Question 3

The third research question was "What kind of data was gathered in order to determine whether the goals were achieved, and how do the data reflect the types of learning outcomes that were addressed and assessed in the *Cultura* project?" A wide variety of data was gathered, both online and offline. Online data produced during the exchanges included postings in questionnaires, forums, text chats, wikis, blogs, and videoconferences and video recordings of online communication. Offline data included class presentations and discussions, learner diaries, worksheets, essays, reflective reports, self-assessments, and post-project surveys and interviews.

The above data helped the respondents assess the students' learning gains, and respondents cited almost as many gains in linguistic skills, knowledge, and attitudes as gains in cultural skills, knowledge, and attitudes.

In addition, responses to open-ended questions revealed overall teacher and student satisfaction and enthusiasm for the *Cultura*-inspired projects as well as a number of challenges and recommendations for future projects. The most commonly mentioned challenges involved instructional alignment between partner classes, logistics and management of the exchange, and integration into the respective courses, all of which in turn had direct effects on student motivation and participation. Further specifics of the challenges and recommendations are presented below in the Discussion section.

Discussion

The findings for each of the research questions were summarized at the end of each of the subsections above. This section will integrate the results across the research questions and will provide representative comments from the respondents that suggest how to improve upon their generally favorable experiences.

Survey findings for the first research question about the goals that led instructors to adopt the *Cultura* model and the desired learning outcomes revealed both external motivations, such as the opportunity to participate in a *Cultura*-based project, and internal motivations, such as the desire to provide their students with an intercultural learning opportunity. Specific internal motivations included the expectation that such an intercultural exchange would help students improve both their linguistic skills (reading, writing, communicating) and their cultural knowledge, awareness, and openness, along with skills of analysis, reflection, abstraction, and exploration. Although cultural learning was deemed to have a relatively higher priority than language learning, the findings for the third research question suggested that the *Cultura*-inspired projects met the instructors' initial goals and in fact enjoyed almost as many linguistic gains as cultural gains.

Respondents commented in the open-ended question about their overall impressions:

> I really embrace this model as a good tool for learning language and culture.

> [It] would have maximized the potential of the online activity if this was the main vehicle for teaching and improving language proficiency.

One respondent noted that students felt the project was "fun" and provided "more free and authentic language." Another stated that students "all felt they'd improved their confidence and fluency and learnt both about themselves and about others." In contrast, although one respondent deemed the exchange to be very worthwhile, it was felt that "students need convincing that this is all relevant for 'language learning.'"

The great majority of the respondents taught in 4-year universities and conducted the exchanges with intermediate to advanced second language students. One respondent noted that the exchange worked very well, serving as the focus for content of an advanced level culture course. Only one of the 18 respondents, a high school teacher whose students' L2 level was Novice High on the ACTFL scale, indicated that they would do a future exchange with more advanced students:

> It was a valuable experience, but would have gone better if the students were at a higher level.

Most of the respondents had had multiple previous experiences using a *Cultura*-inspired model, so the findings of this study reflect the opinions and recommendations of this select group of experienced instructors. Despite the fact that eight different L2s are represented, one common observation was that there was a large gap in L2 proficiency between the two partner classes; it was primarily the case that American students' L2 proficiency was much lower than their partners' L2 English proficiency. This reflects a common reality that studying foreign languages in the US lags greatly behind foreign language learning in other parts of the world, such as Europe and Asia.

With regard to prior cultural experience and exposure, findings for the first research question indicated that the majority of the students were not heritage learners, nor had they visited a country where the L2 was spoken. This limited prior exposure may explain why the results for the third research question were overwhelmingly positive when it came to the success of culture learning.

Survey findings for the second research question revealed great variability in the kinds of tools, media, and activities that were used in the online exchanges and in the face-to-face classrooms. This richness allowed for collection of multiple kinds of data that could be used to assess whether the goals of the projects were reached.

Specific suggestions from students with regard to the activities in the exchange include the following:

> My students... suggested one-on-one email exchanges rather than whole group forums. They also suggested video chats (e.g., via Skype) rather than just text chats.

> Some students wanted more time to interact with the other cohorts and have more control in topics discussed.

> They don't always have the feeling they learn something; they need some follow-up.

Instructors also had recommendations for improving activities in the exchanges:

> Overall, I think the exchange could've used more in-depth discussions. I think more in-depth face-to-face classroom discussions with instructors would have really created more meaningful online discussions with other cohort sites.

> The compare and contrast tasks should have been facilitated and supported by the instructors, since they appear to be difficult for the students.

Answers to the open-ended questions at the end of the survey, in fact, supported the overall success of most of the projects, with some strongly recurring themes: (a) There needs to be close alignment of instructor/course/curriculum goals, requiring careful planning and communication, for example, whether the tasks and activities are mandatory for both/all partner classes, and level of commitment of both teachers and students, as this has direct consequences on learner motivation and participation; (b) A certain amount of teacher involvement is necessary, for example, follow-up in the face-to-face classrooms for more in-depth discussions, organization and coordination of each aspect of the exchange; (c) The need to convince students, colleagues, and administrators alike of the benefits of *Cultura*-like projects; and (d) The flexibility to choose appropriate activities and tools/modes of interaction for the particular partners in an exchange, including seeking and following recommendations from students.

Two representative responses first expressed enthusiasm for the project and also contained recommendations for ensuring success:

I think this is a fantastic project and a very worthwhile experience, but it is so vital to make sure the partner is completely on board and fully committed to the project, and sometimes one only finds that out once the project is underway.

My partners and I have truly enjoyed the implementation of our *Cultura* project. We have observed the positive effects of the project on our students and learned to gradually integrate the feedback and creative ideas from our students to make the project even more interesting and meaningful to them.

Recommendations for future *Cultura*-inspired projects and conclusions

Based on the results of the extensive survey and the comprehensive responses of 18 instructors who completed the survey, it is clear that *Cultura*-inspired projects can successfully provide L2 learners with very rich opportunities for both linguistic and cultural experiences. Learners' confidence is increased, their fluency is improved, and they thoroughly enjoy learning about both themselves and about others. However, upon careful analysis of the survey data, it is also necessary to be fully aware of the caveats of this generally successful model and the potential for unanticipated occurrences that could hinder success. The follow recommendations are offered:

In setting goals for an online cultural exchange, be realistic both about the goals and about what is achievable with your specific learners and their abilities/proficiency. As one respondent commented, "I wish I was able to do this again, maybe with a simpler set of goals and activities. I would also do it with higher level students." It appears that exchanges of this type are most successful with advanced and intermediate L2 learner but challenging for beginning or novice learners.

Planning, planning, planning. This is certainly applicable to almost every pedagogical endeavor, but perhaps even more important in an online exchange where there not only are two or more classes involved but they are physically distant as well. Of particular importance are,

- Discussing and agreeing upon goals, both with your partner teacher(s) and with your own students. Students who are used to L2-only classrooms may not understand the value of or the rationale for communicating in both L1 and L2.

- Having similar curricular commitments (e.g., integration with the rest of the curriculum) and requirements for the students (e.g., mandatory, not optional, assignments). As one respondent commented, "One last challenge that was faced by our group was how the project was integrated into each site's respective curriculum."

- Adapting the model to your particular needs and choosing appropriate activities for your students (e.g., less proficient students may be more comfortable with forum postings and text chats rather than video chats or video conferencing; more proficient students may prefer video chatting and one-on-one correspondence rather than more anonymous forums or text chatting)

- Agreeing upon the scope of the project in advance, both with supervisors and with partner teachers, so that enough time can be devoted to the planned, agreed upon activities. This instructional alignment was one of the most frequently cited components for success.

- Being flexible during the exchange, in particular, allowing students to provide input and reactions so that they have meaningful experiences. If student motivation wanes, either because their partners are not responding in a timely manner or because they are not interested in the topics under discussion, the success of the exchange will be decreased.

Follow up on online activities. Simply allowing students to interact with each other online does not ensure learning or understanding. It is even conceivable that stereotypes could be created or reinforced if students misconstrue what their partners have written or said. It is imperative for teachers to monitor and discuss what happens online so as to avoid misunderstandings that might arise from lack of linguistic proficiency or cultural knowledge. In-depth discussions in the classroom are valued by both teachers and students to follow up on the sometimes superficial exchanges that can be typical of brief online postings.

In conclusion, some of the positive results of *Cultura*-inspired projects are that learners reflect on their own and on another culture, gain new and authentic linguistic and cultural knowledge, and develop new attitudes towards themselves and others. The utmost care must be taken in the planning of the exchange, in particular, in aligning the respective instructional goals and curriculums of the partner classes. One tangible so-called "proof of the pudding" was expressed by one of the survey respondents who wrote about general impressions of the exchange citing the outcome that students were building on the relationships they had developed online:

> Absolutely positive… As many of the students in the U.S. were planning to spend some of their junior year in Italy, it became clear that true relationships had been created when many of the students planned to meet up.

Acknowledgments

I would like to thank Yukiko Watanabe for her significant contributions to the first phase of this meta-synthesis. She helped design the questionnaire and the coding procedures we used for the analyses of the answers to the open-ended questions in the questionnaire. I am very grateful for her gracious assistance.

References

Bauer, B., deBenedette, L., Furstenberg, G., Levet, S., & Waryn, S. (2006). The *Cultura* project. In J. A. Belz & S. L. Thorne (Eds.), *Internet-mediated intercultural foreign language education* (pp. 31–62). Boston, MA: Thompson Heinle.

Byram, M. (1997). *Teaching and assessing intercultural communicative competence.* Clevedon, England: Multilingual Matters.

Chun, D. M. (2011). Developing intercultural communicative competence through online exchanges. *CALICO Journal, 28*(2), 392–419.

Chun, D. M., & Wade, E. R. (2004). Collaborative cultural exchanges with CMC. In L. Lomicka & J. Cooke-Plagwitz (Eds.), *Teaching With technology* (pp. 220–247). Boston, MA: Heinle.

Furstenberg, G., Levet, S., English, K., & Maillet, K. (2001). Giving a virtual voice to the silent language of culture: The *Cultura* project. *Language Learning & Technology, 5*(1), 55–102.

Liaw, M. (2006). E-learning and the development of intercultural competence. *Language Learning & Technology, 10*(3), 49–64.

Liaw, M., & Bunn-Le Master, S. (2010). Understanding telecollaboration through an analysis of intercultural discourse. *Computer Assisted Language Learning, 23*(1), 21–40.

O'Dowd, R. (2003). Understanding the "other side": Intercultural learning in a Spanish-English e-mail exchange. *Language Learning & Technology, 7*(2), 118–144.

Suárez García, J., & Crapotta, J. (2007). Models of telecollaboration (2): *Cultura*. In R. O'Dowd (Ed.), *Online intercultural exchange: An introduction for foreign language teachers* (pp. 62–84). Clevedon, England: Multilingual Matters.

Appendix A. Survey instrument

Consent Form

Thank you for your willingness to participate in this survey. Please read the following "Consent Form" and then indicate whether you would like proceed.

CONSENT FORM
1. PURPOSE:
The purpose of this survey is to gather information about Cultura projects in language programs.

2. PROCEDURES:
You will respond to questions about the Cultura project practices in your program by selecting or typing answers.

3. DISCOMFORTS and RISKS:
There are no known risks involved in completing this survey.

4. BENEFITS:
Your responses will benefit those who wish to adapt the Cultura model to their own educational context. The survey results will be disseminated an edited book, which will be published through the National Foreign Language Resource Center at the University of Hawaii.

5. DURATION:
It will take approximately 20 minutes to complete the survey.

6. CONFIDENTIALITY:
The survey elicits general information about the Cultura-inspired project in your program. The data will be collected on a secure webserver and saved separately from any personally identifiable information such as email addresses. Your responses will be assigned a non-recognizable identification number. Only project personnel will have access to the study data. Findings will be disseminated in aggregate form, with no information identifying individuals or individual programs.

7. RIGHT TO ASK QUESTIONS:
Contact Dorothy Chun (dchun@education.ucsb.edu) with any questions about the survey. If you have questions about your rights as a participan contact the University of California Office of Research (805-893-3807, or email graham@research.ucsb.edu).

8. COMPENSATION:
There is no compensation for completing this survey.

9. VOLUNTARY Participation:
You are not required to participate in this study. You can stop your participation at any time.

Please indicate below whether or not you consent to participate, then click "Next".

○ I consent to participate.
○ I do not consent to participate.

Your background

Please answer a few questions about yourself.

1. What is your primary work setting?

○ High school   ○ 2-year community/junior college   ○ 4-year university

Other (please specify)
[   ]

2. What is your language background?

Native language(s): [   ]
Second/foreign language(s) (advanced-level): [   ]
Second/foreign language(s) (intermediate-level): [   ]

Cultura-inspired projects

1. Why did you choose Cultura as a model?

[   ]

2. How many times have you implemented a Cultura-based/inspired project into your course? Please write in numerical numbers.

[   ]

3. Please provide your and your partner's institution name as well as the most recent project starting date.

Note: Institution names are used to simply match project partners. Your institutional name will not be associated with your responses.

Your institution: [   ]
Partner institution: [   ]
Most recent project starting date: [   ]

If you implemented a Cultura-based (or Cultura-inspired) project multiple times in the past, for the rest of the survey, please provide information about your MOST RECENT project.

Program context

Please answer a few questions about the program context where you implemented the Cultura Model. **If you implemented the Cultura model multiple times in different courses, please respond to the survey for the mos recent course.**

1. In which course did you apply/adapt the Cultura Model? Please specify the language and the level of the course.

Language: [   ]
Course level: [   ]

2. Did you implement the Cultura project in multiple sections of the course?

◯ Yes   ◯ No

If "yes," please indicate how many sections you had.
[   ]

3. What was students' target-language proficiency in your course?

If the target language is a language other than English, please choose the average proficiency level of your students using the ACTFL scale OR the CEFR scale.

	ACTFL	Common European Framework of Reference
Language other than English:	[▼]	[▼]

If English was the target language, please state the test name (e.g., TOEFL) and approximate average score of your students.

Name of the test [   ]
Average score or level [   ]

4. What were your students' cultural experience and exposure? Please rate the proportion of students who had the following experience and cultural background.

	Your students
Visit to a country where the target-language is spoken	[▼]
Heritage language/cultural background	[▼]

5. Did you feel there was a large gap in L2 proficiency between your students and your partner's students?

☐ Yes   ☐ Not sure
☐ No

Please explain

[ ]

6. Which features/activities in Cultura did you use in your project?

☐ questionnaires   ☐ newsstand   ☐ library
☐ forums   ☐ data
☐ films   ☐ images

Any other online activities you incorporated? Please list them below.

[ ]

Student learning outcomes

1. What did you want students to gain through the Cultura project (e.g., language proficiency, cultural awareness, sense of learning community)? Please describe the student learning outcomes you anticipated for the Cultura project.

[ ]

2. What was the relative importance of language learning versus cultural learning in the Cultura project?

○ Language learning was more important than cultural learning
○ Cultural learning was more important than language learning
○ Language and cultural learning were equally important

3. What were some of the greatest student learning gains you observed through the Cultura project?

[ ]

4. For the learning outcomes described above, what kind of information did you gather to determine the degree to which students were able to perform the outcomes?

[ ]

Implementation of the Cultura Model

Please explain the way the Cultura Model was adapted to your programs' contexts.

1. How was the Cultura project integrated into existing courses? Please provide information about your and your partner's courses.

	Modes of instruction	Cultura exchange as...
Your course	[dropdown]	[dropdown]
Partner 1's course	[dropdown]	[dropdown]
Partner 2's course	[dropdown]	[dropdown]

2. What modes of interaction were used for the online exchange? (Check all that apply.)

- [ ] audio-only chat
- [ ] text-based chat
- [ ] voice recordings
- [ ] text-based forums
- [ ] video chat/conference
- [ ] other

3. What was the language(s) of the online exchange?

- ○ Students sent in L1, received in L2
- ○ Students sent and received in L1
- ○ Students sent and received in L2
- ○ A combination: students sent and received in both L1 and L2

Other (please specify)
[_____]

4. What types of activities took place face-to-face in class?

- [ ] discussion of online questionnaires
- [ ] discussion of online forums
- [ ] discussion of films, newsstand, images, data
- [ ] student presentations on Cultura exchange
- [ ] other

5. How many weeks in total did the exchange last? Please give number of weeks and whether or not the exchange was uninterrupted or interrupted (e.g., by breaks, weeks when no Cultura-based/inspired activities were done).

[_____]

6. To what extent was the teacher (you) present in the online exchange (i.e., discussion forums, etc.)?

○ Not at all   ○ A little   ○ Somewhat   ○ A lot

7. What role did the teacher (you) take online? Choose all that apply.

☐ Discussion facilitator   ☐ Model provider   ☐ Language feedback   ☐ Content feedback

Other (please specify)

8. Were there any non-text based materials used in the exchange?

○ Yes   ○ No

If "yes," please explain which media were used and WHY.

Evaluation of the Cultura-inspired project

1. What were your overall impressions of the exchange?

2. What were the overall reactions from the students?

3. What were some of the challenges you encountered implementing the Cultura-inspired project in your course? (e.g., timeframe, finding a partner, tasks, online management, design, integration into existing curriculum, technology, size of the forum, etc.)

Final thoughts and comments

1. Any other comments you wish to share about your Cultura project experience?

2. Do you know of any individuals who have implemented a Cultura-based/inspired project, so we can contact them for further insights? Please provide name and email address if possible.

Thank you!

Thank you for responding to our survey. If you are finished answering all of the questions, please click the "Done" button below.

If you did not finish but would like to return and complete the survey at a later date, please click on "Exit this survey" in the top right corner, and what you have completed so far will be saved.

Appendix B. Codes for motivation for choosing *Cultura* model as an instructional approach

code #	categories
external	
1a	had an opportunity to learn about the *cultura* model
1b	had available technology
1c	recommended by a colleague
1d	invited by a colleague to participate as a partner program
internal	
2a	have belief/buy-in/interest
2b	bring innovation to the program
2c	provide additional inter-cultural learning opportunity
2d	provide autonomous learning opportunity
2e	expand exposure to target culture and language
2f	aligned with what was already in place (or what was previously done)

Appendix C. Codes for expected learning outcomes

code #	categories	label
language		
3a	skill	language proficiency (fluency), writing fluency, summarizing, skills in communicating in target language (TL), ability to discuss cultural issues
3b	knowledge	vocabulary
3c	attitudes	confidence in TL use, confidence in TL communication, increase in motivation to communicate in the TL, openness to language variety (accepting of other's L2), language appreciation
culture		
4a	skill	analytic observation, abstraction of cultural features, identify similarities and differences between own and target cultures, ability to reflect (skill of reflection), ability to discuss cultural issues
4b	knowledge	cultural knowledge, knowledge of cultural practices
4c	attitudes	(cultural) awareness, own values and assumptions, openness and willingness to express oneself, awareness of the variability within culture
other		
5a		sense of learning community
5b		meaningful exchange, collaboration with students from the target culture
5c		problem solving skills, critical thinking
5d		life changing experience
5e		plan to work and study abroad
5f		ability to relate to students their own age

Appendix D. Codes for evaluation, challenges, recommendations and comments

code #	categories
O	success/positive
X	not successful/negative/many challenges
XO	mixed evaluation
NA	no judgment or neutral
REC	recommendations mentioned

Appendix E. Codes for causes/sources of evaluative judgments, challenges, recommendations and comments

code #	categories
a	instructional alignment and integration
b	language learning
c	culture learning
d	learning community
e	management/logistics
f	technology
g	student motivation/interest/needs
h	student participation/responsiveness
i	training students
j	advocacy
k	finding a partner
l	activities
m	attitudes towards the model

Part II:
Research on Acquisition of Intercultural Communicative Competence in *Cultura*-Based Models

A Tale of Two Cultures

Meei-Ling Liaw
National Taichung University

Kathryn English
Université de Paris II, Panthéon-Assas

This chapter describes the evolution of an ongoing computer-mediated project between French and Taiwanese ELF (English as Lingua Franca) students engaged in intercultural learning via the different communication modes afforded by the Internet and real-life exchanges. National Taichung University in Taiwan hosts an Internet-based exchange program with the University of Paris II (Panthéon-Assas) and the Ecole Polytechnique in France. In this chapter, we first present the theoretical framework of the project, the Lacanian concept of extimacy, and Bakhtin's concept of exotopia. Next, we review related studies on Internet-mediated intercultural projects to highlight the significance of conducting the current study. Third, we describe the project website and the rationale underlying the design of the tasks. Fourth, findings from the analysis of specific data collected from students' works are presented. Finally, pedagogical implications are discussed in the conclusion.

Introduction

Learning and teaching English as a foreign or second language has been a major academic and commercial activity since the Industrial Revolution. Due to globalization and the Information Revolution, today more people study English as a foreign language than speak it as a mother tongue. However, the value system that underpinned the Industrial Revolution may no longer hold in the Information Age. Given the many varieties of English across the world today, the vision of a native speaker as being a constant reference with his or her value systems dominating

---

Liaw, M.-L., & English, K. (2014). A tale of two cultures. In D. M. Chun, (Ed.), Cultura-*inspired intercultural exchanges: Focus on Asian and Pacific languages* (pp. 73–95). Honolulu: University of Hawai'i, National Foreign Language Resource Center.

seems pre-Information Age. Value systems and prior knowledge that determine what is right and how things should be understood vary across cultures. As such, teachers' pedagogical decisions when designing English language courses should reflect the needs and values of today's learners. Hence there is a need to explore not only how English could be taught, but to explore our students' value systems rather than refer them to one system of reference, even though the system is actually managed by the many varieties of English.

To take advantage of information technology and link the language learning process to intercultural awareness, the researchers/instructors set up a yearlong intercultural communication course between Taichung National University in Taiwan and the Université de Paris II/Ecole Polytechnique in France. Instructors designed tasks that would stimulate observation skills and help intercultural similarities and differences emerge, while fostering communication in a sustainable way.

Students first were engaged in description of their individual current, past, and future interests; participated in a spontaneous word association exercise designed to show the contrasts and similarities of their cultures; then selected and explained a work of art that exemplified their cultures. They completed the virtual phase of the project by selecting and sharing articles from the press that illustrated current events in their countries. Throughout the project, the students exchanged ideas on the course website, hosted in Taiwan, using text, images, PowerPoint presentations, videos, and videoconferencing. This led to a real life exchange when two Taiwanese students travelled to Paris to experience first hand the cultural elements that had been discussed online. Subsequently, more Taiwanese students travelled to Paris and French students travelled to Taiwan.

We quantitatively analyzed the language they wrote with *Linguistic Inquiry and Word Count* software (Pennebaker, Francis, & Booth, 2001) and qualitatively discussed their observations within the framework of two concepts. First, French psychoanalyst Jacques Lacan's (1986) *extimacy* was used to explore individual perceptions via the notion of "self" and "other." Next, we contrasted the atomistic vision of extimacy with more collective perceptions of *exotopia*, a concept put forth by Russian philosopher Mikhaïl Bakhtin (1984). Students experienced the development of a virtual language class into a real exchange as the instructors observed how teaching could be adapted to the multiple versions of intercultural understanding.

Theoretical framework of the project

Globalization has transformed English into today's *lingua franca* (Crystal, 2003; Graddol, 2006). At the same time, the expansion of information technology further accelerates this transformation process now that online communication is mostly in English and most English speakers in the world are not native speakers, but are rather those who use English as a foreign or a second language (Crystal, 2004; Graddol, 1997).[1]

As speakers of English in the world change, the approaches and references we use to teach English cannot and should not stay the same. In teaching English as a lingua franca (ELF), we need to realize that its speakers are not obedient learners striving to conform to native speaker (NS) norms but are, first and foremost, users

---

[1] According to Internet World Stats, English is the top language of the Internet in terms of number of users (http://www.internetworldstats.com/stats7.htm).

of the language whose main objective is functional effectiveness, not formal correctness (Seidlhofer, 2008). Rather than try to communicate with NSs and approximate the NSs' variety of English, non-native speakers' (NNSs') main focus is on understanding and being understood by other NNSs (Jenkins, 2004). Instead of striving to replicate idealized NS usage, English teaching should work on learners' real-life needs and perceptions to prepare them for intercultural encounters. ELF speakers need to be sensitized to interpersonal aspects of language pragmatics because intercultural encounters are significantly more unpredictable when interactions take place between NNSs rather than with NSs of English (Mauranen, 2003).

It is also worth noting that ELF speakers of different cultural backgrounds may rely on different cultural schemata when using the common language, English, to interact, or even to describe common objects. A schema is an abstract mental structure that develops in the context of one's basic experiences in order to make the world more understandable (Shaghasemi & Heisey, 2009; Yule, 1996). Cultural schemata are conceptual structures that enable an individual to store and interpret culturally specific perceptual and conceptual information as well as experiences and expressions (Malcolm & Sharifian, 2002). They play an important role in intercultural understanding. In intercultural encounters, speakers' cross-cultural schemata are activated and then distorted because they are grounded in the source culture of the speaker. This distortion can be detrimental to meaningful intercultural communication. In line with the beliefs of ELF teaching and learning stated above, what matters most, in our opinion, is therefore appropriateness, not normative grammaticality. The challenge faced by instructors then is to come to grips with what is and what is not appropriate, as well as how the cultural schemata held by the different cultural groups achieve equilibrium in the course of communication.

To date, little research on appropriateness of cultural schemata in the intercultural language classroom has been conducted. More precisely, no study has been conducted to look into how language and cultural schemata underlying its usage interact concretely in intercultural encounters between French and Taiwanese ELF speakers. We hope to begin to fill this gap by examining two concepts applied to the design and analysis of encounters between our students: the Lacanian (1986) concept of *extimacy* and Bakhtin's (1984) concept of *exotopia*. *Extimacy*[2] comes from a French neology, *extime*, formulated by the French psychoanalyst Jacques Lacan to describe the most intimate aspect of "being." According to Lacan's seminar XVI, the notion of extimacy relates to those things that can affect people the most, the things that touch their inner self and yet which they hope to find in resonance outside of themselves, in, what Lacan referred to as "*l'Autre*," or the "Other." In short, it could be seen as the quest for oneself outside of oneself. In cross-cultural situations this could be seen as looking for an idealized other. For this study, the researchers deem it as the opportunity for the participants to become aware of the potential value of otherness. The contemporary French psychologist Serge Tisseron (2001) suggests that extimacy requires initial self-identification and subsequent exteriorization to someone else who we consider initially as our

---

[2] *Extimacy,* derived from the Lacanian notion of *extimité*, refers to a psychoanalytical concept in which the center of the individual subject is projected to the exterior, the center is outside the individual. Also intimate thoughts and beliefs are projected onto another (person or idea) and these may or may not resonate with them and thereby create meaningful and innovative interaction.

"double." Only then can we perceive, access, and accept his or her perspectives. It is the difference in exchanged, yet not necessarily shared, perspectives that allow an enriching dialogue to ensue. This is why it is essential to recognize and acknowledge non-native speakers' needs and perceptions in a respectful and unique dialogic situation.

In this theoretical framework, we suggest that extimacy could go hand-in-hand with the concept of exotopia. According to Bakhtin (1984), exotopia is a powerful tool to understand culture. A foreign culture can only be unveiled through its discovery by another culture. Meaning here is fully understood when a familiar concept is confronted with different understandings of a parallel concept, which then sets a limit or clearly defines the contours. In a culture foreign to one's own, an individual will ask different questions, activate his/her existing schemata, and thereby construct a new framework of understanding.[3]

The interaction of extimacy and exotopia then would describe communication on a personal, extimate as well as a collective, culture-bound exotopic level. We suggest that the interaction of these two theoretical notions could foster a more productive way to understand the dynamics of intercultural communication than the normative opposition of NNS versus NS grammatical correctness. We thus designed the tasks of our project within the framework of these two theoretical concepts. As such, by working collaboratively on the prescribed tasks, our ELF students were provided with multiple opportunities to look into their cultural schemata via experiencing the processes of extimacy and exotopia.

Review of studies related to Internet-mediated intercultural contacts

The advent of the Internet presents unprecedented opportunities for people in far-flung locations to connect and facilitates intercultural interaction. The Internet provides language teachers with a host of tools, such as e-mail, chats, instant messaging, online telephony, and videoconferencing, to link students across geographic boundaries (O'Dowd, 2007). Internet-mediated communication has been used to create interactive learning environments in which students go beyond a checklist approach to cross-cultural knowledge and literacy (Belz, 2004; Felix, 2002; Finkbeiner & Koplin, 2002; Furstenberg, Levet, English, & Maillet, 2001; Liaw, 2007; Rogerson-Revell, 2003; Shawback & Terhune, 2002). Some of these studies have favored a native-speaker language approach on the premise that students can best express themselves within the intimacy of their mother tongue (e.g., the *Cultura* project, Furstenberg et al., 2001). Others took advantages of interacting with native speakers for meaningful target language practice.

There are also studies that reported benefits of linking groups of non-native speakers for intercultural communication via the Internet. For example, Fedderholdt (2001) arranged a group of Japanese university students and a group of Danish students to engage in online communication with the aim to increase their motivation for writing and their awareness of culture where English is not the first language. In another telecollaborative project implemented by Keranen and Bayyurt (2006), Spanish-speaking in-service teachers and Turkish-speaking pre-

---

[3] For example, the particularity of the French, 2-hour, three-course lunch takes on full meaning when compared not to the lighter French breakfasts or dinners but when contrasted with the way Taiwanese students nibble throughout the day and gather to snack at night markets. Perceptions need to be put in the perspective of the "other's" eyes.

service teachers were linked for intercultural communication. They found that the participants shared features of their own cultures, engaged in conversations, and demonstrated interest and willingness to express personal opinions.

Studies have found that online communications between groups of different nationalities provide opportunities to negotiate differences in English. For example, Louhiala-Salminen, Charles, and Kankaanranta (2005) examined the discoursal similarities and differences between Swedish and Finnish interactants by looking into the email communication between the two groups in a post-merger business context. They found that the adoption of business ELF has helped some employees cope with the challenge in cross-cultural settings and that a "Culture Three," that is, a culture that was neither Swedish nor Finnish, was created to facilitate communication between both groups.

Studies have also been conducted to probe into how the use of ELF on the Internet crosses paths with local practices of English. For example, Lam (2000) examines a Chinese immigrant teenager's correspondence with a transnational group of peers on the Internet and how this correspondence related to his identity formation and literacy development in ESL. Another study by Lam (2004) documents the socialization of two bilingual immigrant Chinese girls in a chat room in which participants developed a hybrid language variety that set them apart from both their English-only peers and their Cantonese-only peers. Bloch (2004) shows how Chinese learners of English incorporate Chinese rhetorical forms in English when communicating in a Usenet group, thereby creating a hybrid form of "World Rhetoric" (p. 78).

To continue to advance in examining NNS-NNS online interactions, we designed a series of tasks via a telecollaborative project which would allow ELF students to work on their common target language, English, within a neutral "Third Space" and develop their *extimate* and *exotopic* awareness of self and otherness. Byram and Fleming (1998) define "intercultural speakers" as people who can "establish a relationship between their own and the other cultures, to mediate and explain differences—and ultimately to accept that difference and see the common humanity beneath it" (p. 8). We hoped that the students of the project would have the opportunity to become what Byram and Fleming refer to as "intercultural speakers." In this optic we also visualized that the concepts of extimacy and exotopia would help us understand how the two groups of ELF speakers achieve intercultural schematic equilibrium through the interaction of extimacy and exotopia.

To bridge the gap between the subjective analysis of extimacy and exotopia and what new technologies can tell us about languages and the way people interact across cultures, a concrete, word frequency approach was also adopted. The word frequency approach examined students' actual writings online and analyzed not only what they said but also how they said it and how they structured their interaction. This approach allowed further examination of the social process of negotiating meaning and re-construing semantic networks on the individual and collective levels.

Word frequency is considered a powerful tool in understanding the psychological and sociological profiles of individuals and groups (Pennebaker, Francis, & Booth, 2001). Especially the uses of social words (i.e., words referring to talk about the process of communication and that make frequent references to "friends," "family," and other people) and pronouns have been found to be culturally related (Matsumoto, Yoo, & LeRoux, 2005; Setlock, Fussell, & Neuwirth, 2004; Setlock, Quinones, & Fussell, 2007). Investigations into the uses of social words have been carried out to understand people's social connectedness (Burke & Dollinger, 2005). Social process words are considered to express a relational self-concept where individuals define themselves in terms of their connections to other people. Pronoun uses are also important in evaluating social processes (Campbell & Pennebaker, 2003). How individuals use pronouns may vary by degree of social relatedness. Thus, people may show their sense of connectedness to others by greater use of first-person plural pronouns such as "we" and "us" (Berry, Pennebaker, Mueller, & Hiller, 1997; Pennebaker, 2002; Pennebaker & Lay, 2002). In writing and natural language use, first-person singular pronouns are linked to self-focus and a more personal style of writing (Campbell & Pennebaker, 2003; Rude, Gortner, & Pennebaker, 2004; Stirman & Pennebaker, 2001), whereas first-person plural pronouns appear to characterize a collective focus (Berry et al., 1997; Pennebaker, 2002; Pillsbury, 1998). In addition, in terms of different writing genres, pronouns are less common in academic than personal writing (Carroll, 2007). Information on the uses of social words and personal pronouns will provide triangulation (Dezin, 1978) of the findings from the qualitative discussion of extimacy and exotopia and a deeper insight into the participants' awareness of self and otherness.

Context of the project and focus of the study

As stated above, access to information technologies for language training has created advantages to develop authentic communication in the target language. Access to intercultural learning situations via computer networks is virtually unlimited. The ensuing dialogic situations however often lack the sustained motivation for interaction when students who do not know each other, nor sincerely have the desire to communicate, are put into the same virtual classroom. On the other hand, students may share intimate thoughts since they are not competing with each other and will not experience immediate consequences. We thus thought that an *extimate* approach could enhance the awareness of self and other as well as increase interaction.

The challenge in designing virtual environments for real people in far-flung locations to foster authentic communication is to develop tasks which are not only meaningful to the students but provide a forum which respects both their different cultural identities and adheres to institutional requirements.[4] In addition institutions have different semester schedules, priorities given to language acquisition, and divergent assessment criteria. At the same time, learners in these different institutions need a coherent structure to help them learn aspects of language with tools to measure their individual progress. Learners need to be aware of the progress they are making, otherwise they may lose motivation in spite of the interaction. Also, the exams provided for validation of language acquisition are based on the linguistic production of idealized native speakers. In other words, they tend to be normative rather than generative. This is the quandary ELF speakers face while trying to participate in communicative tasks

---

[4] It should be noted that such activities or tasks will rarely provide the structure needed for institutional exams or TOEIC, TOEFL, and other internationally-validated exams. This conflict in objectives is often an inhibiting factor when attempting to set up intercultural courses.

with native speakers because the learner is situated outside the circle of putatively acceptable language production. Interaction with native speakers can put the non-native at a disadvantage, which diminishes extimacy awareness. On the other hand, the difficulty that ELF speakers face is that meaning, structure, "otherness," and "oddness" are constantly negotiated variables and are unfortunately perceived by many as having somewhat less prestigious linguistic value than NS production. It is within this context of striving for both measurable accuracy and at the same time developing communicative fluency that this project was designed. Our study explores the application of the two theories (i.e., the Lacanian concept of *extimacy* and Bakhtin's concept of *exotopia*) in the design and analysis of the encounters between our students.

Data collections and analyses

To understand the assumptive frameworks held by the students and how extimacy and exotopia interacted during both ELF groups' encounters, the deductive content analysis method was employed (Mayring, 2000). The works submitted by students, including PowerPoint files, graphs, Word documents, word lists, and journal entries, were carefully read by the two researchers/instructors of the project looking for manifestations of extimacy and exotopia. The identifications were discussed for agreement to ensure reliable categorization.

In addition, a text analysis software program, *Linguistic Inquiry and Word Count* (LIWC, 2001), designed by James W. Pennebaker, Martha E. Francis, and Roger J. Booth, was used.[5] The LIWC analysis of social process words and pronouns yields additional information on the participants' perceptions of self and otherness and their possible change during the course of intercultural communication. The social processes category comprised words relating to communication and references to friends, family, and humans (e.g., *mate*, *talk*, *they*, and *child*). Personal pronouns included first and third person pronouns in both singular and plural forms. In adding the quantitative analysis to our qualitative interpretations, we try to explore what they mean by what they don't say.

A telecollaborative project between Taiwan and France

The design of the Taiwan-France telecollaboration website

The project website (http://candle.ntcu.edu.tw:8080/project2010/) provided a multimodal environment where ELF students from Taiwan and France interacted in a common language, English. The French students in this project were either engineering or management students while Taiwanese students were English majors. Because the students had different majors, the instructors designed tasks that would provide a convergence of interest to foster the synergy necessary for sustainable communication. The course is centered on developing communication skills as well as learning English via asynchronous text, graphic, and audio/video exchanges.

To foster communication that would be perceived as meaningful, rather than present lists of vocabulary, reading, or viewing items either on-line or "ex-cathedra," a

---

[5] The program allows the analysis of written text on a word-by-word basis, calculating the percentage of words in the text that match each of up to approximately 80 output variables as a text file that can be read into application programs, such as SPSS for Windows and Excel. A complete description of LIWC can be found at http://www.liwc.net/liwcdescription.php.

task-based approach was adopted (Nunan, 2004). This was to give the students purposeful, hands-on practice. The tasks started at an intimate, potentially *extimate*, individual level and progressed to more collective and interactive accomplishments. The tasks are described below.

Project tasks

"About-Me Bags" activity

The first task was a self-introduction activity known as the "About-Me Bag."[6] In this exercise, the students described three items which embodied their past, present, and projected future. They then wrote several paragraphs to describe the objects and, most importantly, they discussed why these objects were important to them. This was done individually as homework. In class, students presented their objects to other classmates in small groups. After receiving feedback from their real-life peers, students posted their revised paragraphs or PowerPoint presentations on the common website to share with their international partners. This activity was designed to stimulate the students' exploration and awareness of values.

Word associations

Similar to the *Cultura* Project (Furstenberg et al., 2001), students responded individually to word association questions posted on the website. Results were made available once the students posted their responses. This activity was meant to prompt the students to notice how the same words could evoke different conceptual representations. The words chosen were *individualism, creativity, ecology, leisure, beliefs, trade, family, school, poverty, wealth, globalization,* and *crisis*. Students were led to encounter a collective vision as compared to the individual perception in the "About-Me Bags."

Art selection and explanation

The third task involved the collective presentation and explanation of a selection of culturally meaningful art. This was a group activity, similar to the IMRAC project (Johnson & English, 2003) where group members selected a series of paintings or sculptures that they considered representative of their cultures. It involved first finding the cultural artifacts they wished to present, then presenting them in class, and finally negotiating which ones would be posted on the website. The selection was to be seen as a gift presented to their partners. It was assumed that the students' partners would not necessarily know much about their artistic selection.

The selection of art from the foreign partners was then projected and used to encourage class discussions. The uses of form and color were discussed in terms of difference and what they represented. Similar to the way both the *Cultura* Project and IMRAC were designed, the goal of this task was to help students move from the individual "About-Me Bag" or discrete word association, both seen as semantic cultural building blocks, to the collective cultural output. In this way, the students moved from individual identities and word items to collective visions and cultural productions. It was equally essential to situate students' individual identities within a common cultural framework and subsequently validate or invalidate student hypotheses as to why specific cultural art forms were coherent within their assumptive frameworks or not. This led to class discussion on the complexity of art

---

[6] We wish to thank Dr. Susan Bunn from Sam Houston University for suggesting an initial version of this activity.

interpretation and meaning and how, from the outsider's perspective, different forms of art led to different experiences of interpretation.

Online reading and forum discussions

Two newspaper articles[7] were posted for the participants to read. An asynchronous online discussion forum served as a common space for exchanging and debating viewpoints presented in the articles. It was hoped that exchanging viewpoints would deepen the understanding of the students' own culture as well as the other, foreign culture. Similar to the considerations taken in the IMRAC and *Cultura* projects, the instructors did not post on the forums themselves or comment on the content of postings, to allow students to control the conversations.

Real-life exchanges

Following their multimodal, computer-mediated interactions, and to conclude the project, two Taiwanese students visited their partners in France. This provided real-life contacts and the students then were able to provide an enhanced, firsthand account of their visit as cultural informants. They shared their observations by posting text and visual logs on the project website and invited comments from their peers.

Findings and discussions

"About-Me Bag"

For the Taiwanese students, the selections from their past were items from their childhood and high school, for example, photos with their parents, siblings, or friends, favorite toys, high school uniforms and school bags, and so forth. It was interesting to note that the items that were most meaningful to them were mostly electronic devices, such as cell phones, cameras, iPods, MP3 players, and computers. Repeated mentioning of diaries and calendars also suggested an active lifestyle. As for the future, many of them chose world maps, pictures from far away places, postcards from foreign countries, train tickets, road signs, telescope, and so forth, indicating their desire to connect to the world.

Many of the French students, however, provided an item from their past, from an old hobby or a musical or sporting interest. Others used this exercise to explore ongoing situations within their families and their pets. In each case, the exercise led to the deepening of self-knowledge for each student and a successful activity in getting to know the other students in the group.

This activity led to considerable introspection that provided an excellent introductory activity for the new class. Students developed their intimate ideas associated with each object and then set this in an *extimate* perspective. However, students were introducing themselves as individuals and comparing themselves within their own educational and cultural schemata. At this stage, they were not interacting with their foreign peers. The juxtaposition of these personal items provided a uniquely personal insight to collective culture because it was introduced as fragments of collective culture. Similar to Furstenberg et al. (2001), students needed the vision, the linking of artifacts to consider the value

---

[7] The first article was about the Taiwanese Health Minister's offer to step down from the post for lifting the ban on U.S. beef without the parliament's consent. The second article was related to the famous roquefort cheese and how the US agreed to drop the 300% super tax on the French blue cheese in exchange for higher EU beef imports.

of concepts, from a person abroad in order to see their own worlds through different lenses.

Word association

Following the idea initiated in the *Cultura* Project, the authors selected similar words for free association. As Korshuk (2005) put it,

> The premise is that as associations show links between words, they reflect relations between notions and life experiences. If an association is evoked, the link is quite stable and is of relevance for the object. Languages reflect and shape cultures, hence links between words also reflect cultural patterns (e.g., if a subject responds "respect" to stimulus "old man" it may show positive value of age, past time orientation, as well as hierarchy principle in that society).

The intention of this activity was to probe into students' cultural values and observe whether the responses from the two groups would be different or not.

Interestingly the Sino-French responses for the concept "individualism" were somewhat similar. This provided a stark contrast with results from Furstenberg, et al. (2001) in which Franco-American responses were almost antonymic. Throughout the nearly 10 years of the French-American exchanges, the word *individualism* was associated with words that had positive connotations for Americans: Words such as *creativity, self, uniqueness, independence, freedom, choice,* and *capitalism* came up frequently and therefore were highly predictable. Each time it was a surprising discovery for the students, one which led to interesting forum discussions. The French responses were frequently words with negative connotations: *égoisme, solitude, capitalisme*. The difference in positive or negative connotations in associated words revealed the difference in values attributed to these concepts.

In this project, the Taiwanese students, in spite of a few positive words (e.g., *freedom, confident*), seemed to significantly share the French vision of individualism. Words such as *selfish* and *solitude* were frequent. The result seemed to confirm that Taiwanese culture is more collective rather than individualistic (Fan, 2000; Hofstede, 1986, 1982; Hsu, 2004). Being influenced by Confucianism, Taoism, and Buddhism, Taiwanese people view collectivism as a virtue, whereas individualism is usually associated with being selfish or egotistic (Wang, 2005). However, interestingly, while the French continued to associate the word *capitalism* with individualism, the Taiwanese associated nearly antonymic words *socialism, Marx,* and *totalitarianism*. These results gain meaning when considered in relation to American answers in the *Cultura* Project among which *socialism* was a frequent response to the prompt *Solidarity*. Several American students did not answer the prompt for *solidarity* or even ask what it was. Others provided responses such as *evil*.[8]

Another interesting word association for analysis was *Taiwan* since the words written by the Taiwanese students would be projections of individual extimate perceptions while French students' associations would provide more limited, stereotypical views of Taiwanese culture. This would contradict the Taiwanese vision of Taiwan and produce a vision of exotopia.

---

[8] The authors acknowledge that considerably more research should be conducted into the analysis of the cross-cultural word association responses.

In the Taiwanese students' associations, *island*, *small*, *beautiful*, *mountains*, and *Formosa*, appeared most frequently. Also repeatedly occurring were words related to the political scene, such as *country*, *free*, *election*, *independent*, and *democracy*. Words related to food, for example, *delicious*, *fruit*, and *night markets* also recurred often. Words such as *culture*, *aborigines*, *dialects*, and *foreign laborer* indicated the diversity in Taiwanese culture.

Interestingly, *island* was also the most frequently written word in French students' association. *China*, a word not found at all in the association made by Taiwanese students, was the second most frequently associated word in the French students' list. Different from Taiwanese students' associations, however, the words that French students repeatedly brought up, such as *made in Taiwan*, *electronics*, *technology*, and *competitive* could not be found on the associated word list of the Taiwanese students.

In comparing the associated word lists, the words written by Taiwanese students presented a collective self-perception of Taiwan as a small, beautiful island with rich and diverse cultures. People in Taiwan enjoy freedom, democracy, and good food. Its delicate political relationship with China was only hinted in the selected word *independent*. Its image as being competitive in the global economy with electronic and technological products had a more prominent impression on the French students than on the Taiwanese students themselves.

This difference in looking through cultural lenses was noted in Taiwanese students' comments after reviewing the word lists:

> Taiwanese almost talk about the politics and geography. We are Taiwanese, so we always think of the things close to our life and understand more about what Taiwan has and what situation we are in...They think we have high technology and succeed in economic. Somehow, our group has the same opinion that foreign people really don't know much about Taiwan...The government in China has a powerful influence in the world, so some foreign people think that Taiwan is similar to China.

The cultural and political vision of students reflected the value systems that were activated by these prompt words. Concepts are not free-floating entities but are grouped within semantic networks, or word webs. As such, one idea is associated with another to form a coherent structure for each individual. These networks can then be construed collectively to provide a collective cultural vision. The networks are not set in stone either. Frequently meaning will change over time and according to global events.

Art selection and explanation

Art selections made by Taiwanese students

The Taiwanese students were very enthusiastic about the art selection activity. They felt that this would allow them to collectively construct a "cultural self-portrait" to present to their French partners. Merely one work of art was not enough, so they negotiated and ended up selecting several. They included a folk song, two paintings, a cartoon art, a hand puppet, temple parade characters, a series of sculptures, a metal mosaic, and two architectural monuments.[9] Similar to the

---

9   They were 1) the song, 望春風, by 鄧雨賢 and 李臨秋; 2) the ink painting, Lotus Pond by 林玉山; 3) the oil painting, Chiayi Park, by 陳澄波; 4) cartoon art, *A Fish With a Smile*, by 幾米;

"About-Me Bag" activity, selecting and explaining artworks gave the participants a chance for externalization of collective extimacy. However, this activity moved beyond the interpersonal level to the collective level.

The students' written explanations of their choices clearly indicated that they wanted to send messages to their French partners. They were searching for a resonance in the eyes of the *other*. In this way the foreign students' perceptions and reactions would validate and contrast with the Taiwanese vision of themselves. They were eager and proud to show the wealth and uniqueness of their culture:

> It is very special and unique culture in Taiwan, even in the world… we want to let people all over the world know more about the culture in Taiwan and which is different from theirs.

Also, as indicated in the explanation of selecting the folk song, they wanted to share something "beautiful" with their French friends:

> This traditional song is so popular that almost every person in Taiwan has heard of it and even can sing it out. We'd like to share this beautiful song with French friends and hope you can enjoy it.

In addition to sharing something "beautiful," the students purposefully selected a variety of artworks reflecting the wide spectrum of Taiwanese culture that were in line with its historical and societal changes. There were works dated in the Japanese occupation era, pieces influenced by traditional Chinese ink art, folk performances accompanying religious rituals, pop-art most favored by the younger generation, and a temple hundreds of years old, as well as the modern skyscraper that challenged the most advanced architectural technology. All of these selections are well known to the Taiwanese and are parts of their daily lives. As students explained their reasons for choosing one of the paintings and the hand puppet, their intention was to show how their culture extended from the past to the present and continued to evolve:

> The ink painting [style][10] represents the past, however, the [scene in the] drawing represents the present. I regard both aspects of the drawing, the old style and the modern construction, important to understanding Taiwanese culture.

> And most importantly, we can see Taiwanese traditional image and personality of Taiwanese through puppet show. Indeed, it also changed and grew with development of Taiwan. Although animations are widespread and popular nowadays, the puppet show still plays an essential role in Taiwanese culture because we Taiwanese people like and treasure its uniqueness very much.

Art selection by French students and responses by Taiwanese students

The French students collectively selected the painting by Eugène Delacroix, *Liberty Leading the People* (see Figure 1). The Taiwanese students commented on the painting and asked questions. This exercise revealed remarkable aspects of the Taiwanese students' vision of France and also revealed aspects of their own self-perception. This is an excellent example of collective extimacy and touches upon exotopia.

---

5) hand puppet, 史艷文; 6) temple parade characters, Eight Generals; 7) sculptures, the Tai-chi series by Ju Ming; 8) metal mosaic 九份礦坑 by 胡達華; 9) the temple, 三峽祖師廟; and 10) the skyscraper Taipei 101.

[10] The words in brackets are added by the authors for clarity.

Figure 1. *Liberty Leading the People* by Eugène Delacroix

The image represents a bare-breasted woman as the central figure that prompted many questions from the Taiwanese students, who were mostly women. The following is a typical reaction:

> Why did he (the artist) want to paint a woman with bare breast, not with any clothes?

Such examples of women figures are very frequent in France and the leading symbol of the nation is a woman, Marianne, so this kind of nudity was neither surprising nor shocking to the French students. Here, what was "normal" in one culture is not in another. Once again, Bahktin's exotopia was a useful tool for developing awareness of what was "normal" or "appropriate" and what the connotations in one culture might be when set in relation to another. The kind of questions the Taiwanese asked were most useful to the French students who learned about the specificity of their own culture. In Delacroix's painting, the French students said that the woman's bare breast was a metaphor for strength as breasts are such a common artistic element in painting, sculpture, and even architecture in France. They did not perceive it as something sexual.

Beyond nudity the idealized vision of woman led to a discussion about gender equality. Taiwanese students wrote,

> …we think the painting shows some messages, including the equality of men and women the courage to fight for freedom.

None of the French students perceived one their national symbols as representing gender equality. This projection is more a statement about Taiwanese culture, although the French painting served as a prompt to trigger an internalized emotion. As Hofstede (2005) described in his five-dimensional model, Taiwan not only has a collective culture, it also is a feminine society where men and women's social roles overlap and women tend to have the same caring values as men. The Taiwanese students' response to the female figure leading the people might have reflected its feminine cultural value. In other words, in this case, the visual characteristics of the painting worked the way word associations had earlier in the course to reveal specific, hidden or internalized aspects of culture.

Beyond this, a projection of values that were not part of an initial interpretation by the French reflected the idealized student-authors' vision as much, if not much more, than what the French students wrote to describe this painting.

> …she represented the homeland, the sweet-natured that could tolerate the different aspects like politics, strategy, society culture and accepted people's voices. She is a symbol of mother nursing the young generation and the whole country France.

In this passage, we can see how the idea of exotopia could allow French students to become aware of cultural perceptions of nudity and vision of gender as well as projections onto women while for the Taiwanese students, extimacy allowed them to evaluate the projections of what they may not have realized was actually an intimate, internalized vision.

A Taiwanese student who had studied the painting in history class several years earlier provided a third example of extimacy. This student referred to the painting:

> …French people's passion for pursuing liberty, which might be one of their internal characteristics.

This process of discovery using the formulation of a hypothesis led to the very productive maieutic form of questioning that was used throughout the *Cultura* project. In this case, French history had been learned at school and was presented as an interpretation which in turn corroborated an earlier statement from a Taiwanese peer learner.

> In our opinion, the most striking feature of this painting is the bared female, who the artist spotlighted on, and made her a leading figure instead of a sexual one.

The process of using famous visual prompts to formulate, validate or invalidate hypotheses led to a discovery process that revealed hidden characteristics of culture to French students via exotopia while, at the same time, allowed Taiwanese students to explore their own internalized thoughts via extimacy. Computer-meditated communication facilitated this back and forth expression—to integrate extimacy and exotopia to provide a rich format for language learning as well as cultural exploration.

Forum discussions

To analyze the forum entries, a computational word frequency count method was adopted using the text analysis software program Linguistic Inquiry and Word Count (LIWC; Pennebaker, Francis, & Booth, 2001). The analysis findings give additional information on the social process approaches taken by the two groups of participants as well as their perceptions of self and otherness during the course of intercultural communication. In other words, we can analyze what they say and try to estimate what we think they mean by what they say. The additional word count and turn-taking statistics may shed some light on what they mean by what they don't say.

The LIWC output of the social process words used by students reveals that French participants used lower percentages of social process words in the postings related to both the first and the second articles (see Table 1). Further statistical analysis shows that the Taiwanese students' uses of social process words were significantly higher than those of French participants in their forum entries discussing both articles: Article 1, $F(1,37)=4.22$, $p<.05$; Article 2, $F(1,29)=6.580$, $p<.05$. This means that in comparison to their French counterparts, the Taiwanese wrote more about their family, friends, and other people, suggesting a higher degree of interpersonal connectedness and personal-emotional identification with the messages they wrote. It also suggests that the Taiwanese participants focused more on forming trust and solidarity with team members than their French counterparts. Thus, an examination of the uses of social words shows a difference between French and Taiwanese students' writing as what was desirable when engaged in intercultural communication.

Table 1. Participants' uses of social process words

linguistic category	article	Taiwan		France	
		M	SD	M	SD
social processes words (e.g., mate, talk, they, child)	1	10.84	3.81	8.23	3.60
	2	9.21	2.68	6.09	2.67
family	1	0.52	0.85	0.10	0.26
	2	0.56	0.82	0.00	0.00
friends	1	0.32	0.59	0.07	0.18
	2	0.11	0.24	0.00	0.00
humans	1	1.25	1.07	0.83	0.85
	2	1.10	0.90	1.01	0.63

note: Variables expressed as a percentage of total words used.

As for the uses of pronouns, LIWC output of pronoun analysis shows that French participants had lower percentages of total pronouns, personal pronouns, as well as first person singular and plural forms of pronouns than the Taiwanese participants. The less frequent uses of pronouns by the French participants may also suggest that they placed less emphasis on interpersonal relationship building than their Taiwanese counterparts when engaged in intercultural forum discussions. Further statistical analysis provided interesting additional information. While the Taiwanese students did use more pronouns than their French counterparts, the differences were only significant in the uses of personal pronouns and first person singular pronouns when they were discussing Article 1: personal pronouns, $F(1,37)=7.11$, $p<.05$; first person singular pronouns, $F(1,37)=5.60$, $p<.05$. None of the uses of pronouns between the two groups was significantly different in the discussion of Article 2. This result might be an indication of convergence in styles as communication continued. The LIWC output of the pronoun uses by the participants is listed in Table 2.

Table 2. The uses of pronouns by the participants

		Taiwan		France	
	article	M	SD	M	SD
total pronouns	1	15.23	3.67	13.29	4.86
	2	13.43	3.38	11.97	3.85
personal pronouns	1	9.42	3.35	6.56	2.72
	2	7.57	2.42	5.27	4.02
first person singular (e.g., I, me, mine)	1	5.49	2.28	3.67	2.23
	2	3.14	1.12	2.63	2.19
first person plural (e.g., we, us, our)	1	1.24	1.49	0.72	0.59
	2	1.71	1.48	1.38	1.43

note: Variables expressed as a percentage of total words used.

The quantitative analysis findings suggest a rich amount of extimacy demonstrated by the Taiwanese participants on the personal as well as collective level. This communication approach was not immediately reciprocated by their French counterparts. Nevertheless, as the interaction intensified, interpersonal relationships began to form and deeper levels of extimacy and exotopia were enjoyed by both groups.

Real-life exchanges

Two Taiwanese students visited French students during the Christmas holidays. They posted observations and photos of their visit on the project website as well as exchanged views on what they were experiencing as if they were taking their Taiwanese peers on a virtual journey with them. Over 100 written entries were posted in the week of the two students' visit. However, since, by that time, the semester for the French students was already almost over and they were taking their final exams, they did not have the chance to participate in the web discussion.

An analysis of what was posted by the Taiwanese students revealed cross-cultural insights and changes in perceptions. Their writings are witness to developmental stages they went through and their experiences of extimacy and exotopia.

The journal entries started with exhilarating sensory impressions of traveling abroad. On the first two days, the two Taiwanese students excitedly described the beautiful sceneries of Paris (e.g., Eiffel Tower, Galeries Lafayette, Montmartre, the Christmas market) and repeatedly used words such as "amazing," "grand," "awesome," "great," "romantic," and so forth. Hyperbolic expressions like, "the most famous," "the most beautiful," and "I love it" were also common. Their excitement was echoed by their Taiwanese peers' uses of "cool," "wow," "splendid," "OMG," and numerous exclamation marks in their responses. The signs of a honeymoon stage of intercultural encounters were prevalent. On day two, in addition to praising the street scenes and architectures, they started to take note of people's behaviors. Two things that they observed were how "strange" it was that French kissed each other on cheeks when greeting and how "annoying" that most shops closed very early. On day three, they continued to rave about the beauty and romantic atmosphere of Paris. Interestingly, a photo of a classroom at Paris II University stirred up a debate. Some exclaimed in disbelief, "It's just like a classroom in the movie!!" or "That's what we called a classroom in a university!!" and hoped that "one day I really can sit in that kind of the classroom and learn something!" However, others were too overwhelmed and even questioned its appropriateness:

> The classrooms there seem to be so splendid that I can't believe students all take courses in that artistic atmosphere. And such a classroom also shows the emphasis on learning that must be regarded as solemnity.
>
> Oh! The classroom looks so beautiful!! ummm...it looks like a church to me! xD
>
> Their classroom is so different from ours. It looks just like a conference hall here in Taiwan
>
> Don't you think it looks more like a court or something? I'm wondering if everyone can see the professors clearly or they simply listen during classes? After all, it's so spacious there.

About the same time the students expressed their uncertainty about the excessively spacious and elaborate classrooms of French universities, they also became aware and proud of their ability to move in and out of their own culture and the host culture. The two visiting students described their exploration all over the city with French students, the jokes they made, and the French dessert they much enjoyed. Their peers in Taiwan keenly took note and commented on their "becoming French" and a visiting student responded proudly, "I took it as a compliment." This sense of self-confidence that came from discovering their adaptability increased as they spent more days in Paris. By day five, one of them declared, "I feel like a Parisian now!"

Although feeling like new immigrants, the two students still looked at the host culture through their own cultural lenses. They observed how the French concepts of time were different from those of the Taiwanese:

> It is interesting that most of the clerks in French shops will take their time at the counter, no matter how many customers are standing in lines waiting. They just put our stuff in the bag slowly and give us the change slowly. That is quite different from Taiwan.
>
> The funny thing we discovered these days by taking the Metro and the bus is that French people would not wait for two minutes for the next bus which has more space but spend two hours having lunch and chatting with each other. They would squeeze onto the bus no matter how crowded it is.

After day 6, one of the Taiwanese students finished her visit and left Paris. The solitude seemed to have allowed the remaining student to have more room for self-determination of what was meaningful to her. She wrote,

> Actually, I am pretending I am a Parisian now since I live in the centre of Paris and lead a simple life here. In this trip, I would suggest that I see the practical side of Paris. It is more like the real life than in the movies or the books about this fantastic city! Anyway, I am having my own "Paris, Je T'aime."

She went back to most of the sites where she had visited with her Taiwanese and French peers and took more photos. She posted the photos and expressed a renewed appreciation of Paris:

> I took a lot of pictures of Paris by night. Tonight, I went to Champs Elysees and L'Arc de Triomphe. It is so amazing to take a walk on Avenue Champs Elysees at night. Everyone has his or her own pace. It doesn't matter if they walk super fast or slow. It is the pace of Paris's own kind.

Finally, she ended her journal entry asserting the value of the visit:

> You would learn more about their culture once you live in here for a period, like me. If you pay attention to their daily lives, you would know that it is not that romantic as in movies, they are quite practical, I would say!

After taking a close look at the posted entries, we found that the two students went through stages of being external tourists, cross-cultural observers and informants, and finally intercultural speakers. The real-life exchange allowed the two students to immerse themselves in the culture, thereby lending a greater depth of meaning to the intercultural experience. As for the Taiwanese students who remained in Taiwan and followed the two on the virtual tour, they also joined in the process of understanding French culture via extimacy; the French students in turn had renewed insights into their own cultural characteristics through exotopia. In fact, the French students may have gained as much as the Taiwanese guests by observing how they reacted, for example, to the university lecture halls they visited together. The Taiwanese thought they were beautiful while the French really remember a lack of heating and hard wooden benches. The same situation applied to the use of public transportation. French students cram onto crowded metros everyday so they no longer "see" them. Hearing what the Taiwanese had to say and seeing their reactions made the French students experience their own city in a different light.

Therefore, visits proved to be as useful for the visitors as for the hosts in terms of accessing the exotopic aspects of both target and host cultures. In this sense, the activities in the classroom that were designed to lead to extimacy and exotopia, allowed both hosting and traveling students to benefit from the exchange.

Conclusions and pedagogical implications

To provide our students with opportunities to develop intercultural competence and to communicate in their common target language, English, a task-based telecollaboration program was carefully designed and implemented. Different from most telecollaboration projects in which students strive for native-speaker norms of communication and linguistic accuracy, the project tasks aimed to foster participants' awareness of cultural identities, willingness to express personal opinions, and knowledge of *self* and *otherness*. Through a website, the students engaged in various types of multimodal, computer-mediated exchanges. Finally, the project concluded with real-life interactions of two Taiwanese students visiting their telecollaboration partners in Paris.

To understand the effectiveness of the project, we adopted the Lacanian (1986) concept of *extimacy* and Bakhtain's (1984) concept of *exotopia* to analyze the participants' interactions. Our analysis shows that the self-introductory activity was helpful for the students to overcome initial inhibitions to communicate with people they were not familiar with. Extimacy was approached by presenting and explaining objects that were very personal. Viewing and comparing the differences between the selected objects facilitated the acknowledging of *otherness*. The juxtaposition of personal items provided insights to collective culture when explained to the whole group. The second task, word associations, revealed shared cultural values (e.g., collectivism) and a refreshed view of one's own culture via exotopia. Similar words had different values. The third task, art selections and responses, also demonstrated excellent examples of collective extimacy and exotopia in terms of what could be considered appropriate. The task allowed the students to form and explain cultural hypotheses and later led to discoveries of cultural schemata.

The fourth task, forum discussion, was analyzed with a computational approach to tap into the desirable goals held by the two groups of participants for online intercultural contacts. Differences in interpersonal communication style were initially pronounced; yet as contact between both sides went on, convergences could also be inferred. This revealed a developing sense of empathy, which requires further research. As we suggested above, communication depends on interpreting what people say and write but also deducing what they may mean from what they don't say.

The final task, real-life contacts, was the highlight and finale of the project. According to Byram's (1997) model of intercultural communicative competence and the guidelines for assessment of intercultural experience (Byram, 2000), one of the criteria for assessing intercultural communicative competence is the ability to cope with living in a different culture. This, in a telecollaborative program, however, is usually not implemented or assessed due to logistic constraints. Again, different from other telecollaborative projects, we extended the teaching and learning of intercultural communication from the "lab" setting to the real world. During their visits, the students put what they had learned to practice and experienced firsthand the meaning of being intercultural speakers.

We understand that the project only involved two groups of ELF participants and its findings may not be generalizable to other populations. At the same time, we are excited over the fruitful outcome and findings. In retrospect, we observe several factors that could have contributed to the positive results and thus carry pedagogical implications.

Careful planning of program objectives and tasks played a very important role in ensuring the active and enthusiastic participation of the students. The program aimed to facilitate students' intercultural communication competence instead of grammatical accuracy, and the assessments of the students' performance were mainly based on participation. This aim and practice not only reflected the reality of international communication but also directed the students' attention to meaningful and purposeful interaction. Communicating with other ELF speakers and knowing that their "not-so-perfect English" would be a common feature in their communication could reduce the students' constant self-consciousness of making language errors. Since the focus of the communication was not on grammatical accuracy, the affective filter of the students could have been lowered and the communication fluency then increased (Krashen, 1981).

In addition, making culture the focus of discussions was a motivating factor for the students to engage in ongoing communication with their foreign partners. The tasks took students' background knowledge into account and all of the students had something to say and could make contributions to the interaction. The outcome of our project was similar to Fedderholdt's (2001) findings of a study arranging for Japanese university students to interact with Danish students: Writing and communicating about one's own culture could facilitate learners' motivation to interact with people they don't know and whose first language is not English. The active participation in the exchanges of our students also echoes Keranen and Bayyurt's (2006) assertion that when participants share features of their own cultures, they are not only willing but enthusiastic in expressing personal opinions. By adopting tasks in which cultures were compared and contrasted, students can have a voice to speak their own minds and gradually develop target language proficiency.

Besides active participation, we observed increased intercultural competence in our students. We believe the extimate approach to tasks took the students from interacting on a personal level to understanding resonance on a collective plane. This allowed them to develop insights into refreshed views on their own cultures. Such is the value of engaging the students' personal extimacy and fostering an awareness of exotopia.

Constant communication between instructors/directors of the project was also crucial. We, the project instructors, were constantly communicating and keeping each other informed of the reactions of students to the tasks. Although we defined our roles as facilitators and tried to be as unobtrusive as possible, we closely monitored the progress of the students and ensured that any technical problem would be quickly resolved and execution of the tasks not impeded.

The need for adequate technical support cannot be overly emphasized either. We have been fortunate to have technical assistants to design and revise the website according to the needs of the project and feedback from our students. By using the project website, the participants could easily share, post, and make comments about text, photos, or video clips. In general, the students were happy with the project website and appreciated our effort of making changes according to their suggestions. Students today are digital natives who grew up with the convenience of easy access to the Internet and may have little tolerance for unfriendly website and technical breakdowns. Accepting student suggestions and making the website as interactive as possible so that they can easily make contributions to the content of the website can give students a sense of ownership of the project website and the project itself.

Our study made an attempt to look into the language patterns in ELF interactions and had interesting findings. As ELF speakers increasingly use online communication to serve their various purposes, we need to better understand how ELF is used or formed during intercultural contacts. We urge further study of ELF patterns, given the implications for future design and implementation of multimodal interactions for ELF learners whose interaction increasingly defines the global educational mainstream.

References

Bakhtin, M. (1984). *Esthétique de la création verbale [Aesthetics of verbal creation]*. Paris, France: Gallimard.

Belz, J. (2004, July). Telecollaborative language study: A personal overview of praxis and research. In *Selected papers from the 2004 NFLRC Symposium:*

Distance education, distributed learning, and language instruction. Honolulu: University of Hawai'i National Foreign Language Resource Center. Retrieved from http://www.nflrc.hawaii.edu/networks/nw44/belz.htm

Bloch, J. (2004). Second language cyber rhetoric: A study of Chinese L2 writers in an online usenet group. *Language Learning and Technology, 8*(3), 66–82. Retrieved from http://llt.msu.edu/vol8num3/bloch

Byram, M. (1997). *Teaching and assessing intercultural communicative competence.* Sydney, Australia: Multilingual Matters.

Byram, M. (2000). Assessing intercultural competence in language teaching. *Sprogforum, 18*(6), 8–13.

Byram, M., & Fleming, M. (Eds.). (1998). *Language learning in intercultural perspective.* Cambridge, England: Cambridge University Press.

Campbell, R. S., & Pennebaker, J. W. (2003). The secret life of pronouns: Flexibility in writing style and physical health. *Psychological Science, 14*, 60–65.

Carroll, D. W. (2007). Patterns of student writing in a critical thinking course: A quantitative analysis. *Assessing Writing 12*, 213–227. Retrieved from http://www.elsevier.com/authored_subject_sections/S06/S06_345/misc/assessing_writing1.pdf

Crystal, D. (2003). *The Cambridge encyclopedia of the English language* (2nd ed.). Cambridge, England: Cambridge University Press.

Crystal, D. (2004). *English as a global language* (2nd ed.). Cambridge, England: Cambridge University Press.

Dezin, N. K. (1978). *The research act: A theoretical introduction to sociological methods.* New York, NY: McGraw-Hill.

Fan, Y. (2000). A classification of Chinese culture. *Cross Cultural Management, 7*(2), 3–10.

Fedderholdt, K. (2001). An email exchange project between non-native speakers of English. *ELT Journal, 53*(3), 273–280.

Felix, U. (2002). The web as a vehicle for constructivist approaches in language teaching. *ReCALL, 14*(1), 2–15.

Finkbeiner, C., & Koplin, C. (2002). A cooperative approach for facilitating intercultural education. *Reading Online, 6*(3). Retrieved from http://www.readingonline.org/newliteracies/finkbeiner

Furstenberg, G., Levet, S., English, K., & Maillet, K. (2001). Giving a virtual voice to the silent language of culture: The *Cultura* project. *Language Learning & Technology, 5*(1), 55–102.

Graddol, D. (1997). *The future of English? A guide to forecasting the popularity of the English language in the 21st century.* London, England: The British Council. Retrieved from http://www.britishcouncil.org/learning-elt-future.pdf

Graddol, D. (2006). *English next.* London, England: The British Council. Retrieved from http://www.britishcouncil.org/files/documents/learningresearchenglishnext.pdf

Hofstede, G. (2005). *Cultures and organizations: Software of the mind.* London, England: McGraw-Hill.

Hsu, J. (2004). Going online to Chinese audiences: The role of culture. *Issues in Information Systems, V*(2), 516–522. Retrieved from http://www.iacis.org/iis/2004_iis/PDFfiles/Hsu.pdf

Jenkins, J. (2004). ELF at the gate: The position of English as a lingua franca. *The European English Messenger,*13(2), 63–69.

Johnson, S., & English, K. (2003). Images, myths and realities across cultures, *The French Review, 76*(3), 492–506.

Korshuk, A. (2005). Learning more about cultures through free word association data. *Intercultural Communication, 8.* Retrieved from http://www.immi.se/intercultural/nr8/korshuk.htm

Krashen, S. (1981). *Second language acquisition and second language learning.* Oxford, England: Pergamon Press.

Lacan, J. (1986). *Le Séminaire [The Seminar]* (7th ed.). Paris, France: Editions du Seuil.

Lacan, J. (2006). *Séminaire XVI [Seminar XVI].* Paris, France: Editions du Seuil.

Lam, W. S. E. (2004). Second language socialization in a bilingual chat room: Global and local considerations. *Language Learning and Technology, 8*(3), 44–65. Retrieved from http://llt.msu.edu/vol8num3/pdf/lam.pdf

Liaw, M.-L. (2007). Constructing a virtual "third space" for EFL learners: Where language and cultures meet. *ReCALL, 19*(2), 224–241.

Louhiala-Salminen, L., Charles, M., & Kankaanranta, A. (2005). English as a lingua franca in Nordic corporate mergers: Two case companies. *English for Specific Purposes, 24,* 401–421.

Malcolm, I. G., & Sharifian, F. (2002). Aspects of aboriginal English oral discourse: An application of cultural schema theory. *Discourse Studies, 4,* 169–181.

Mayring, P. (2000). Qualitative Content Analysis. *Forum Qualitative Sozialforschung [Forum: Qualitative Social Research], 1*(2), Art. 20. Retrieved from http://www.qualitative research.net/index.php/fqs/article/view/1089/2385

Nunan, D. (2004). *Task-based language teaching.* Cambridge, England: Cambridge University Press.

O'Dowd, R. (2007). Evaluating the outcomes of online intercultural exchange. *ELT Journal, 6*(1/2), 144–152.

Pennebaker, J. W. (2002, August). *Expressively easing trauma.* Paper presented at the 110th annual convention of the American Psychological Association, Chicago.

Pennebaker, J. W., Francis, M., & Booth, R. (2001). *Linguistic inquiry and word count: LIWC 2001.* Mahwah, NJ: Erlbaum Publishers.

Pennebaker, J. W., & Lay, T. C., (2002). Language use and personality during crises: Analyses of Mayor Rudolph Giuliani's press conferences. *Journal of Research in Personality, 36,* 271–282.

Pillsbury, G. (1998). First-person singular and plural—strategies for managing ego—and sociocentrism in four basketball teams. *Journal of Contemporary Ethnography, 26,* 450–478.

Rude, S. S., Gortner, E. M., & Pennebaker, J. W. (2004). Language use of depressed and depression-vulnerable college students. *Cognition & Emotion, 18,* 1121–1133.

Seidlhofer, B. (2008). Introducing English as a lingua franca (ELF): Precursor and partner in intercultural communication. *Synergies Europe, 3,* 25–36.

Setlock, L. D., Fussell, S. R., & Neuwirth, C. (2004, November). Taking it out of context: Collaborating within and across cultures in face-to-face settings and via instant messaging. *Proceedings of CSCW 2004* (pp. 604–613). New York, NY: ACM Press.

Setlock, L. D., Quinones, P.-A., & Fussell, S. R. (2007, January). Does culture interact with media richness? The effects of audio vs. video conferencing on Chinese and American Dyads. *Proceedings of the 40th Hawai'i International Conference on System Sciences* (p. 13).

Shaghasemi, E., & Heisey D. R. (2009). The cross-cultural schemata of Iranian-American people toward each other: A qualitative approach. *Intercultural Communication Studies, XVIII1*, 143–160.

Shawback, M. J., & Terhune, N. M. (2002) Online interactive courseware: Using movies to promote cultural understanding in a CALL environment. *ReCALL, 14*(1), 85–95.

Stirman, S. W., & Pennebaker, J. W. (2001). Word use in the poetry of suicidal and non-suicidal poets. *Psychosomatic Medicine, 63,* 517–523.

Tisseron, S. (Ed.). (2001). *L'intimité surexposée [Intimacy overexposed]*. Paris, France: Ramsay.

Wang, Q. (2005). Different ethical values in Chinese and American cultures. *US-China Foreign Language, 3*(5), 55–60.

Yule, G. (1996) *Pragmatics*. Oxford, England: Oxford University Press.

Developing Intercultural Communicative Competence Through Online Exchanges

Dorothy M. Chun
University of California, Santa Barbara

Based on Byram's (1997) definition of Intercultural Communicative Competence (ICC) and specific types of discourse analysis proposed by Kramsch and Thorne (2002) and Ware and Kramsch (2005), this chapter explores how online exchanges can play a role in second language learners' development of pragmatic competence and ICC. With data obtained from an intercultural exchange between students learning German in an American university and students studying English at a German university, we illustrate how culture is embedded in language as discourse, how "language learners have to negotiate new ways not only of interpreting the content of utterances, but also of navigating interactional pragmatics" (Ware & Kramsch, p. 201), and how advanced learners of German as a foreign language and English as a foreign language employ different discourse styles in their online postings as they seek to understand the discourse genres of their partners.

Introduction

The fields of second language acquisition (SLA) and foreign language education (FLE) both recognize the importance not only of linguistic and communicative competence but of intercultural competence as well. In theorizing about SLA, functionalist approaches focus on how language is used primarily for

---

[1] This chapter originally appeared as Chun, D. M. (2011). *Cultura*: Developing intercultural communicative competence through online exchanges. *CALICO Journal, 28*(2). It is reprinted here with the permission of the author and of *CALICO Journal*. The article appears as it did in the original with the addition of appendices plus minor changes to correct typographical errors and to bring it in line with the formatting conventions of this series.

communication and therefore must incorporate multiple levels of language, including pragmatics (Bardovi-Harlig, 2007). The focus of functionalist theories is on the linguistic resources used to make meaning and entails analysis of how learners' language constructs meaning (Chapelle, 2009). Many scholars have argued that language and culture must be treated as inseparable constructs (Byrnes, 2002; Kramsch, 1993), and recent work focuses on the pedagogies that seek to develop intercultural competence. Byrnes (2009) examines three documents, the *Standards for Foreign Language Learning* (ACTFL, 2006), the *Common European Framework of Reference* (CEFR; Council of Europe, 2001), and the report by the Modern Language Association Ad Hoc Committee on Foreign Languages (2007) entitled "Foreign languages and Higher Education: New Structures for a Changed World," which indicate a shift in the foreign language profession as it pertains to the role of culture. Each document "assumes that language use must be seen as embedded in diverse social activities in the lives of people and peoples around the globe" (p. 316) and subscribes to the idea that the goal of FLE is to develop speakers who have deep translingual and transcultural competence.

Studies focusing on how computer-mediated communication (CMC) or telecollaboration can contribute to the development of pragmatic competence and ICC are emerging (e.g., Belz, 2007; Kramsch & Thorne, 2002; Schneider & von der Emde, 2006; Ware & Kramsch, 2005). Belz reviews the work on the role of computer mediation in the development of pragmatic competence, stating that "there is a general consensus among scholars that *pragmatics* involves the study of communicative language use in sociocultural context" (p. 45) and citing studies of collaborative interaction that have investigated, for example, variations in conversational style, the performance of apologies, the presentation of opinions, and the negotiation of positive and negative face. The present study examines the discourse produced by L2 learners in asynchronous forum discussions and synchronous text chats and reports on the interactional pragmatic abilities exhibited by the learners in these different types of computer-mediated communication (CMC) environments that reflect different levels of ICC.

Review of studies on CMC for ICC

This section reviews previous work in three areas: first, in defining what intercultural communicative competence (ICC) entails; second, in documenting how different types of computer-mediated communication (CMC) can be leveraged to help learners develop pragmatic competence and ICC; and third, how the acquisition of ICC can be assessed.

ICC

The interculturally competent speaker, as defined by Byram (1997), is able to effectively exchange information with members of the target culture and does so by displaying attitudes of curiosity and openness, by demonstrating knowledge of how language and culture are related in the target culture, by possessing skills of interpreting and relating, and by being able to use in real-time an appropriate combination of knowledge, skills and attitudes to interact with interlocutors from a different country or culture. If interlocutors want to maintain conversational involvement, they must be aware of the other's socio-cultural background as well as the linguistic practices used to express that background or culture. Successful intercultural communication requires interlocutors to understand the differences in interactional norms between different speech communities and the ability to "reconcile or mediate between different modes present" (Byram & Fleming, 1998, p. 12). In addition, ICC involves an understanding not only of the culture and language being studied but also the readiness to suspend disbelief and judgment about the other culture (Culture 2 or C2) and the willingness to reflect on one's own culture (Culture 1 or C1) and question the values and presuppositions in one's own cultural practices. Through comparing and contrasting, learners can become more deeply aware of their own belief system and ideological perspectives, which are often unconscious. They understand how aspects of their own culture are perceived from the other's cultural perspective and how this link between the two cultures is fundamental to interaction.

CMC to develop ICC

The use of online telecollaboration between individuals or groups in different locations has been documented with both successful and failed exchanges. For example, Abrams (2002), Furstenberg, Levet, English, and Maillet (2001), and Kramsch and Thorne (2002), to name but a few, have shown that online exchanges can raise learners' cultural awareness. Other studies by Belz (2003), Chun and Wade (2004), Müller-Hartmann (2000), and Wade (2005) report on successful development of some aspects of intercultural competence. But success cannot be taken for granted in telecollaborative exchanges, and even the aforementioned studies discuss a wide range of sociocultural and intercultural pragmatic factors that can hinder success.

In a comprehensive review of existing research on the use of telecollaboration in language and culture learning, O'Dowd and Ritter (2006) provide and describe 10 different factors at four levels (individual, classroom, socioinstitutional, and interaction), which help to explain "failed communication" in online exchanges. The fourth level, the interaction level, refers to "the misunderstandings and tension which arise from cultural differences in communicative style and behavior" (p. 634), reflecting a focus on intercultural pragmatics.

Just as in face-to-face communication, Internet users bring with them their own culturally specific communicative norms and modes of behavior, and in an intercultural exchange, they must determine whether their norms and behaviors are compatible with those of their partners. The study by Kramsch and Thorne (2002) investigates the use of synchronous and asynchronous communication between French learners of English in France and American learners of French in the US and finds different discourse styles between the two groups. "Most of the French interlocutors used factual, impersonal, dispassionate genres of writing" (p. 94), whereas most of the American students' postings reflected an "oral style... full of questions and exclamation marks, [which] suggests a high degree of affective involvement and emotional identification" (p. 95). Different expectations of each group about the relative focus on information exchange versus on personal engagement provide "a strong example of the challenges inherent to cross cultural interaction while illustrating little in terms of interlanguage pragmatic development" (Thorne, 2003, p. 45), using Boxer's (2002) distinction between cross cultural and interlanguage pragmatics.

Ware and Kramsch (2005) also advocate examining language as discourse, looking at interactional structures in addition to linguistic structures. They describe an extended episode of misunderstanding between two students in an asynchronous CMC project, and suggest that online intercultural exchanges "afford both students and teachers the opportunity to learn more about historical facts, linguistic features of speech, and discourse pragmatics, as well as about the expectations of genre and the constraints of the medium" (p. 202). Students can explore the nature of language and communication across cultures and can be encouraged to reflect on both their and their interlocutors' utterances.

In addition to the potential problem of differing discursive styles in intercultural CMC, different cultures-of-use of the Internet communication tools can help or hinder communication (see Ware and Kramsch's, 2005, reference above to the constraints of the medium). Based on three case studies, Thorne (2003) concludes that the tools are not neutral media. E-mail was found to be a constraining variable in the intercultural communication process, as students perceived it to be a tool for communication between power levels and generations (e.g., students to teachers, children to parents); students much preferred IM (instant messaging) for communicating with their peers. Not only is the asynchronous versus synchronous nature of the CMC tool an issue, but as Herring (1999) suggests, the structural properties of CMC systems have an effect on interactional coherence, specifically, on turn-taking and exchange structures. In synchronous text chats, for instance, there is a high degree of "disrupted adjacency, overlapping exchanges, and topic decay" (p. 1). The choice of CMC tool can therefore be important in how successful an intercultural telecollaboration is.

As Belz (2003) recommended, tensions within telecollaboration often "constitute cultural rich-points that we want our students to explore" (p. 87), and this sentiment is echoed by Schneider and von der Emde (2006), who acknowledge that intercultural conflicts will never disappear and the solution is not to teach students sociocultural strategies for more "effective" communication that avoids conflict, but rather help students to deal with the conflict as a learning opportunity. O'Dowd and Ritter (2006) advise educators to take "an on-going action research approach to their classes which involves collecting and analyzing online interactions and subsequent feedback from their students" (p. 639). This proposal is expanded upon in the next section on how to assess ICC.

Assessment of ICC

Although intercultural competence has gained importance in foreign language curricula, there are few comprehensive treatments of the assessment of ICC outcomes (Sinicrope, Norris, & Watanabe, 2007). Schulz (2007) proposes a set of fundamental objectives for cross-cultural awareness and understanding and recommends the use of portfolio assessment for tracking learners' development, since acquiring ICC is an iterative process. Program-specific questionnaires, self-assessments, and interviews can also be used for assessing ICC outcomes. In addition to a renewed understanding of language within an intercultural orientation, Scarino (2009) suggests a reconceptualization of the assessment process, proposing that it involves several dimensions: (a) communication in the target language, in which students negotiate meaning through interpreting and using language in diverse contexts; (b) understanding how students' dynamic and developing enculturation affects how they see and interpret the world; (c) eliciting students' meta-awareness of how language, culture and meaning are interrelated; and (d) positioning students as both language users and learners/analyzers (p. 328).

Research questions

The research questions investigated in this study are

RQ1: How does the choice of Internet tools (specifically asynchronous forum discussions and synchronous chats) contribute to the style of language produced by the learners? In particular, (1a) Is there a difference in the percentage of statements versus questions used by both the American and German students? and (1b) What types of speech acts are used to convey pragmatic ability and the development of ICC?

RQ2: How does discourse analysis of our data contribute to "an empirically informed Internet pragmatics"? Specifically, how do learners demonstrate their pragmatic ability to perform various types of speech acts in their online postings, for example, express facts, express opinions, express curiosity or interest, negotiate meaning, seek to understand the other, save face, hedge, and reflect on their own or the other culture, all components of ICC?

Method

Participants

The participants in this study were (a) students in an upper division German sociolinguistics course at a large western state university and (b) students in an English class for math, physics, and geoscience majors at a university in northern Germany. Twenty-three students were enrolled in the German course, and 23 students attended the English class intermittently. In both classes, the online exchange was a part of the course but not a central component of the course. It is important to note that the students in the German course had regular, required assignments, including requirements to answer the online questionnaires and post in the online forums. In contrast, the students in the English course were strongly encouraged, but not required, to participate in the online exchange. This difference in course requirements is common and often unavoidable in these types of exchanges (O'Dowd & Ritter, 2006). The exchange took place over a 10-week period during the course of an American trimester.

Materials and procedures

Word associations and asynchronous forum discussions

The exchange began following the procedure used by Furstenberg et al. (2001) in their *Cultura* project (http://cultura.mit.edu/). The students were asked to fill out a word association questionnaire, consisting of 12 words/phrases chosen by the two course instructors. Students were asked to write 3–5 words or phrases in their respective L1 that they associated with the 12 words/phrases (listed in their L1). Four of the 12 words were related to "language" so that they might be relevant to the sociolinguistics course (left column of Table 1). The other 8 words/phrases were thought to be topics or concepts of interest to university students (right column of Table 1).

Table 1 List of words/phrases in the word associations

language-related words	other words of interest	
language/*Sprache*	alcohol/*Alkohol*	quitting time/*Feierabend*
dialect/*Dialekt*	homeland/*Heimat*	night life in city X/*Nachtleben in der Stadt X*
slang/*Umgangssprache*	order/*Ordnung*	recycling/*Recycling*
Denglish/*Denglisch*	work/*Arbeit*	climate change/*Klimaänderung*

The entries for the word associations formed the basis of discussion in the subsequent online forum discussions. Students in both courses were instructed to view the word associations online, where the answers for each word/phrase were shown side-by-side; the U.S. answers were in the left column, and the German answers were in the right column (see Table 2).

Table 2. Answers for word associations: "Dialect/Dialekt"

dialect	Dialekt
a language spoke in a certain region	Akzent, Plattdeutsch, Tonakzent, Änderung der Tonhöhe, Morphem
a more specific form of communication, but not considered "official" or "standard"	(accent, Plattdeutsch, tone accent, change in pitch, morpheme)
a way of speaking, or a language sub-group	
Aachener Platt, Bavarian, cowboy accent	Eigenart, regional, lustig
accent, region, language	(idiosyncrasy, regional, funny)
Boston and Chicago	Einge Formen von Sprachen
differences in saying the same thing	(own form of language)
grammar, diction, geographical regions	Hannover dialektfrei witzig regional
grammar, geographical region, diction	(Hannover, dialect-free, funny, regional)
neat to hear, german dialect, cultural	Regionale Verbundenheit
Plattdeutsch, Bairisch, Westfaelisch (Plattdeutsch, Bavarian, Westfalian)	(regional bonds)
pronunciation, geography, diversity, history, expressions	regionaler Unterschied innerhalb der selben Sprache
region	(regional difference within the same language)
region, accent, sound	Verschiene Tonhöhe einer Sprache, (different pitches of a language), language of people not from your home town, a different form of your language that is spoken in certain area of your country, sometimes the same words may have different meanings then
region, slang, intonation	
switzerland, diglossia, culture,	
twang, regional, changing	
unique, familiar, cultural	
what defines an autochthonous inhabitant	
a labeling force	

For each of the word associations there was a separate forum. Students were instructed to choose several word associations of interest and write comments of approximately 50 words in German in each respective forum, comparing the answers of the students in the US (at UNIV-A) with the answers of the students in Germany (at UNIV-G) and noting what they found especially interesting (see Table 3 for a sample forum discussion about the word associations for the words "dialect/Dialekt").

Table 3.	Forum discussion "Dialect/Dialekt"

Please type your answers directly in the forum window—DO NOT cut and paste from Microsoft Office or another rich text application, as this can introduce corrupted characters into the post. Thank you!

Schreiben Sie ca. 50 Wörter auf Deutsch. Vergleichen Sie die Antworten der UNIV-A Studenten mit den Antworten der UNIV-G Studenten. Was finden Sie besonders interessant daran?

(Write approximately 50 words in German. Compare the answers of the UNIV-A students with the answers of the UNIV-G students. What do you find especially interesting?)

Dorothy Chun, Apr 24, 2009

Was fuer mich am interessantesten waren zwei Sachen; Erstens keine negative Woerter wurden damit (Dialekt) verbunden. Zweitens, diese Idee von Semiotics, d.h von Bezeichner und Bezeichnetes.

Ich fand es interessant, dass am "schlimmsten" wenn man das so beschreiben darf, wir haben solche woerter benutzt wie "lustig," "witzig" statt "idiotisch," proletenhaft, voll asi usw. Keine negative Woerterassoziationen, keine Verurteilungen...wir sind schon unterwegs wahr? Es gab noch einen Punkt: Bezeichner und Bezeichnetes. Wir verwenden manchmal verschiedene Woerter oder sprechen die Komplett anders aus, wann das Objekt das selbe Objekt in einer andere Sprache ist.

(What was most interesting for me were two things: First, no negative words were associated with it (dialect). Second, this idea of semiotics, i.e., of signifier and signified. I found it interesting, that the "worst," when one can describe it that way, we used such words as "funny," "humorous" instead of "idiotic," working class/crude, [profanity], etc. No negative word associations, no convictions... we are already on our way, yes? There was one more point: signifier and signified. We sometimes use different words or say them completely differently, when the object is the same object in another language.)

Brian (UNIV-A), Apr 27, 2009

Ich denke, wir alle stimmen eine generelle Definition von einer Dialekt ein. Ich habe festgestellt, Kommentare wie "innerhalb der selben Sprache" und eine Art der "Verbindung." Wie wir in der Klasse diskutiert haben, die Kriterien, an der man definiert, was eine Sprache ist oder was bindet Menschen bei regionalen Sprach ist sehr subjektiv. Persönlich bin ich nicht für die Idee der Dialekte. Ich denke, es ist wichtig, zu vereinheitlichen Sprachen zusammen, oder zumindest einige Basis-Sprache. Eine Region, die nicht, dies zu tun, auch nicht für die Kommunikation mit dem Rest der Welt und wird nicht als Wirtschaft existieren.

(I think we all agree about a general definition of a dialect. I have noticed comments like "within the same language" and a kind of "connection." As we discussed in class, the criteria by which one defines what a language is or what connects people through a regional language is very subjective. Personally, I am not for the idea of dialects. I think it is important to unify languages, or at least a basic-language. A region which doesn't do this also [cannot have] communication with the rest of the world and will not exist as an economy.)

Charlie (UNIV-A), Apr 29, 2009

Akzent ist für uns akziptierbar. manchmal es läßt uns lachen manchmal läßt uns beneiden. Aber all in positivem Sinne. Wenn man sich an eine Person erinnert, erinnert er sich auch an ihren Akzent, falls diese Person einen hat. Also, der Akzent zeichnet nicht eine Persönlichkeit aus aber macht sie in der Erinnerung noch lebendiger und kann auch ein charakteristisches Merkmal sein.
Solange man sich verständigen kann, ist Akzent noch ok. Aber wenn man einen anderen nicht mehr so gut versteht...ich weiß nicht, wie geduldig wir sein können...

(Accent is acceptable for us. sometimes it makes us laugh and sometimes it makes us envious. But all in a positive sense.
As long as one can make oneself understood, [having an] accent is ok. But when one can't understand the other well, I don't know how patient we can be...)

Mani (UNIV-G), May 07, 2009

Synchronous chat session

Towards the end of the course, a synchronous text chat was scheduled between the two groups. Students in the US went to a computer lab during their normal class hour, and students in Germany were asked to go to a computer lab at a later hour than their class usually met. Students were told that they could write in whichever language they chose (German or English). Since only seven German students were present for the online chat, students in the US paired up in order for all of the students to be involved. They were instructed to chat about anything that had been posted previously online (see Table 4 for an excerpt, completely in English, of a chat about dialects in Germany).

Table 4. Excerpt of a chat discussion: Sam and Niko: Dialects/High German

Sam (UNIV-A) is an American student with Swiss parents.
Niko (UNIV-G) was born in Vietnam and emigrated to Germany with his parents.

Sam:	is the type of German which you speak in Hannover much different than in other parts of Germany?
Niko:	oh yes
Sam:	how so?
Niko:	yes we talk high german in Hannver
Sam:	do you find it a pretty type of German?
Sam:	do you like it?
Niko:	it's like the kind of german you hear in the News on TV
Sam:	i see
Niko:	in the other part of germany people talk it with a lil bit more accents
Sam:	what do you think about low German, such as what they speak in Munchen or Switzerland
Sam:	?
Niko:	i like it very much
Niko:	we're proud of our high german
Sam:	Have you ever been to Switzerland?
Niko:	not yet, i have a friend there and will probbably go there this summer
Niko:	if i have sime money
Sam:	yes, i understand

Data analysis

The data produced by the students is analyzed in three ways. First, numerical tallies of the number of words written in the asynchronous online forums and in the synchronous text chats are made. Second, macro-level tallies of statements and questions and mean length of these statements and questions is calculated in order to compare the different genres of forum discussion versus chat. Third, a finer-grained micro-level discourse analysis, investigating the language used to show interest/curiosity and to perform facework (hedging, avoiding conflict; expressing disagreement) is presented, as these types of speech acts could contribute to development of pragmatic competence and intercultural communicative competence (ICC; Koike, 1989). As Bardovi-Harlig (2001) states,

"Although it is not the only way of viewing pragmatics, speech act research has been well represented in crosscultural and interlanguage pragmatics research" (p. 13). In his description of what is required for ICC, Byram (1997) states that "the efficacy of communication depends upon using language to demonstrate one's willingness to relate, which often involves the indirectness of politeness, rather than the direct and 'efficient' choice of language full of information" (p. 3) and which is a component of performing facework.

Student assessment of success of chat

At the end of the course, students in the U.S. class were asked via a written questionnaire to evaluate the success of the online exchange, with particular regard to the text chat. The responses of individual students is compared with the actual text chat in which the student participated, and the discourse analysis of the text chat and the level of satisfaction expressed about the chat provide two different means of determining or explaining what constitutes a "successful" intercultural exchange.

Results and discussion

Participants

It is important to note that most of the participants on both sides are multilingual and multicultural to varying degrees. Of course, the students in the US were all studying German, and the students in Germany were all taking an English class so they all were bilingual in German and English. A number of the students grew up bilingual. Five of the students in the US grew up as English/German bilinguals, two of the students were raised bilingually in English and Vietnamese, three were raised as English/Spanish bilinguals, and one was a Romanian/German bilingual. Among the students in Germany who participated in the forum discussions and chats, one was raised bilingually in German and Vietnamese, one was a Chinese/German bilingual, and one was a Spanish/German bilingual. Many of the students had lived or studied abroad. Although the multilingual backgrounds of the students present a potentially confounding variable, it is increasingly the case that today's students are bi- or multi-lingual to varying degrees, and it is nearly impossible to find monolinguals who are also monocultural.

Word associations

For each of the 12 English words/phrases, 18 (sometimes 19) students in the US posted anonymous entries. For each of the 12 German words/phrases, 7–8 students in Germany posted anonymous entries (see Table 1 for entries for the words "dialect/Dialekt"). These numbers indicate that a great majority of the 23 students in the US wrote word associations, while only about a third of the students in Germany made postings.

Asynchronous forum discussions

To answer RQ1, the first type of analysis is a tally of the number of entries posted, along with the total number of words in each forum, the average number of words per entry, and the average number of words per sentence (see Table 5). A very low number of forum entries was written by the students in Germany: Only 4 students made a total of 10 posts. In contrast, 58 posts were made by the U.S. students, an average of 3 posts per student. The word associations in **boldface** are the ones with forum entries from the students in Germany.

Table 5. Number of entries in the forum discussions about the word associations

forums about word associations	no. of U.S. entries	no. of words	average words per entry	average words per sentence	no. of German entries	no. of words	average words per entry	average words per sentence
language/*Sprache*	2	167	84	14	0			
dialect/*Dialekt*	3	395	132	17	1	87	87	15
slang/*Umgangssprache*	3	204	68	15	0			
Denglish/*Denglisch*	6	487	81	16	0			
alcohol/*Alkohol*	9	696	77	19	0			
homeland/*Heimat*	5	499	100	15	0			
order/*Ordnung*	5	408	82	18	0			
work/*Arbeit*	5	425	85	15	1	53	53	27
quitting time/*Feierabend*	8	509	74	13	0		0	
nightlife in city X/*Nachtleben in der Stadt X*	7	582	78	14	2	123	62	18
recycling/*Recycling*	2	232	116	17	1	59	59	20
climate change/*Klimaänderung*	2	123	62	13	5	373	75	19
averages	5	394	87	16	2	139	67	20

To answer RQ(1a), the second type of analysis of the forum discussions is a tally of the number of questions versus statements in the entries. One of the reasons for such a tally is to obtain an overall idea of the global syntactic types of entries in an asynchronous forum, which can then be compared with the types of entries in a synchronous chat. Table 6 shows the number of questions posed versus statements made in the forum discussions for each of the word associations. The word associations in **boldface** are the ones with forum entries from the students in Germany.

Table 6 Number of questions vs. statements in the forum discussions

forums	no. of questions in U.S. entries	no. of statements in U.S. entries	no. of questions in German entries	no. of statements in German entries
language/*Sprache*	0	12		
dialect/*Dialekt*	1	21	0	7
slang/*Umgangssprache*	1	13		
Denglish/*Denglisch*	5	27		
alcohol/*Alkohol*	0	46		
homeland/*Heimat*	0	31		
order/*Ordnung*	3	25		
work/*Arbeit*	0	21	0	2
quitting time/*Feierabend*	1	38		
nightlife in city X/*Nachtleben in der Stadt X*	0	40	2	5
recycling/*Recycling*	0	14	0	3
climate change/*Klimaänderung*	0	11	0	19
totals	11 (4%)	299 (96%)	2 (5%)	36 (95%)

As the data in Table 6 show, statements comprise 96% of the entries made by the students in the US and 95% of the entries made by the students in Germany, which is not surprising for asynchronous forums.

To answer RQ(1b), a third, finer grained analysis beyond tallying entries, word counts and syntactic types examines the posting from all the forums. The goals of this discourse analysis are to determine, on the one hand, the linguistic means used to state facts, make less definitive statements, make observations, and express opinions, and on the other hand, the types of pragmatic speech acts used to exchange information, display attitudes of interest or curiosity, suspend disbelief about the other culture (C2), or to reflect on one's own culture (C1), all hallmarks of ICC.

Tables 7–9 show that the advanced learners of German employ many of the same linguistic means and speech acts as the students in Germany for stating facts, making definitive statements, mitigating statements, speculating, and expressing opinions. The examples are representative of all of the students in the fourth-year sociolinguistics class, not just a few.

Table 7. Examples of typical statements in the forum discussions

American students' typical statements	German students' typical statements
Für die amerikanischen Studenten... (For the American students...) *Aber für die deutschen Studenten...* (But for the German students...) *Die Deutschen sagen, dass...* (The Germans say that...) Die Amerikaner glauben, dass... (The Americans think that...) *Man merkt...* (One notices...) *Die Studenten beschreiben...* (The students describe...) *Ich habe bemerkt, dass...* (I noticed that...)	*Die amerikanischen Studenten haben mehr geschrieben, wie..., während die mesiten deutschen Studenten...* (The American students wrote more about..., whereas most of the German students...) *Das zeigt, dass...* (That shows that...)

In the definitive statements in Table 8, note in particular the use of particles (in **boldface**) such as *doch* (really, very) and *wohl* (surely, very), and the use of adjectives and adverbs, such as *wirklich* (really), *klar* (clearly), *genau* (exactly), and *unbestreitbar* (indisputable).

Table 8. Examples of definitive statements in the forum discussions

American students' definitive statements	German students' definitive statements
*Die Eintraege von dieser Thema ist **doch** ja getraennt...* (The entries for this topic is **very** distinct...) *Der Unterschied... ist **genau** erkennbar* (The difference... is **exactly** discernible) *Man kann sehen, dass es **wirklich** ein Unterschied...* (One can see, that there **really** is a difference...) *Klar, dass...* (**Clear** that...) *Es ist **unbestreitbar**...* (It is **indisputable**...)	*Uns ist das Thema **wohl** bewusst,...* (We are **very** aware of the topic...)

As can be seen in Table 9, the linguistic means used to make statements less definitive or speculative include the words *vielleicht* (perhaps) and *anscheinend* (apparently) and the verbs *scheinen* (to seem) and *aussehen* (to appear, look like), and these words were used in multiple postings.

Table 9. Examples of less definitive statements in the forum discussions

American students' less definitive statements	German students' less definitive statements
***Vielleicht** ist es nicht so in Deutschland...* (**Maybe** it is not that way in Germany...) *Es **scheint**, als ob...* (It **seems** as if...)	*Das liegt **vielleicht** daran, dass...* (That is **perhaps** because...) ***Vielleicht** hängt es aber auch damit zusammen, dass...* (But **maybe** it is also related to the fact that...)

Als Amerikaner **scheint** *es mir zu sein...*
(As an American, it **seems** to me to be...)
Die Amerikaner/Studenten **scheinen**...
(The Americans **seem**...)
...auf jeden Fall **sieht es so aus**,...
(in any case **it looks**...)

...aber es **sieht so aus**, *dass...*
(...but **it looks/seems** that...)
...in Amerika aber **anscheinend**...
(...but in American **apparently**...)

In terms of expressing opinions, the most commonly used phrases (in **boldface**, see Table 10) were *ich glaube/denke/meine* (believe/think/mean), with 26 occurrences on the American side and 3 occurrences on the German side. The second most common comments were variations of *ich finde/fand... interessant* (I find/found... interesting), with 19 occurrences on the American side and 3 on the German side. Less commonly used expressions included *meiner Meinung nach* (in my opinion), *persönlich* (personally), *ich weiß nicht* (I don't know), *ich bin mir nicht sicher* (I'm not sure). Adjectives used to express opinions included *lustig* (funny) with 4 occurrences, *typisch* (typical), *komisch* (funny, odd), and *ironisch* (ironic).

Table 10. Examples of expression of opinion in forum discussions

American students' expression of opinion	German students' expression of opinion
Ich **denke/glaube/meine**,... (I **think**...)	*Ich* **denke**... (I **think**)
Ich **finde** *es besonders* **interessant**... (I **find** it especially **interesting**...)	*Ich* **finde**... (I **find**...)
Ich **finde** *die unterschied...ganz* **interresant** *und manchmal auch* **kommisch** (I **find** the difference...very **interesting** and sometimes also **funny**)	*Allerdings ist es* **interessant**... (It's certainly **interesting**...)
Ich **finde** *die unterschied* **interestant** *aber* **typisch** (I **find** the difference **interesting** but **typical**)	*Aus der amerikanischen Seite kam mehr..., was ich eigentlich* **gut finde** (From the American side came more..., which I actually **think is good**)
Was fuer mich **am interessantesten** *war...* (What was **most interesting** for me was...)	...***ich weiß nicht***, *wie geduldig wir sein können...* (I **don't know** how patient we can be...)
Meiner Meinung nach... (**In my opinion**...)	*Was mich aber* **wirklich aufgeregt** *hat, war...* (But what **really upset/annoyed** me was...)
Persönlich *bin ich nicht für die Idee...* (**Personally**, I'm not for the idea...)	
Ich **bin mir nicht sicher**, *ob...* (**I'm not sure** if/whether...)	
Wie **lustig**, *dass viele von uns glauben...* (How **funny**, that many of us think...)	
Aber es ist ganz **ironisch**... (But it's really **ironic**...)	
Es freute mich *zu sehen...* (**It pleased me** to see...) emotion?	
Diese Assoziation **gefaellt mir** *mehr als unsere* (I **like** this association more than ours)	

As an example of how these types of statements and opinions are manifested as reflections on students' own culture (C1) or the other culture (C2) and comparisons of the two cultures (C1 and C2), see Table 11, which is the forum discussion for the topic "Work/Arbeit" (speech acts are in **boldface**).

Table 11. Forum discussion on word associations: "Work/Arbeit"

discussion	speech acts
Ich glaube, dass die meisten UNIV-A Studenten eine mehr negative Verbindung mit Arbeit haben, **es schaint als ob** sie UNIV-G Studenten mehr an eine gute Zukunft denken, wo Arbeit Geld, Spaß und Kollegen bedeutet. **Die UNIV-A Meinung**, dass Arbeit langweilig ist und nur da ist um man Geld zu verdienen, kommt von den Erfahrungen mit "High School und College jobs", die man nur hat um Taschengeld, Essen oder Rente zu bezahen. Die Arbeit ist aber nur fur eine kleine Zeitspanne und bringt wenig Geld. **Was die meißten UNIV-G Studenten beschreiben ist die Zukunft, wo Arbeit auch Spaß machen kann und soll, die UNIV-A Studenten warten auf das auch wenn das Studium fertig ist.** (**I think** that most of the American University students have a more negative connection with work, **it seems as though** the German University students think more about a good future, where work means money, fun, and colleagues. **The American University opinion** that work is boring and is only there so that one can earn money comes from the experiences with "high school and college jobs," which one has in order to have pocket money and pay for food or rent. Work is but for a short time span and brings in little money. **What most of the German University students describe is the future, where work can and should also be fun, the American University students are also waiting for that when their studies are done.**) Daniela (UNIV-A), Apr 26, 2009	statement of opinion; less definitive statement; reflection on C1; comparison of C2 and C1
Die UNIV-A Studenten sehen ihre Arbeit als was negatives, aber auch als etwas was ein Teil des Lebens ist. **Die UNIV-G Studenten scheinen** ein bisschen mehr positiv darüber zu sein. Sie beschreiben die Arbeit als "motivitation" und als "notwendig". Sie beschieden die Arbeit auch als etwas was einem Geld verdient. **Ich glaube** der Unterschied zwischen den Antworten hat damit zu tun das die Wörter "work" und "Arbeit" sehr anders von einander sind. "Work" in der Amerikanischer Kultur wird meistens mehr als eine Belastung gesehen. (**The American University students see their work as something negative**, but also as something that is a part of life. **The German University students seem** to be a bit more positive about it. They describe work as "motivation" and as "necessary." They describe work as something that earns you money. **I think** that the difference between the answers has to do with the fact that the words "work" and "Arbeit" are very different from each other. "Work" in the American culture is mostly seen as more of a burden.) Lynda (UNIV-A), Apr 27, 2009	reflection on C1; less definitive statement about C2; opinion/reflection on C1
Ich denke, das Wort "Arbeit" wird im Deutschen tatsächlich direkter mit einem Beruf verbunden als mit der Aktivität "arbeiten". **Allerdings ist es interessant**, dass die Studenten der UNIV-G die Arbeit fast einheitlich mit "Geld verdienen" verknüpfen, während Studenten der UNIV-A "work" mehr differenzieren und eine große Bedeutung bis hin zum Lebensinhalt zukommen lassen. (**I think** the word "Arbeit" in German is in fact more directly tied to a profession than with the activity of "working." **It is certainly interesting** that the students of the German University almost uniformly link work with earning money, while the students of the American University differentiate work more and afford it a larger meaning in terms of purpose of life.) Uwe (UNIV-G), Apr 27, 2009	opinion about C1; interest in comparison of C1 and C2

Die Studenten von UNIV-G denken viel uber das Geld, das in Beziehung zu Arbeit ist. **Ich dachte** die Amerikanern liebeten Geld viel mehr, weil ich die Leute hier einkaufen lieben weiss. **Oder wollen wir nicht Arbeit fur das Geld, wie die Deutsch. Vielleicht** alle die Leute lieben und brauchen Geld ebenso. (**The students of the German University think** a lot about money in connection to work. I thought that Americans loved money much more because I know that people here love to shop. **Or we don't want work for money, like the Germans. Maybe** all people love and need money equally.) Andrew (UNIV-A), Apr 28, 2009	reflection on C2; opinion/reflection on C1 and C2; speculation about C1 and C2
Viel von den UNIV-A studenten sagten, dass Arbeit stressvoll ist. Aber die Studenten von UNIV-G sagten, dass Arbeit soll spass machen. Das ist einen **interessanten Unterschied** zwischen Ami und Deutsche kultur. Im durchsnitt sagten viel studenten von UNIV-A, dass arbeit etwas negatives ist. Aber die Studenten von UNIV-G sagten, dass sie arbeit geniessen mochten. **Interessant** ist auch wie viele Studenten von UNIV-G an das Geld denken. **Ich meine**, dass nur Amis immer an Geld denken. (**Many of the American University students said that work is stressful. But the students from the German University said that work should be fun**. That is an interesting difference between American and German culture. On average many students from the American University said that work is something negative. But the students from the German University said that they want to enjoy work. It is also **interesting** how many students of the German University think about money. **I think** that only Americans are always thinking about money.) Sam (UNIV-A), Apr 28, 2009	comparison of C1 and C2; interest in the differences and similarities of C1 and C2; reflection on C1

In an asynchronous forum, it can be difficult to engage in dialogue, given the nature of the forum and the fact that there can be great time lags between posts. However, in one forum on "climate change/Klimaänderung," students on both sides made attempts to engage their partners, in contrast to all of the other forums in which students on each side simply made statements without attempting to interact with each other. Table 12 shows the entire forum discussion, including the speech acts (in **boldface**) that were employed in the asynchronous postings. This forum discussion was unique among the forum discussions, mainly because it had the greatest participation by students in Germany, and it provides a glimpse into how interactive such online forums could be.

Table 12. Forum discussion: "Climate Change/Klimaänderung"

discussion	speech act
Interessant ist, dass fast alle Studenten der UNIV-A die Klimaänderung als eine Bedrohung sehen. Leider gibt es nur wenige Antworten aus Deutschland, aber **es sieht so aus**, dass das Thema von Studenten der UNIV-G weniger emotional betrachtet wird. **Das liegt vielleicht daran**, dass der Klimawandel in Deutschland schon seit vielen Jahren ein Thema ist und mittlerweile die möglichen Folgen nicht mehr so stark diskutiert werden. **Vielleicht hängt es aber auch damit zusammen**, dass die Medien in den USA gut darin sind, den Menschen Angst zu machen.	opinion about C2; speculation, less definitive statement; speculation, less definitive statement

(It is **interesting** that almost all of the students at the American University see climate change as a threat. Unfortunately, there are only a few answers from Germany, **but it looks as though** the topic is viewed less emotionally by the students at the German University. **Maybe that is due to the fact** that climate change has been a topic [of interest] for many years in Germany and in the meantime the possible consequences are not being discussed so strongly any more. **Maybe it is also related to** the fact that the media in the USA are good at frightening people.)

Uwe (UNIV-G), Apr 27, 2009

Ich denke das Medien trägt einen großen Teil dazu bei Umweltbildung verbreiten und damit die Menschen umweltbewusster zu machen. Denken wir an die großen Waldbrände in Kalifornien und sogar direkt in Santa Barbara im Sommer 2008. Tagelang wurde im Fernsehen Polizei- und Feuerwehr- sowie Zivileinsätze gezeigt, wie sie mit dem Feuer kämpfen. Und da hat Klimawandel sicherlich mehr oder weniger damit zu tun. Total schreckliche Bilder, **die es selten bei uns in Deutschland zu sehen gibt, weil wir eben den Ausmaß des Klimawandels in Deutschland nicht so stark "sprüren" müssen. Uns ist das Thema Klimawandel wohl bewusst, jedoch müssen wir noch nicht mit Umweltproblemen so wie die Kollegen in USA konfrontieren.**	opinion; reflection on C1; comparison of C1 and C2

(**I think** that media contribute a large part to spreading education about the environment and thereby making people more environmentally conscious. Think of the huge wildfires in California and in fact directly in Santa Barbara in the summer of 2008. For days the police, fire department and civilian operations were shown on television fighting the fire. And surely climate change had something more or less to do with it. Totally awful images, **which are seldom to be seen here in Germany, because we don't have to "experience" the full extent of climate change in Germany. We are well aware of the topic of climate change, but we don't yet have to confront environmental problems like our colleagues in the USA.**)

Niko (UNIV-G), Apr 27, 2009

Ich stimme zu. Fast alle Studendten der UNIV-A haben "scary", "threat", und "end days" oder etwas aenliches geschrieben. Fuer uns wird Klimaaenderung eng mit Bedrohung verbunden. **Ich glaube** das Medien hat etwas damit zu tun. Besonderes wenn Klimaaenderung heutzutag so eine politische "talking point" ist... DREI Studenten haben "Al Gore" gescrieben!! **(Fuer unsere Freunden aus Deutschland, die ihn vielleicht nicht kennen: Al Gore hat den global-warming Film "An Inconvenient Truth," gemacht.) Leider ist Klimaaenderung fuer viele Leute in den USA nur politisch und sensationell.**	direct response to previous posting; opinion; statement directed at German partners ("friends"); opinion/reflection on C1

(**I agree.** Almost all the students from the American University wrote "scary," "threat", and "end days" or something similar. For us, climate change is tied closely to threat. **I think** that the media have something to do with it. Especially because climate change these days is such a political "talking point"... THREE students wrote "Al Gore"!! **[For our friends from Germany, who perhaps don't know him: Al Gore made the global-warming film "An Inconvenient Truth."] Unfortunately, climate change is for many people in the USA only political and sensational.**)

Ashley (UNIV-A), Apr 28, 2009

Es sieht so aus, wie alle Studenten angst haben von GLOBAL WARMING. Leider sind unsere **westlichen Lebensstile** veranwortlich fur es. **Ich finde es auch interessant**, dass Studenten von UNIV-A und von UNIV-G an Al Gore denke wann sie dieses Wort "Klimaaenduring" lesen. (**It looks as though** all students are afraid of GLOBAL WARMING. Unfortunately, our western life styles are responsible for it. **I also find it interesting** that students from both the American University and the German University think of Al Gore when they read this word "climate change.") Sam (UNIV-A), Apr 28, 2009	less definitive statement; reflection on C1; opinion
Noch was dazu: von den Antworten **ist die Einsicht zu vermitteln**, dass die **westliche Lebensweise** ein Auslaufmodell ist. Die wachstumsorientierte kapitalistische Wirtschaftsweise ist nicht nur unter dem Eindruck der aktuellen Finanzkrise sondern auch wegen der nachhaltigen Wirkung auf unser Klima grundsätzlich in Frage zu stellen. (**Something else to add:** from the answers **we get the sense** that the **western way of life** is an obsolete model. The growth-oriented capitalistic economic model is not only under the effect of the present financial crisis but also should basically be questioned because of its lasting effect on our climate.) Niko (UNIV-G), Apr 28, 2009	additional comment to further the discussion; less definitive statement; reference to previous posting about the "western lifestyle"
Ich denke, das jeder Mensch auf der Erde die Gefahren einer globalen Erwärmung sieht und sich gegen Verschwendung von Ressourcen ausspricht. Aber wenn es dann auf persönlichen Verzicht ankommt, relativieren sich die Meinungen.... (**I think** that every person on the earth sees the dangers of a global warming and speaks out against waste of resources. But when it then comes to personal renunciation, the opinions become relative...) Tom (UNIV-G), Apr 28, 2009	opinion
Aus der UNIV-A-Seite kam mehr sentimentale Reaction, was ich eigentlich gut finde. Unsere Studenten habe auch tolle Antwort dazu mit bisschen mehr Gelassenheit. Meinstens arbeiten die Menschen unter Druck noch mehr effizient. 5 Jahre vorher konnte man andere Antwort finden und in 5 jahre sehen die Antwort bestimmt wieder anderes aus. **hoffentlich denkt man nicht nur automatisch an Al Gore** und einen Hausaufgabe, sondern auch noch dran, Gott, wie viel CO2 habe ich heute noch produziert, muss schon wieder für den Überschuss teuer bezahlen?) (**From the American University side there were more sentimental reactions, which I actually find good. Our students also have great answers with a bit more dispassionateness/equanimity.** Generally, people under stress work more efficiently. 5 years ago you could find other answers and in 5 years the answers will surely look different again. **hopefully one doesn't think automatically of Al Gore** and of an assignment, but rather also, God, how much CO2 have I produced today, I will have to pay dearly for the excess.) Mani (UNIV-G), May 03, 2009	opinion; reflection on C2 and C1; direct reference to previous posting about Al Gore

Synchronous chat session

A total of 8 (of the 10) chats were saved (the remaining two were not saved due to technical difficulties), totaling over 6,450 words, for an average 807 words per chat discussion over a 50-minute period. On average, the forum discussions contained 490 words per discussion. All eight chats were analyzed, but only three will be discussed here, as they represent both the less successful attempts at interaction as well as the more successful exchanges between the chat partners. To answer RQ1, Table 13 shows basic information about each of the three chats. Striking, but not surprising, is the average number of words per sentence/entry in these chats. Whereas the average number of words per sentence in the forum discussions was 16 for the students in the US and 20 for the students in Germany, the average in the chat was 6 words per chat entry for students in both countries. This is typical of chat style, where the idea is to "hit return often," as will be seen in the examples. This means that turns are often very short and multiple turns are strung together in quick succession (Herring, 1999).

Table 13. Synchronous chat quantitative data

chat	no. of words in U.S. entries/ average per entry	no. of words in German entries/ average per entry
#1 Lynda & Karen (UNIV-A) and Tom (UNIV-G) (35 min.)	118/5	136/5
#2 Sam (UNIV-A) and Tom (UNIV-G) (53 min.)	314/8	384/8
#3 Cara & Daniela (UNIV-A) and Tom (UNIV-G) (42 min.)	398/6	486/7
averages	277/6.2	335/6.5

To answer RQ(1a), unlike the forum discussions, where 95–96% of the entries were statements, the percentages are very different for the chats, again, as was expected. Table 14 shows that 66% of the U.S. entries were statements, as compared with 75% of the German entries. The students in the US *quantitatively* asked a higher percentage of questions (34%) than their German chat partners (25%). (These percentages correspond almost exactly to those compiled for all 8 chats.) In fact, students who found the chats less successful commented that the German partners did not seem interested in chatting with them and did not ask many questions. However, for students on both sides, the percentage of statements was much higher than the percentage of questions. This important point will be discussed further below.

Table 14. Synchronous chat quantitative data

chat	no. of questions in U.S. entries	no. of questions in German entries	no. of statements in U.S. entries	no. of statements in German entries
#1	12	5	12	13
#2	19	12	24	37
#3	15	16	53	47
totals #1–#3	46 (34%)	33 (25%)	89 (66%)	97 (75%)
all 8 chats	125 (33%)	121 (26%)	257 (67%)	336 (74%)

The excerpt from Chat #1 (see Table 15) is an example of a less successful chat, in the sense that basic (mundane) questions are asked and the discussion consists of many short questions and answers (and some expansions on answers). Considering that the learners on both sides are advanced L2 learners, the language they employed is basic and simple. The English-German American bilingual student (Lynda) who was typing the chat entries for herself and her American classmate, has excellent German competence, but the questions she posed are not very advanced linguistically. In fact, her reaction to the chat was that it was problematic because their partner was not very talkative; she claimed that they asked him questions but that he posed very few questions to them. Her American classmate (an English-Vietnamese bilingual) lamented that it was difficult to begin the chat and that for the most part, they asked questions and their partner asked the same questions back.

Table 15. Chat #1: Excerpt about the German language

Lynda [typist] and Karen (UNIV-A): bilingual English-German speaker, bilingual English-Vietnamese speaker
Tom (UNIV-G): German student who had been to the US once for three weeks

[...]

Tom:	do you like the german language ?	interest
L&K:	ja die Sprache gefaellt uns ganz gut. ich bin eigentlich zweisprachig aufgewachsen (yes we really like the language. I actually grew up bilingual [Lynda].)	(answer + additional information)
Tom:	but in the us or in germany ?	clarification question
L&K:	in Kalifornien (in California)	
L&K:	wann hast du englisch gelernt? (when did you learn English?)	interest
Tom:	since 5th grade	
L&K:	und gefaellt dir die englische sprache? (and do you like the English language?)	(same question as above)
Tom:	and since when do you speak german	interest
Tom:	i love it	opinion
Tom:	it is simpler than german	
Tom:	and i can talk to every freakin person in the whole wide world	(expansion)
L&K:	seit ich Kind war (since I was a child)	
Tom:	you are lucky to be native speakers	
L&K:	haha ja das stimmt (haha, yes that's right)	opinion
L&K:	thanks	
L&K:	sprichts du auch andere Sprachen ausser Deutsch und Englisch? (do you also speak other languages besides German and English?)	curiosity

continued...

Table 15. Chat #1: Excerpt about the German language *(cont.)*

Tom:	no	
Tom:	but i would like to learn spanish before finishing my diploma	
L&K:	was studierst du? (what are you studying?)	
Tom:	german: wirtschaftsingenieurwesen (industrial engineering with business studies)	
L&K:	wow	
L&K:	und gefaellt dir dieses Fach? (and do you like this subject?)	interest
Tom:	i like it	
Tom:	but it would be better if we could talk over skype	(new topic)
L&K:	see each other and talk	
L&K:	hmm our professsor won't allow it	
L&K:	we tried but your lab and our lab have had problems with it. skype is prohibited at UNIV-A	
L&K:	it would be better though	
L&K:	wir haben Klasse dieser Stunde. bist du an der Uni auch? (we have class at this time. are you also at the university?)	
L&K:	es ist fast 21 Uhr bei dir? (it is almost 9 p.m., there?)	
Tom:	yeah that right	
L&K:	du hast jetzt noch Unterricht?! (you still have class now?)	
Tom:	it is a free course	
L&K:	ach so (oh, I see)	

From a discourse or pragmatics perspective, asking questions is not the only way to indicate interest or curiosity, and while one of the Americans (Lynda) said that Tom did not ask many questions (though he did), the other American (Karen) said that Tom asked them the same questions that they asked him. Although this may simply be due to the task structure, what is interesting is that both Lynda and Karen felt that the chat had not been successful, despite their opposite assertions about how many questions their German partner posed.

Similarly, in the excerpt in Table 16 from Chat 2, which is entirely in English, the chat consists of short and basic questions followed by short and "perfunctory" replies. In the post-chat evaluation, the American student (an English/Swiss German bilingual) commented that the chat was about "really basic topics," that it was "interesting yet a bit awkward," and that it seemed that his partner "was not interested/bored by the topic" of the type of German he speaks.

Table 16. Chat #2a: Dialects/High German

Sam (UNIV-A): American student with Swiss parents
Niko (UNIV-G): Born in Vietnam, emigrated to Germany with his parents

[…]

Sam (UNIV-A):	is the type of German which you speak in Hannover much different than in other parts of Germany?	interest
Niko (UNIV-G):	oh yes	(short answer)
Sam (UNIV-A):	how so?	interest
Niko (UNIV-G):	yes we talk high german in Hannver	(short answer)
Sam (UNIV-A):	do you find it a pretty type of German?	curiosity
Sam (UNIV-A):	do you like it?	(short question)
Niko (UNIV-G):	it's like the kind of german you hear in the News on TV	
Sam (UNIV-A):	i see	
Niko (UNIV-G):	in the other part of germany people talk it with a lil bit more accents	(expansion)
Sam (UNIV-A):	what do you think about low German, such as what they speak in Munchen or Switzerland	curiosity
Sam (UNIV-A):	?	
Niko (UNIV-G):	i like it very much	(simple answer)
Niko (UNIV-G):	we're proud of our high german	reflection on C1
Sam (UNIV-A):	Have you ever been to Switzerland?	curiosity
Niko (UNIV-G):	not yet, i have a friend there and will probbably go there this summer	(short answer, no details)
Niko (UNIV-G):	if i have sime money	
Sam (UNIV-A):	yes, i understand	

To answer RQ2, in the same chat between Sam and Niko, there is a second excerpt that contains a more involved discussion about American and German culture (Table 17). The turns are a bit longer, and there is evidence of curiosity and interest in the other culture, reflection on one's own culture, and some hedging and facework being performed. The American student (Sam) commented in the post-chat evaluation that he felt he had obtained an "authentic German perspective" (despite having chatted with a partner [Niko] who had been born in Vietnam but emigrated to Germany years ago with his parents).

Table 17. Chat #2b: USA/Germany/American/American culture

Sam (UNIV-A): American student with Swiss parents
Niko (UNIV-G): Born in Vietnam, emigrated to Germany with his parents

[…]

Sam:	warum mochtest du an die USA kommen. mir gefallt die USA meistens gar nicht (why do you want to come to the USA. for the most part I don't really like the USA)	curiosity, reflection C1

continued…

Table 17. Chat #2b: USA/Germany/American/American culture *(cont.)*

Niko:	ich glaube es ist immer so, man will immer wo anders hin, hauptsache weg (I think it's always like this, you always want to go somewhere else, as long as you can go away)	opinion
Niko:	ich finde es gibt so viele zu entdeken in USA (I think there are so many things to discover in the USA)	interest in C2
Sam:	jaa.... aber manchmal mag ich die Leute and das Kultur einfach nicht (yees...but sometimes I just don't like the people and the culture)	hedging; reflection C1
Sam:	amerikaner sind im durchschnitt sehr bloed (on average the Americans are very stupid)	reflection C1 (strong statement)
Sam:	find ich... (I think...)	hedging
Niko:	das ist auch normal so, wenn du ne Weile hier wohnst wirst du wahrscheinlich auch das Gleiche empfinden (that's normal, after having lived here for a while you'll probably feel the same way)	facework (doesn't disagree outright)
Niko:	was mgst du so nicht an den Leuten und der Kultur? (what don't you like about the people and the culture?)	curiosity
Sam:	amis haben kein richtigen kultur. der kultur in den alle glauben ist oberflaclich...es geht nur um viel geld und material dinge (Americans don't have a real culture. the culture everybody believes in is superficial...everything just revolves around money and material things)	reflection C1, solidarity with Niko(?)
Sam:	was denkst du uber deutscher kultur? (what do you think about german culture?)	curiosity

The final chat excerpts exhibit evidence of more engagement and interaction between the interlocutors (Tables 18 and 19). As is true of all of the more engaged chats, multiple, sequential turns can be found, often several statements that expand on the interlocutor's thoughts or position, and there are fewer simple question–simple answer sequences.

Table 18. Chat #3a: Politics (Torture: Guantanamo Bay)

Tom (UNIV-G): German student who had vacationed once in the US for thee weeks
Cara (UNIV-A): American student who had studied for a year in Germany

[…]		
Tom:	can i ask you what you think of guantanamo bay?	(polite) curiosity
Cara:	aber ich glaube es ist so einfach eine regierung zu kritizieren wenn wir nichts wirklich alles wissen (but I think it's so easy to criticize a government when we don't really know everything)	expansion of earlier post
Cara:	na ja also ich weiss es genauso nichtich meine eine sland sollte eigentlich eine protection agency haben oder? (well I don't really know I mean a country should have a protection agency, right?)	hedging (bit defensive?)
Cara:	aber ich weiss es nicht ob gitmo die richtige antwort ist (but I don't know if gitmo is the right answer)	reflection C1
Tom:	but why guantanamo bay and not palm beach ?	interest
Cara:	what... gitmo=palm beach for terrorist	

Tom:	why outside of the usa	negotiation of meaning
Cara:	ahh	
Cara:	dass meinst du (that's what you mean)	
Cara:	ummm ja, kein plan, ich hab es selber nicht gemacht (ummm yes, no plan, I didn't make it myself)	hedging
Tom:	you got one of the best constitution in the world	
Tom:	but that the way betray it	
Cara:	hmmm?? das versteh ich nicht (hmmm?? I don't understand that)	negotiation of meaning; facework (question instead of statement)
Tom:	if you are going outside the us you don't have to stick to your constitution, right ?	
Tom:	thats why they were going "international"	
Cara:	also.. ja (well...yes)	hedging
Cara:	ja, also ich weiss was du mit gitmo meinst (yes, well I know what you mean about gitmo)	
Tom:	don't get me wrong, i really like the us	facework (avoiding conflict)

Table 19. Chat #3b: Politics (collective guilt)

Tom (UNIV-G): German student who had vacationed once in the US for 3 weeks
Cara (UNIV-A): American student who had studied for a year in Germany

[...]

Cara:	also was findest du am besten bei euch (so what do you like the most over there)	curiosity
Tom:	in germany?	negotiation of meaning
Cara:	ja, die uni (yes, the university)	reflection on C1
Cara:	deutschland, eure regierung (germany, your government)	
Tom:	they do things more quietly, and they have to be more careful about certain issued, because we started WW II	curiosity
Cara:	yeah, we are kinda in the same boat huh??	negotiation of meaning
Tom:	we did some really horrible things in the past	reflection on C1
Tom:	no we were worse	
Cara:	ja ich weiss, ihr wisst dass, die ganzes welt wisst dass (yes I know, you [guys] know that, the whole world knows that)	negotiation of meaning
Cara:	aber du hast dass selber nicht gemacht (but you didn't do yourself)	
Cara:	also, ich finde diese kollektive schuld total bloed (so, I find this collective guilt totally stupid)	(strong opinion statement)
Tom:	but it is frightening that such things can happen with "educated people" at that time	
Cara:	ja.. stimmt (yes...that's true)	facework? (agrees)

The American student Cara commented that she enjoyed the chat about culture, Germany, and American politics, noting that "Germans like to talk about politics." But she also stated that it would have been better if the Germans had shared more of their ideas rather than just asking questions. This is an interesting comment because the actual chat data reveal that Tom shared his ideas and did not pose that many questions.

Summary and conclusions

To recapitulate, RQ 1 was "How does the choice of Internet tools (specifically asynchronous forum discussions and synchronous chats) contribute to the style of language produced by the learners?" The data in this study reveal that as Thorne (2003) found, different Internet tools are not neutral media in that each fosters a different kind of syntactic and pragmatic style: Asynchronous forum entries contain longer, more syntactically complex statements, whereas synchronous chat entries are short, reactive, and less formal. From multiple past experiences (e.g., Chun & Wade, 2004), asynchronous forums often lack true interaction unless learners can be trained to respond to previous postings, which takes constant and repeated admonition on the part of the instructors. In following Scarino's (2009) suggestion that assessment of intercultural competence entails understanding how students' dynamic and developing enculturation affects how they see and interpret the world and positioning students as both language users and language analyzers, this study examined the forum and chat transcripts both quantitatively and qualitatively and triangulated this data with the students' post-exchange evaluations about the success of the exchange. Future research might employ corpus analysis for more precise collocation data.

To answer RQ(1a) "Is there a difference in the percentage of statements vs questions used by both the American and German groups?" and (1b) "What types of speech acts are used to convey pragmatic ability and the development of ICC?" in the chats, the American students quantitatively asked a higher percentage of questions than the German students (33% to 26%, respectively). This could explain the expectation on the part of some American students that one shows interest by asking questions, and in fact, in their post-chat evaluations these students stated that they were disappointed that the Germans did not seem to be interested in their thoughts or that their partner seemed bored by the topic because they did not ask many questions. The chat transcripts of these American students, however, revealed simple question-answer sequences, without in-depth expression of opinions or curiosity. These particular students, incidentally, possessed advanced linguistic ability, but they ostensibly did not appear to have the pragmatic ability to realize that it is not only through questions that one signals interest or curiosity. Instead, they perceived a lack of interest on the part of the German students despite the fact that the German interlocutors did ask questions, albeit not to the same extent as the American students. In addition, their own postings lacked expansion of their thoughts and opinions.

The data show, on the one hand, that students from the two classes interacted according to their own pragmatic norms, sometimes resulting in a clash of expectations (so-called "cross-cultural pragmatics" as defined by Boxer, 2002). On the other hand, RQ2 "How do learners demonstrate their pragmatic ability to perform various types of speech acts in their online postings?" can be answered with the observation that some students' chat entries revealed their emerging "interlanguage pragmatic" ability, reflecting Boxer's concept of "interlanguage pragmatics" that "it is the task of the language learner or newcomer to acquire the norms of the host community" (p. 151). These students demonstrated ICC as they were able to use in real-time an appropriate combination of knowledge, skills, and attitudes to interact with interlocutors from a different country or culture, maintaining conversational involvement by making additional statements to indicate interest instead of only posing questions. Their chat transcripts revealed more involved sequences in which both interlocutors posted several comments in succession, expanding on their thoughts and opinions.

In other words, qualitatively comparing the types of discourse produced in the chats with the students' end-of-the-quarter reactions to the exchange revealed that when certain types of discourse were present in the chats, learners judged the chats to be "successful" while other types of discourse often resulted in dissatisfaction with the chat. As stated above, in several chats, students showed curiosity and interest in the other culture and reflected on their own culture (components of ICC described by Byram, 1997) not only by asking questions, but also by contributing unsolicited thoughts and opinions. In addition, they appeared to keep the conversation flowing by hedging, avoiding conflict, and performing facework. These students subsequently had positive reactions and felt they "gained an authentic perspective" of the other culture and that their "partner was interesting because he wanted to know about us."

The discourse analyses of the data suggest that students who were satisfied with the chats tended to have had extended discussions with their partners about cultural and political topics, whereas students who found the chats "awkward" or difficult to start used brief questions and answers about mundane topics similar to face-to-face "small talk." There was ample evidence of many students' emerging ICC (e.g., they showed curiosity, suspended disbelief about the other culture, and reflected on their own culture), and the types of speech acts that these advanced learners used were sophisticated and nuanced, particularly in how they performed facework. The discourse of the synchronous chats reflected much more engagement and evidence of developing ICC than the entries in the asynchronous forum postings. However, there were also examples in the forum postings of students' reflecting on their own culture and changing their attitudes, "I [used to think] that Americans... but maybe we are more similar to the Germans [after all]."

To conclude, this study has corroborated previous research by Kramsch and Thorne (2002) with regard to different discourse styles and Ware and Kramsch (2005) with regard to students reflecting on discourse pragmatics (with varying degrees of success). It is hoped that the types of discourse analyses in this article can contribute to understanding how L2 learners develop interactional pragmatic abilities and might eventually contribute to an empirically informed Internet pragmatics for L2/C2 learners. Learners today participate in diverse social activities online, and such intercultural exchanges can help them gradually develop translingual and transcultural competence, despite the pragmatic hurdles that need to be overcome in the process.

References

Abrams, Z. I. (2002). Surfing to cross-cultural awareness: Using Internet-mediated projects to explore cultural stereotypes. *Foreign Language Annals, 35*, 141–160.

ACTFL. (2006). *Standards for foreign language learning in the 21st century* (3rd ed.). Yonkers. NY: National Standards in Foreign Language Education Project.

Bardovi-Harlig, K. (2001). Evaluating the empirical evidence: Grounds for instruction in pragmatics? In K. R. Rose & G. Kasper (Eds.), *Pragmatics in language teaching* (pp. 13–32). Cambridge, England: Cambridge University Press.

Bardovi-Harlig, K. (2007). One functional approach to second language acquisition: The concept-oriented approach. In B. VanPatten & J. Williams (Eds.), *Theories in second language acquisition: An introduction* (pp. 57–76). New York, NY: Routledge.

Belz, J. A. (2003). Linguistic perspectives on the development of intercultural competence in telecollaboration. *Language Learning & Technology, 7*(2), 68–117. Retrieved from http://llt.msu.edu/vol7num2/belz/

Belz, J. A. (2007). The role of computer mediation in the instruction and development of L2 pragmatic competence. *Annual Review of Applied Linguistics, 27*, 45–75.

Boxer, D. (2002). Discourse issues in cross-cultural pragmatics. *Annual Review of Applied Linguistics, 22*, 150–167.

Byram, M. (1997). *Teaching and assessing intercultural communicative competence.* Clevedon, England: Multilingual Matters.

Byram, M., & Fleming, M. (Eds.). (1998). *Language learning in intercultural perspective.* Cambridge, England: Cambridge University Press.

Byrnes, H. (2002). The cultural turn in foreign language departments: Challenge and opportunity. *Profession 2002*, 114–129.

Byrnes, H. (2009). Revisiting the role of culture in the foreign language curriculum. *The Modern Language Journal, 94*(2), 315–336.

Chapelle, C. (2009). The relationship between second language acquisition theory and computer-assisted language learning. *The Modern Language Journal, 93*, 741–753.

Chun, D. M., & Wade, E. R. (2004). Collaborative cultural exchanges with CMC. In L. Lomicka & J. Cooke-Plagwitz (Eds.), *Teaching with technology* (pp. 220–247). Boston, MA: Heinle.

Council of Europe. (2001). *Common European Framework of Reference for languages: Learning, teaching, assessment.* Cambridge, England: Cambridge University Press.

Furstenberg, G., Levet, S., English, K., & Maillet, K. (2001). Giving a virtual voice to the silent language of culture: The *Cultura* Project. *Language Learning & Technology, 5*(1), 55–102.

Herring, S. C. (1999). Interactional coherence in CMC. *Proceedings of the 32nd Hawaii International Conference on System Sciences* (pp. 1–13). Los Alamitos, CA: IEEE Computer Society Press.

Koike, D. A. (1989). Pragmatic competence and adult L2 acquisition: Speech acts in interlanguage. *The Modern Language Journal, 73*(3), 279–289.

Kramsch, C. (1993). *Context and culture in language teaching.* Oxford, England: Oxford University Press.

Kramsch, C., & Thorne, S. (2002). Foreign language learning as global communicative practice. In D. Block & D. Cameron (Eds.), *Language learning and teaching in the age of globalization* (pp. 83–100). London, England: Routledge.

Modern Language Association Ad Hoc Committee on Foreign Languages. (2007). Foreign languages and higher education: New structures for a changed world. *Profession, 2007,* 234–245.

Müller-Hartmann, A. (2000). The role of tasks in promoting intercultural learning in electronic learning networks. *Language Learning & Technology, 4*(2), 129–147. Retrieved from http://llt.msu.edu/vol4num2/muller/

National Standards in Foreign Language Education Project. (1999). *Standards for Foreign Language Learning in the 21st Century.* Yonkers, NY: National Standards in Foreign Language Education Project.

O'Dowd, R., & Ritter, M. (2006). Understanding and working with "failed communication" in telecollaborative exchanges. *CALICO Journal, 23*(3), 623–642.

Scarino, A. (2009). Assessing intercultural capability in learning languages: A renewed understanding of language, culture, learning, and the nature of assessment. *The Modern Language Journal, 94*(2), 324–329.

Schneider, J., & von der Emde, S. (2006). Conflicts in cyberspace: From communication breakdown to intercultural dialogue in online collaborations. In J. A. Belz & S. L. Thorne (Eds.), *Internet-mediated intercultural foreign language education* (pp. 178–206). Boston, MA: Heinle & Heinle.

Schulz, R. A. (2007). The challenge of assessing cultural understanding in the context of foreign language instruction. *Foreign Language Annals, 40*(1), 9–26.

Sinicrope, C., Norris, J., & Watanabe, Y. (2007). Understanding and assessing intercultural competence: A summary of theory, research, and practice. *Second Language Studies, 26*(1), 1–58.

Thorne, S. L. (2003). Artifacts and cultures-of-use in intercultural communication. *Language Learning & Technology, 7*(2), 38–67. Retrieved from http://llt.msu.edu/vol7num2/thorne/

Wade, E. R. (2005). Enhancing German language learners' intercultural communicative competence through the on-line exchange project ICE (Unpublished doctoral dissertation). University of California, Santa Barbara.

Ware, P., & Kramsch, C. (2005). Toward an intercultural stance: Teaching German and English through telecollaboration. *Modern Language Journal, 89*(2), 190–205.

Part III:
Best Practices in Implementing the *Cultura* Model for Asian and Pacific Languages

Intercultural Learning on the Web: Reflections on Practice

Song Jiang, Haidan Wang, & Stephen Tschudi
University of Hawai'i at Mānoa

This chapter offers an overview and analysis of trial results using a web-based platform for intercultural dialogue developed at the University of Hawai'i at Mānoa, the "China-USA Business Café." The Café features a series of online interactive tasks designed to teach culture to Chinese and American business students, including word association, sentence completion, situational response, comparison of and reflection on authentic materials, and free discussion forums. Assessment performed on trial implementation of these tasks shows that this web-based teaching platform can help minimize cultural barriers and bridge the cultural gap, while at the same time pointing to needed improvements in the design of the exchange. Through completion of culturally focused interactive tasks followed by reflection and discussion in the web-based intercultural exchange described, Chinese and American learners deepen mutual understanding and enhance their interpretive and expressive abilities in each other's target language.

Role of cultural knowledge in second language teaching

In recent years, the integration of the teaching of culture into the practice of teaching language has received increasing attention. Research on teaching second language and culture has shown that the integration of culture into study of the second language can provide critical support for learners' successful completion of communicative tasks in the target language environment (Lange & Paige, 2003). For second language educators, the most challenging aspect of integrating culture in language courses lies in how to effectively overcome culturally-based barriers to communication and build communicative bridges spanning the cultural gap between their learners and speakers of the target language. As the Internet comes of age, the capabilities of the traditional classroom are being extended and expanded into the online universe, offering unprecedented possibilities for the teaching of the culture of second languages.

Language and culture

The definition of "culture" has been a subject of some academic controversy. As early as the 19th century, the British anthropologist E. B. Tylor was already applying a very broad definition of culture: "that complex whole which includes knowledge, belief, art, morals, law, custom, and any other capabilities and habits acquired by man as a member of society" (Tylor, 1871/2010, p. 1). In the 20th century, the role of culture became a focus of many of the social sciences. Anthropologists, sociologists, linguists and language educators all tried to define and interpret culture and its effects from the perspective of their own discipline. Brooks (1968) defined a broad concept of culture encompassing the following five areas: biological growth, personal refinement, literature and the fine arts, patterns for living, and the sum total of a way of life. As a language educator, Brooks stressed the direct relevance of the "patterns for living" aspect of culture to the teaching and learning of language. He defined "patterns for living" as the thoughts, beliefs, language, and corresponding range of behavior expected in the context of a person's social group in any of a number of typical scenarios. Kramsch (1998) further elaborated the inseparability of language and culture, expressing their relationship as follows: Language expresses cultural reality; language embodies cultural reality; language symbolizes cultural reality. Lange (1998) asserted that, from the perspective of foreign language teaching, culture is a part of language, and language is part of culture.

Integrating cultural and language instruction

Based on the close association of language and culture, Krasner (1999) clarified that communicative competence reflects a combination of mastery of grammatical form and its practical application within the framework of a society's cultural values governing the use of language, or "linguaculture" (p. 81). Mastery of grammatical form and structure does not guarantee successful practical application. To achieve successful communication, one must combine the use of language with appropriate cultural behavior. In the mid–1990s, the National Standards for Foreign Language Learning were developed under the auspices of the American Council on the Teaching of Foreign Languages (ACTFL). These standards proposed an increased emphasis on the integration of culture into foreign language teaching, privileging Cultures as one of the "5 Cs"—Cultures, Communication, Connections, Comparisons, and Communities—proposed as a framework for the country's objectives in foreign language education. These standards focus on the mastery and understanding of the target culture through the learning of its language, representing a paradigmatic shift away from the focus on grammatical form as the main target of language teaching. In the new paradigm, culture has been elevated to equal status with grammatical forms, and the standard for judging learners' mastery of a second language has been extended to include mastery of the culture in which that language is embedded (American Council on the Teaching of Foreign Languages, 1996).

State of cultural instruction in Chinese language teaching

Since the publication of the ACTFL National Standards for Foreign Language Learning, language educators have begun to pay attention to the integration of culture into curriculum and language teaching activity design. But even as culture begins to penetrate educators' consciousness as a desirable element to include in actual teaching practice, the adoption of culture as a formal curricular target in the field overall still has a long way to go, as evidenced in the content of current textbooks. Yu (2009) analyzed the treatment of culture in seven popular elementary Chinese textbooks. The results showed that although these textbooks include culture to differing degrees, on the whole, culture in textbooks is still relegated to "Notes" status and is still far from being integrated as a core element of the curriculum. This situation shows that the teaching of culture in Chinese language in general is still rather weak.

Directions for better integration of culture into Chinese language teaching

The authors' view is that the greatest challenge in integrating culture into language teaching is how to identify those cultural elements hidden behind grammatical forms that can determine the success or failure of communicative exchanges—in other words, the "silent language" identified by Edward T. Hall (1956)—and reveal these hidden cultural elements to the learner. This challenge is particularly great for Chinese language teaching, which is still in its developmental stages. Revealing how culture intersects with linguistic forms is a key element for successful language teaching. Kramsch (1993) opined that in the process of integrating culture into language teaching, foreign language educators must take care not to simply convey their own subjective judgments regarding the target culture to students, but should make the language classroom an open cultural laboratory enabling learners to form their own perceptions of the target culture through exploration, discovery, and reflection on similarities and differences between the target and native cultures. Advances in Internet-based technology, which have extended the reach and capabilities of the classroom, offer new possibilities for realizing the principles advocated by Kramsch for the teaching and learning of culture in language education.

New approaches integrating cultural and language instruction

Cultura: A web-based model for teaching culture

Among various projects in the research and practice of teaching culture using the Internet, the intercultural communication project (Furstenberg, Levet, English, & Maillet, K., 2001), developed at the Massachusetts Institute of Technology, stands out as a model worthy of emulation. The original *Cultura* linked language students in the United States and France who were respectively studying French and English, using an intercultural web-based communication platform on which students complete task-based online interactive activities. The activities are designed to lead students toward discovery, apperception, and reflection on similarities and differences between the cultures of their first language and the target language, with the ultimate goal of achieving deep understanding of differences in cultural attitudes, beliefs, communication styles, and world view. As expressed in the motto on the *Cultura* website (cultura.mit.edu), *Cultura* is designed to help students "see the universe through the eyes of others." Using this platform, students in the United States and France complete interactive tasks based on their reactions to media, text, images, movies, and linguistic phenomena. These tasks are designed to guide students toward discovery of both the target culture and how their own culture appears to others. Interaction between the two sides of the exchange is accomplished through making postings, reading others' postings, reflection, and discussion about cultural differences.

Task design in *Cultura*

Development of the awareness of cultural contrasts is a core motivating element in the design of tasks in the *Cultura* model. The developers of *Cultura* feel that language forms fully reveal their culturally based meanings only when placed in a dynamic interactional relationship with another culture. Contrast is an effective way to reveal cultural connotations. Using a web-based platform, *Cultura* juxtaposes similar information, such as newspaper ads, pictures, and words from different cultures, in a way that that highlights their hidden cultural content and heightens learners' awareness.

Language use in *Cultura*

Cultura differs in one important respect from many other models for online exchange among language learners: When making postings, each participant uses his or her native language. This provides students the opportunity to fully express their ideas while also providing direct and relevant contact in the exchange with students using the target language, whose postings serve as source material for language learning. In other words, American students post in English and French students post in French, then they read and discuss each other's postings, each side in the discussion maintaining the use of its mother tongue. One advantage of this design is that on the network platform, the principle of authentic input is maintained: All postings are in authentic native language, thus ensuring the linguistic quality of postings, since all students are experts in their own language. The difficulties in communication that are seen in language exchanges in which the target language is used are avoided, since students are not posting in interlanguage. At the same time, students can make use of language from the target-language postings they have read as material for study in class.

Student autonomy in *Cultura*

In addition, *Cultura* also conforms to an important principle expressed by Kramsch (1993), namely that the teaching of culture should allow for autonomous learner discovery and apperception. The communicative tasks in *Cultura* are designed using a constructivist approach to learning. The purpose of these tasks is not the simple transmission of cultural knowledge, but rather the *discovery* by learners themselves, working as a community, through observation, comparison, and analysis of linguistic, visual, or multimedia materials with implicit cultural content, followed by reflection and discussion. This process of co-construction of cultural knowledge abandons the mechanical method of one-way transmission of cultural knowledge found in the traditional foreign language classroom and attempts to lead students toward independent, self-motivated discovery, awareness, and sharing of cultural connotations encountered during the task process and integration of this discovered knowledge into their own interlanguage system.

Design and testing of the "China-USA Business Café"
A *Cultura*-inspired model for Chinese language instruction

Taking its cue from the successful track record of *Cultura*, a team at the University of Hawaiʻi at the beginning of 2008 launched the "China-USA Business Café" (CUBC) web-based intercultural exchange project to promote the teaching of Chinese culture in an online environment. Research and development on this project was performed by the authors in the context of a Business Chinese language program offered by the Department of East Asian Languages and Literatures at the University of Hawaiʻi. This web-based exchange was established with the goal of exploring best practices in teaching Chinese as second language using an online platform, with a view to fostering the cultural component of students' communicative competence in Chinese.

The *Cultura*-based teaching model adopted in CUBC, emphasizing cross-cultural learning through exploration and discovery, consists of the following five steps: 1) accessing cultural material, 2) posting personal responses to the material, 3) observing and analyzing others' responses to the material, 4) engaging in exchange and discussion based on one's analysis, and 5) self-reflection.

BRIX platform

The CUBC project team selected the *BRIX* courseware system, developed by the University of Hawaiʻi National Foreign Language Resource Center (NFLRC), as a web-based platform for foreign language teaching and learning, as its primary medium. *BRIX* features several capabilities that make it particularly suitable for language teaching applications, including,

- a vocabulary tool that enables the class, as a learning community, to contribute and compile lists of related words or sentences, and
- an essay tool that enables learners to work through multiple drafts, publishing each subsequent draft to the group for feedback from peers and the instructor.

CUBC content and task design

In CUBC itself, the design of the main content aimed at maximum effectiveness and practicability while hewing to the principle of teaching culture through exploration and discovery. Accordingly, the following task types were included: (a) word association, in which learners were invited to contribute words they associated with culturally freighted concepts such as *friendship* or *boss*; (b) sentence completion, in which learners completed sentences that elicited cultural attitudes, for example "A good teacher is one who..."; (c) situational response, in which learners indicated how they might react to a situation such as public punishment of a child or a boss showing preferential treatment to an employee; (d) reaction to authentic cultural artifacts, such as a job advertisement; (e) a language clinic; and (f) free conversation in an open forum. The specific design of the activities is detailed below.

Word association

Eliciting word associations for culturally freighted terms is a quick and effective way to reveal cultural differences. People from different cultural backgrounds provided with the same cue words, for example "friendship" in English and 友谊 (*youyi*, friendship) in Chinese, return differing associated words reflecting differing cultural values surrounding the stimulus concept. In the task, students are asked to look at stimulus terms on the website in their own language (L1), and then under each word are asked to type at least five words that immediately come to mind in association with the stimulus term, also in L1. So, in the task Chinese students respond in Chinese, and American students respond in English, yielding two datasets of responses to the stimulus terms. In the Business Café, for example, the sets of stimulus terms in Chinese and English were 关系 (*guanxi*)/relationships, 礼节 (*lijie*)/etiquette, 送礼 (*song li*)/gift-giving, 上司/上级 (*shangsi/shangji*)/supervisor, 老板 (*laoban*)/boss, 同事 (*tongshi*)/colleague, 关系网 (*guanxiwang*) network, 朋友 (*pengyou*) friend, 同学 (*tongxue*) schoolmate/classmate, and 地位 (*diwei*)/status. The word associations submitted by the Chinese and American students on the website were compiled in order of frequency of occurrence with the frequency of each noted, and the results were displayed to all the students as a basis for comparison and discussion between the two sides as a next step.

Sentence completion

In this task in the Café, students are provided with culturally significant unfinished sentences in their own language and are asked to complete each sentence in three different ways, each of which conforms to their own values. This task is also presented in Chinese and English versions. The following are the Chinese and English versions of several of the sentence completion tasks:

1. 怎么样才算一个成功的人？我觉得...
   Zenmeyang cai suan yi ge chenggong de ren? Wo juede...
   A successful person is one who ...

2. 一个理想的工作应该是...
   Yi ge lixiang de gongzuo yinggai shi...
   A good job is one that...

3. 我给礼物的目的是...
   Wo song li de mudi shi...
   The reason I give gifts is ...

4. 谈自己看法的时候，重要的是...
   Tan ziji kanfa de shihou, zhongyao de shi...
   When giving your own opinion, it is important to ....

The sentence completions submitted by the Chinese and American students on the website were compiled and analyzed in terms of the key concepts mentioned, and the results were displayed to all the students, as a basis for comparison and discussion between the two sides as a next step.

Situation response

This task in the Café is carried out in the form of discussion forums. Teachers offer a scenario in both Chinese and English to which members of different cultures might respond differently. Both American and Chinese students are asked to describe, each in their own language, how they would specifically respond to the scenario. For example, under the theme "gifts," teachers offered the following scenario, asking students to respond according to their own ideas.

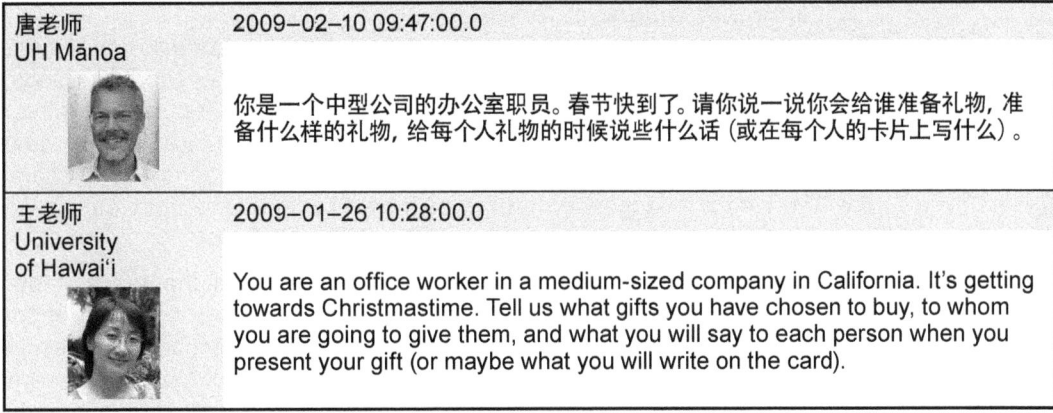

Figure 1. Situation response tasks in Chinese and English

The situation responses submitted by the Chinese and American students on the website were compiled and analyzed in terms of the key concepts mentioned, and students were asked to identify and explore interesting and controversial parts of the responses in an open discussion.

Authentic language materials and reflection

This activity type is based on making cultural comparisons between corresponding authentic cultural artifacts from participants' respective cultural contexts. For example, the designers of the activity might choose images of Chinese people engaging in an activity and American people engaging in a similar activity (such as shopping), a Chinese film and an American film on a similar theme or topic, ads for similar products, and so forth, and ask participants in the two groups to compare and discuss their content, each side using its own language (but reading responses from both sides). By comparing and discussing paired authentic cultural artifacts in this way, and working through any points of difference in their understanding, participants can gain insight into cultural differences.

In this part of the China-USA Business Café, we designed a task asking participants to identify similarities and differences between an American job advertisement and a Chinese job advertisement. The task required students to examine and compare the job ads, and then in several subsequent forums work through distinct tasks that comprised the activity. First, a "Questions about language/语言问题" thread was established so that students could ask questions about Chinese and English words, grammar, usage, and other language-related issues in the advertisements themselves. Next, a "Similarities and differences/相似与分歧" thread was posted to allow participants, using their respective languages, to contribute their observations about differences between the two ads in format, content, style, job requirements, employment conditions, and so forth. Finally, in the "Joint Discussion and exchange/中美双方讨论与交流" thread, Chinese and American students, each using their own language, discussed what they thought were the underlying reasons for similarities and differences between the two ads, how these similarities and differences reflected certain cultural values in Chinese and American society, and how these differing states of mind and differing value systems could be characterized.

"Working with language" forum

The "Working with language" forum is designed to serve as a sort of "advice desk" or place for learners to get answers about grammar, usage, word meanings, or any other aspect of language and language use they encounter during their interaction with authentic materials, including both materials found in task prompts and language found in postings from their exchange partners. One way to characterize the "Working with language" forum would be as a language classroom inside the larger cultural classroom of the China-USA Business Café.

The "Working with language" forum can be adapted to suit the needs of the individual sides of the exchange. If an exchange constitutes a significant portion of class work for one side or the other, the instructor on that side can assign structured tasks as threads in the "Working with language" forum. For example, the instructor might assign a web quest to find and share vocabulary on a topic related to the Café, or might ask students to produce sentences using a challenging grammatical pattern that has appeared in the Café. At all times, however, a thread is available in the "Working with language" forum for learners' open-ended questions about language.

Open discussion area

Inside the Café, there is an open social forum not associated with any task in the exchange. In this "café within the Café," students are welcome to use any language they wish to converse freely on any topic of their choosing or to share links and media related to their interests. Students from both sides of the exchange can treat this forum as a chance to quiz target language and culture "experts"—that is, native speakers—about any question they wish, or can simply engage in social networking and fellowship as an extension of the organized intercultural exchange.

Testing the CUBC model

Cohorts in CUBC testing

After basic construction of the China-USA Business Café was completed using the University of Hawai'i's BRIX courseware, two trials of the Café were conducted in Summer 2008 and Spring 2009.

In Summer 2008, seven students from the United States International MBA Program (USIMBA) at China's Sun Yat-sen University, who had just arrived for a student exchange at the University of Hawai'i, were placed in a trial exchange with 10 students from the University of Hawai'i's Shidler School of Business China International MBA program (CIMBA). The seven students from China all had scores on the Test of English as a Foreign Language (TOEFL) that met or exceeded English proficiency requirements for entering international students enrolled at the University of Hawai'i. The 10 U.S. students had a relatively diverse array of Chinese language proficiency levels: 2 were at the Advanced level on the American Council on the Teaching of Foreign Languages (ACTFL) proficiency scale, while 4 were at Intermediate Mid or Intermediate High, and 4 were at Intermediate Low.

In Spring 2009, 18 students enrolled in Business Chinese classes at the University of Hawai'i were placed in a trial exchange with 15 Chinese sophomores enrolled at China Tianjin Foreign Trade Vocational College. Of the American students, 5 had proficiency levels of either Intermediate High or Advanced on the ACTFL scale, 3 were at Intermediate Mid, and 10 were at Intermediate Low. The Chinese students' program of study included international trade, business logistics, and business

English. All of the Chinese students had passed the College English Test Band 4 (CET–4), designed by the Chinese Ministry of Education to test non-English majors in English listening, reading comprehension, and writing based on a vocabulary of 4,500 English words (Kang & Chen, 2005).

Setting goals for an array of proficiency levels
In view of the wide array of Chinese language proficiency among the American partners in the China-USA Business Café in Spring 2009, three distinct sets of learning goals were established for the three groups of American students in this iteration of the exchange. Students at the Intermediate Low level were required to learn to use at least 10 new Chinese words in each thematic unit and to employ these new words to create complete sentences describing cultural similarities and differences between American and Chinese cultures as seen in the exchange. Students at the Intermediate Mid/High level were required to learn to use at least 20 new Chinese words in each thematic unit and to employ these new words to create a coherent paragraph describing their own reflections on cultural similarities and differences between American and Chinese cultures as seen in the exchange. Students at the Advanced level were required to write a series of linked paragraphs comparing and analyzing differences between American and Chinese cultural phenomena, explaining their personal theory about deeper cultural causes behind these differences, and commenting on how their experience in the Café affected the state of their cultural knowledge and how it might affect their future behavior in the target cultural context.

Results of the exchange

Rather than presenting the entire exchange in full detail, we will discuss results of the exchange in two sections of particular interest: word association and authentic language materials.

Word association results
During the two trial exchanges, word association, including the follow-up discussion, proved to be a very successful activity. Both Chinese and American students were able to observe a large number of cultural phenomena and concepts embedded in the associations both sides made to the stimulus words. In their discussions, through comparative analysis and concrete examples, students came to recognize that the "same" word in different cultures may represent a completely different concept. Words that on the surface serve as translations or glosses of one another may have quite different semantic fields in different cultures. The process of cultural self-discovery by students gave them the motivation to further explore the underlying causes.

For example, for the word pair "gift-giving/送礼" in the word association activity, by working through their collective associational responses, students discovered different cultural significances attaching to the Chinese and English words and advanced a few theories on the reasons for the differences. The process unfolded as follows. At the start of the activity, working in separate web forms, Chinese and American students each contributed up to five separate words they associated with the word "gift-giving" or "送礼," each in their own language. Once the associated words were submitted, the teacher collated all responses into a list showing words with the number of times they occurred, arranged in order of frequency in each language. A portion of the results is shown in Figure 2.

Query 3: gift-giving N=74	Query 3: 送礼 N=85
birthday (7) Christmas (7) caring (4) holiday (4) love (4) generous (4) thoughtful (3) celebration (2) friendship (2) fun (2) gratitude (2) happy (2) kids (2) money (2)	过年过节 (5) 过生日 (5) 礼尚往来 (5) 办事 (4) 谋求 (4) 朋友 (3) 友好 (3) 亲情 (3) 婚姻彩礼 (2) 贿赂 (2) 走后门 (2) 选择 (2) 钱 (2) 串亲戚 (1)

notes: (n)=total number of replies received for each query (each respondent gave a few replies).
过年过节 *celebrating the New Year and holidays* (5), 过生日 *celebrating birthdays* (5), 礼尚往来 *reciprocity* (5), 办事 *getting things done* (4), 谋求 *seeking favors* (4), 朋友 *friends* (3), 友好 *friendliness* (3), 亲情 *family ties* (3), 婚姻彩礼 *wedding gifts* (2), 贿赂 *bribes* (2), 走后门 *taking the "back door"* (2), 选择, *choosing* (2), 钱 *money* (2), 串亲戚 *visiting relatives* (1)

Figure 2. Teacher-compiled "gift-giving/送礼" word association results as displayed to Spring 2009 Chinese and English students

Student observations on different word association responses

By examining the word associations that emerged and the frequency of their appearance, students quickly grasped similarities and differences between the responses of the two sides, began to analyze possible reasons for the similarities and differences, and in turn developed new cultural awareness. Observations from the two sides were largely convergent. For example, an American student shared her[1] observation of the following similarities: "The top two words associated from the American students were 'Birthday' and 'Christmas'; the top two words associated from the Chinese students were 'Celebrating the New Year and Holidays' and 'Birthday.'" The same student also took note of the differences: "The Chinese students made more associations with seeking help or favors, giving bribes, etc., while the American students made associations with emotion, responsibility, etc." Another American student observed, "Chinese students used 办事 [taking care of business, getting things done] in response to gift giving. The association between gift giving and business seems to be stronger in China." A Chinese student remarked, "In the responses to the 'gift-giving/送礼' word association task, Chinese respondents made more associations with taking care of business and with the practice of bribery, while the [Americans] made associations with emotions and with responsibility."

---

[1] The identities and biodata of the students are completely opaque to the researchers; the student subject in question may be male or female.

Student reflections on word association results

While observing differences in the two sides' responses to the word association task, at the same time Chinese students reflected further on reasons for the differences, calibrating their perceptions both of their own culture and of the target culture (in their case, U.S. culture). For example, one of the Chinese students observed,

> Among the Chinese students, many wrote words such as "reciprocity," "bribery," "taking care of business" and other such mercenary and venal concepts. Students from [the US] never gave words such as "bribery," instead coming up with words such as "happy," "fun,'" "thoughtful," and so forth. At a minimum, this shows that, at least in the minds of American students, bribery is rare in their country. That our students so easily come up with such words [as bribery etc.] shows that this phenomenon is very common in China!

Yet another Chinese student wrote,

> This shows that the differences between American and Chinese culture often depend on social conditions, vested interests, and so forth. Chinese people emphasize "reciprocity," that is, paying in the hope of gaining returns. American students place more emphasis on feelings, and their outlook is less utilitarian.

In addition, Chinese students showed awareness of the particular cultural and historical associations that led U.S. students to make certain word associations. One Chinese student remarked, "Under 'relationship/关系,' US students thought of church and God, which shows the importance of religion in their culture." From these forum entries we see that not only did students observe differences in word association responses, they also probed the possible reasons behind such differences.

Student linguistic meta-awareness

In addition to gaining deeper understanding of the cultural implications of words in the word association task, by contrasting Chinese and U.S. culture, students gained fresh insight into features of vocabulary in their respective target and native languages overall. For example, after observing the word associations generated by U.S. students, one Chinese student offered this impression:

> Chinese words tend to have a single clear-cut definition, while it seems that many English words have multiple definitions. The same English words appeared repeatedly in association with different stimulus words. Moreover, due to cultural differences, Chinese and US students' understanding of the "same" words were different.

Plainly, the word association task inspired students to explore deeper significances of words familiar to them, and their encounter with polysemy in English words seems to have had a positive impact, stimulating their desire to know more. For example, in analyzing associations with the words "relationship/关系," a Chinese student noted, "US students used the word 'nature.' I do not understand whether what was meant was the relationship between man and nature or natural and harmonious relationships between human beings. This may also be a reflection of the polysemous nature of English words." The student's process of puzzling through the possibilities and forming a hypothesis seems to convey a sense of freshness when placed aside dominant educational practices in China, which often stress received interpretations.

Language exploration prompted by word association results
Another remarkable effect of the word association exchange was that certain less common word associations posted by Chinese students inspired U.S. students to learn new words and explore the relevant cultural background, thereby increasing their Chinese vocabulary and broadening their knowledge. For example, one of the U.S. students—not a native speaker of English—commented,

> I saw a word "脑白金" [editor's note: *naobaijin*, "brain platinum," melatonin] as a word association in the "gift-giving" query. I asked my Chinese friend what was that [sic]. She told me that is a product which is made in China. It is very famous because of its advertisement[s]. Maybe the advertisement already influenced Chinese people. So, they think "送礼" ="脑白金" ["gift-giving"="melatonin"]. Interesting!

Results from comparison of authentic materials
The section of the exchange based on examination of and reflection on authentic language materials appears to have been quite successful. In this section, students compared job advertisements from the US and China. In the initial discussion portion of the task, Chinese and American students made preliminary comparisons between two job ads, accurately capturing key differences. Among the Chinese students' observations were the following:

> The Chinese-language recruitment ad featured restrictions related to gender, age, marital status, and height, while the ad in English had none of these restrictions.

> Chinese [employers] impose too many conditions [on candidates], including height, marital status, an appealing image, a good temperament, while in the United States, no such requirements appear in the ad. It is quite apparent that the bad practice of hiring people based on appearance is widespread in China.

> Most Chinese companies will recruit only candidates who have relevant work experience, while U.S. companies do not impose this condition. I was quite surprised to find that U.S. companies give employees special training.

> The US ad was more focused on the individual's mastery of language and work skills.

U.S. students observing similarities and differences between the two ads expressed similar thoughts:

> The first thing that struck me about the Chinese ad was that it was biased in wanting a female secretary, whereas the USA ad wasn't as specific. I think the US company was trying to avoid being biased in order not to be blamed for "sex discrimination," since men can be secretaries too.

> The Chinese ad was more concerned about personal qualities, rather than elaborating on the job description.

> Although the USA ad wanted certain job skills, they were willing to train. However, the Chinese ad wanted a secretary with at least one year of experience.

Students' hypotheses regarding observed differences

Based on their discoveries, the U.S. and Chinese students in the cohort undertook further discussions exploring possible sociocultural bases for similarities and differences between the job ads. For example, some Chinese students wrote:

> The differences are related both to current realities and to the traditional culture of the respective countries. Since in China there are many candidates competing for each position, recruiters can be very choosy. And the foreign advertisement [would be] open [to] significantly more [candidates].

> It can be seen in the job advertisements that Westerners focus on practical factors, while the Chinese place emphasis on benefits. The underlying causes of this phenomenon are differences in the standard of living as well as differences in the relationship between superiors and subordinates. This phenomenon is reflected in Chinese [companies'] stress on the use of benefits packages to attract employees to work while Western companies stress capabilities and skills to attract qualified workers. Chinese companies are focused heavily on the financial bottom line, while in the West companies pay more attention to the company's value or strength. Chinese companies focus on immediate practicalities, while in the West the focus is on the development of the enterprise.

Based on their own culture, U.S. students also presented their views:

> I find it interesting that although the students in Tianjin noticed the differences between the job ads regarding personal appearance requirements, none of them mentioned one underlying reason for that difference: namely, that in the United States (and in other industrialized nations) it is illegal to make requirements for job positions that are not related to the job duties themselves. For example, in advertising for a secretary.

> Selecting an individual based on outward appearances is foolish and inefficient. Height, appearance, marital status, and age have no correlation with the ability to produce in the workplace. Using such hiring practices is not only discriminatory but could produce disastrous results as choosing "beauty" over "brains" could directly affect the profit level of a company in a negative way.

Students' reflection on underlying cultural values

The courseware provided an effective platform for the forum exchanges between the U.S. and Chinese students while facilitating development of the discussion from concrete observations towards higher-level critical thinking. For example, in response to a Chinese student's observation that population pressure contributed to intense competition in recruitment in China, a U.S. student extended the discussion toward the relationship between free enterprise and social development:

> I agree with your response that cultural differences were apparent. I think it is interesting that Chinese companies have more freedom to require specific personality traits and physical appearances. It makes me question who is more free to do what. Where we have been restricted, Chinese companies have been given freedom. It seems the meaning of a "free country "is more complex than I once thought. However, in business, sometimes what appears to be "free" is really just a lack of oversight in the regulatory policies of the country. I wonder if this creates problems for different societal groups to find employment, such as

> older generations or less attractive persons. It would be a shame if all industries employed beautiful dummies (like Hollywood does) rather than a group of skilled workers with various physical characteristics.

Through contrasting the Chinese job ad, which was familiar to them, to the relatively new and different English-language ad, the Chinese students achieved a new critical perspective, thereby attaining the desired state of "seeing oneself through the eyes of others." For example, with regard to issues in the Chinese job ad, some of the Chinese students offered the following reflections:

> The foreign ad was relatively humane towards the job-seeker, allowing candidates to see at a glance whether or not they were qualified for the job; it was quite detailed. The Chinese ad was relatively concise; in several places, a few characters sufficed to convey a rich message. But in other places, it was not very detailed and gave the reader an impression of fuzziness.

> In the American job market, more attention is paid to workplace skills and ability in various languages. In this regard, I think China should learn from the US. As we strive for economic and social development, we should not look only at people's appearance; companies should attach importance to a person's ability to create value.

> If every company required one year of work experience, then recent college graduates would have a terrible time finding work; this is a very important issue. Companies only want "ready-made" people with experience rather than training new people so that more people can GET experience. I think this reflects the lack of a sense of social responsibility on the part of companies. The Chinese government should think of ways to change this phenomenon.

An unintended opportunity for language development

The use of authentic material in the Café in some measure made up for the limitations of the textbook language typically seen in language courses. For example, seeing an authentic advertisement in English for the first time, many of the Chinese students, judging by the grammatical standards they had seen in their English textbooks, thought that the language in the ad was in error, and offered suggestions for changing the English wording:

> In standard format, "Date Listed: 02-Jun–08" should be "June 8, 2002."

> "Skill requirements" should be "Skills Required."

> "Computer use" should be changed to "Computer using."

> "Significant [use] of memory" should be changed to "good memory."

> "Experience: Will train" should be "Experience: Have or have not is ok."

Needless to say, the instructors made haste to correct these misconceptions in the Grammar Clinic and to explain the relevant English grammar, usage, and register specific to the advertising domain. The pedagogic effectiveness of the Grammar Clinic is readily apparent in Chinese students' subsequent feedback to teachers:

> Thank you so much for letting us get to know a real ad, it's my first time ever to read a real one, I benefited a lot from your responses, it's a great opportunity for us to learn native things.

> After seeing your explanation that the English advertisement was authentic and accurate, I was very surprised. This reflects our lack of knowledge of the difference between book learning and real-life learning.

Reflections on teaching culture via a *Cultura*-based model

Benefits yielded by the model

Our analysis of our beta test of CUBC shows that a web-based platform inspired by the *Cultura* model can be an effective venue for integrating culture into language instruction along several dimensions.

The web facilitates an exploratory model

Cultura-based models for intercultural learning, such as CUBC, provide a virtual laboratory in which American learners of Chinese and Chinese learners of English can discover culture through exploration, as advocated by Kramsch (1993), moving beyond mere language study into the world of truly intercultural communication.

The teaching of culture in the traditional classroom is often limited to teacher input based in a single cultural perspective. In such an environment there can be no direct collision of or exchange between cultures. In contrast, a web-based cross-cultural environment featuring effectively designed tasks casts each participant in the role of expert in his or her own culture, providing a multitude of cultural "teachers" who are given the responsibility to provide a native perspective for participants in the other side of the exchange. As a result, learners on both sides are given a kaleidoscopic and multi-layered view of the target culture.

Allowing the instructor to "get out of the way"

The web-based platform subverts the traditional role of teachers as cultural authorities and casts them instead in the role of assistants in the cultural exchange. The teacher's attention is devoted to ensuring smooth communication among participants, clearing up misunderstandings, collaborating in learners' own mental construction of the target culture system, and promoting participants' reflection on their own culture from a new perspective. This repositioning of the teacher gives students the space to play a leading role, not only as effective acquirers of the target culture, but also as expert exponents of their own culture in the process of cultural exchange.

Task-based activity design

As vehicles for the teaching of culture in the web-based environment, task-based activities targeted toward teaching the second language and culture play an important role. By completing task-based interactive activities, students on both sides of the exchange deepen their cultural awareness. While exploring, figuring out, and mastering the targeted cultural knowledge, participants simultaneously expand their linguistic knowledge, so that cultural knowledge and language skills are simultaneously increased.

Multivalent learning benefits

The U.S. and Chinese students' in-depth discussions and cultural comparisons also show that cross-cultural, web-based communicative exchanges focusing on cultural comparison help to reveal cultural differences, sharpen learners' awareness of cultural constructions that are closely intertwined with the target language, facilitate the exploration of differences caused by sociocultural factors, and heighten learners' cultural decoding skills.

Areas for improvement

While the beta-testing of the Café demonstrated its considerable potential, it also revealed a number of problems and areas for improvement.

Exclusive L1 use may not be optimal when cohorts are of mixed proficiency

Since participants on each side of the intercultural exchange use their mother tongue to express their ideas, the postings made by both sides feature typical authentic native language expressing relatively complex ideas, and consequently demand a fairly high level of target language reading proficiency from the other side. Target language reading comprehension levels thus become a determining factor in the success or failure of the exchange. In the two trials conducted, insufficient target language reading proficiency level had a certain negative impact on the exchange. The Chinese language proficiency levels of the U.S. students ranged across at least three different levels from Intermediate Low to Advanced, with the result that U.S. students were not able to take part in Chinese language-related activities with a uniform level of competence, and it was not possible to guarantee that all students began in-depth discussion at the same time in the exchange. The English language proficiency of the Chinese students, which was relatively uniform, was significantly higher than the Chinese language proficiency of the U.S. students, so they were better able to understand the U.S. students, while the U.S. students had more difficulty understanding the Chinese students. This situation was disheartening for the portion of U.S. students whose proficiency levels were Intermediate Mid or lower, who could only vaguely understand Chinese students' postings, and whose participation in the discussion was consequently limited. In organizing similar exchanges in the future, the target language level of participants should be taken fully into account and participants with roughly equivalent target language levels selected for participation, in order to avoid these problems and achieve better communicative results.

Organizational challenges

Differences between the Chinese and U.S. sides in terms of academic calendars and time zones also made it difficult to find an ideal time to carry out the exchange. The two trials we were able to conduct were only possible due to the enthusiasm for the project and mutual personal trust shared by the teachers on both the U.S. and China sides. In the future, if exchanges are formalized as part of an educational program, considerable effort will need to be devoted to fostering mutual support and cooperation between institutions, as well as to long-term project planning. The two sides need to coordinate all aspects of project organization, time coordination, teacher training, and training students to use the site. Moreover, particular attention must be devoted to monitoring the quality of students' contributions to online activities. Performance objectives and operating procedures must all be clearly defined.

Insufficiency as a standalone language curriculum

In its current state, the "China-USA Business Café" is not a fully independent web-based culture course, but rather an ancillary tool supporting the teaching of culture in the foreign language education context. Much work remains to be done before the Café can be established as a formal curriculum. The number of task-based activities in the existing Café is relatively small and does not suffice to meet the needs of a formal curriculum over a full semester. In the future, more practical and effective task-based activities will need to be added, and new task types introduced, as time and resources permit.

Conclusion

The *Cultura* model from MIT, developed to highlight the importance of the acquisition of cultural knowledge as an integral component of language learning, represents a constructive challenge to the language teaching field along many dimensions. It dethrones the instructor as dispenser of cultural knowledge and trains learners to act as co-constructors of knowledge through a process of mutual inquiry. It harnesses the power of the web to place native speakers in the role of expert cultural informants and exploratory learners at one and the same time, with the result that participants often succeed not only in learning about the target culture, but in seeing their own culture through the eyes of others. And it provides learners with unparalleled motivation through the exploration of vital, yet often hidden, cultural values that underlie and pervade all linguistic communication. As Chinese language educators, we are inspired by this challenge and we intend to continue testing and improving the implementation of *Cultura*-based projects in our Chinese language teaching.

References

American Council on the Teaching of Foreign Languages. (1996). *Standards for foreign language learning: Preparing for the 21st century.* Lawrence, KS: Allen Press.

Brooks, N. (1968). Teaching culture in the foreign language classroom. *Foreign Language Annals 1*(3), 204–217.

Furstenberg, G., Levet, S., English, K., & Maillet, K. (2001). Giving a virtual voice to the silent language of culture: The *Cultura* Project. *Language Learning and Technology 5*(1), 55–100.

Hall, Edward T. (1956). *The silent language.* New York, NY: Doubleday.

Kang, Y., & Chen, J. (2005). Testing the test: Aspects of CET 4 revisited. *CELEA Journal 28*(2), 21–25.

Kramsch, C. (1993). *Context and culture in language teaching.* Oxford, England: Oxford University Press.

Kramsch, C. (1998). *Language and culture.* Oxford, England: Oxford University Press.

Krasner, I. (1999). The role of culture in language teaching. *Dialog on Language Instruction 13*(1–2), 79–88.

Lange, D. L. (1998). *The teaching of culture in foreign language courses.* Center for Applied Linguistics, Washington, DC. (ED 433726). Retrieved from http://www.eric.ed.gov/ERICWebPortal/contentdelivery/servlet/ERICServlet?accno=ED433726

Lange, D. L., & Paige, R. M. (Eds.). (2003). *Culture as the core: Perspectives on culture in second language learning.* Greenwich, CT: Information Age Publishing.

Tylor, E. B. (2010). *Primitive culture: Researches into the development of mythology, philosophy, religion, language, art, and custom.* Cambridge, England: Cambridge University Press. (Original work published 1871).

Yu, L. (2009). Where is culture?: Culture instruction and the foreign language textbook. *Journal of the Chinese Language Teachers Association 44*(3), 73–108.

UHM-UCLA Filipino Heritage Café and the Fil-Ams' Quest for Identity

Nenita Pambid Domingo
University of California—Los Angeles

The majority of Filipino Americans enroll in Filipino language classes in the hope of retrieving their Filipino identity. This chapter describes the Filipino Heritage Language Café,[1] a collaborative project between intermediate Filipino language students at the University of Hawai'i at Mānoa (UHM) and the University of California, Los Angeles (UCLA). The Café was inspired by the Cultura *model and planning began at the Summer Institute at UHM in 2008. In this chapter, the first iteration of the Café is discussed, and details about the participants, modes of exchange, content and sequence of activities, the students' reflections, the teachers' observations, and the lessons learned are presented.[2] The inaugural exchange in 2008 achieved the general goals of improving Filipino language proficiency and providing a community for students to explore their Filipino identity and culture, and ways to improve such exchanges were also revealed.*

Introduction

Identity. What are my roots? What am I? Who am I? What is my heritage? Jose Rizal, a Philippine national hero, became acutely aware of his ethnicity and identity because he was immersed in foreign cultures most of his adult life while studying in

---

[1] http://nflrc.hawaii.edu/brix/

[2] Since 2008, two additional exchanges have taken place: in Fall 2009 and Spring 2010. The 2009 exchange involved 51 participants: one intermediate class of 32 at UHM, 7 students from the University of the Philippines (UP), and one intermediate Filipino class of 12 at UCLA. The 2010 iteration was between one intermediate class of 24 at UHM, an intermediate Filipino class of 4 at University of Pennsylvania, and an intermediate class of 14 at UCLA, for a total of 42 students.

Domingo, N. P., (2014). UH-UCLA Filipino Heritage Café and the Fil-Ams' quest for identity. In D. M. Chun, (Ed.), Cultura-*inspired intercultural exchanges: Focus on Asian and Pacific languages* (pp. 145–161). Honolulu: University of Hawai'i, National Foreign Language Resource Center.

Europe, traveling in the United States, and practicing medicine in Hong Kong and Germany. He articulated Philippine culture through his research on the Philippines in European archives. The following stanza in praise of one's native language, which is part of a poem that Rizal wrote when he was eight, encapsulates the Filipinos' struggle against colonialism and quest for identity (Romero, Santa Romana, & Santos, 2006).

Ang hindi magmahal sa kanyang salita	One who does not love one's tongue
mahigit sa hayop at malansang isda	is worse than a beast and putrid fish
kaya ang marapat, pagyamaning kusa	and like a truly precious thing
na tulad ng isang tunay na nagpala.	it therefore deserves to be cherished.

The Filipino-American experience, I suggest, is no different from Rizal's predicament for there is language in culture, and culture in language. Knowing the native language of one's progenitors is a definite mark and mooring of one's culture and identity. With this in mind, this chapter will describe the Filipino Heritage Café, an online intercultural exchange between two university Filipino language classes, one at the University of California Los Angeles and the other at the University of Hawai'i at Mānoa. This chapter discusses its inception at the 2008 Summer Institute, the moderators, participants, content, time frame, mode of exchange, and an evaluation of the project based on the first exchange in Fall 2008. A brief description of the Filipino language, a less-commonly taught language in the United States, is given below.

Filipino: The Philippines' national language

Filipino became the national language of the Philippines as mandated by the Philippine Constitution of 1987. It is a vital language based primarily on Tagalog, one of the eight major languages of the Philippines, belonging to the Indonesian subfamily of the Austronesian family of languages. Before Spanish colonial times, it used its own syllabary called the *baybayin,* which has three vowels and 14 consonants. With colonization by the Spaniards, Roman letters replaced the Tagalog syllabary. Filipino also has contributions from 80 or more different extant languages in the Philippines, as well as from foreign tongues, particularly Spanish and English, which were the languages of its colonizers, Spain and the United States of America. It uses the English alphabet plus the Tagalog letter *ng* and the Spanish letter *ñ*. The present alphabet mirrors, in brief, the history of the archipelago, that is, 350 years under Spain and 50 years under the United States. The name of the country itself is a testament to its colonial past: It was named after the Spanish monarch King Philip II.

Birth of the Filipino Heritage Café

The Filipino Heritage Language Café is a collaborative project between intermediate Filipino language students at the University of Hawai'i at Mānoa (UHM) and the University of California, Los Angeles (UCLA). The Café is based on the *Cultura* Project, created in 1997 by Gilbert Furstenberg, Sabine Levet, and Shoggy Waryn of the Massachusetts Institute of Technology (MIT), where an intermediate French language class at MIT was paired with students taking an advanced English class at Institut National des Telecommunications (INT) in France.[3] The students looked at the same materials coming from their own cultures and exchanged views in their native languages, that is, French and English. According to Furstenberg (2003),

---

[3] http://cultura.mit.edu/

"The goal of *Cultura* is to develop in-depth understanding of another culture's concepts, attitudes, values, ways of thinking, interacting and relating to others and one's environment." Furthermore, Furstenberg, Levet, English, and Maillet (2001) suggest that it gives "a virtual voice to the silent language of culture" and enables students to construct their own definition and knowledge of another culture through computer mediated language and culture learning in another part of the globe.

In the summer of 2008, the National Foreign Language Resource Center (NFLRC) at the University of Hawai'i at Mānoa sponsored the Summer Institute for Heritage Cafés for Chinese, Japanese, Filipino, and Samoan languages.[4] The institute was a one-week planning workshop for the language Cafés' curriculum for immediate implementation in August-September of 2008, also sponsored by the NFLRC. The UC Consortium for Language Learning and Teaching (UCCLLT), housed at UC Davis, coordinated UCLA's participation. The Filipino Heritage Café was co-sponsored by the Southeast Asia National Resource Center. During the institute, the designers of the Filipino Heritage Café were Imelda Gasmen (UHM), Lilibeth Robotham (UHM), Jovanie de la Cruz (UHM), and Nenita Pambid Domingo (UCLA).

The group created a planning document that detailed the overall goals, participants, level of language ability, languages of exchange, mode of exchange, motivation for students, role of the teacher, and time frame, and brainstormed on other ideas such as creating a grammar section, guidelines for posting and replying, assessment tools, and the possibility of a final project such as an on-line magazine.

Project

The inaugural exchange took place in Fall 2008. Instruction for Fall Quarter at UCLA started on September 25, and ended on December 5. For University of Hawai'i at Mānoa, the first day of instruction was August 25, and the last day was December 11. Since UCLA had only 10 weeks in the quarter, the instructors identified an overlapping 8-week period at each university during which the Heritage Café activities would take place.

In contrast to the MIT *Cultura* Project, the Filipino Heritage Café's adaptation was between two campuses in the US that teach Filipino language. Both campuses have large enrollments of Filipino Americans whose parents are newly arrived immigrants, including doctors, nurses, technical people, skilled laborers, and professionals, as well as descendants of Filipino plantation workers in the sugar cane fields in Hawai'i and the farm workers in California.

Hawai'i was the site of Filipino sugar cane workers recruited by the Hawai'i Sugar Planters' Association during the first decade of American colonization of the Philippines in the 1900s. With the unrestricted immigration of Filipino cheap labor before 1945, it is not surprising that the Filipino/Tagalog language is the number one language, after English, spoken at home in the state of Hawai'i, and it ranks third in California (U.S. Census Bureau, 2009).

The search for Filipino identity and articulation of Filipino culture was a burning issue among Filipino Americans even before the institution of Ethnic Studies in the United States in the 1960s. Even in their home country—as a result of more than 400 years of western colonization—Filipino intellectuals straddling Western and Eastern cultures have been preoccupied with this issue.

---

[4] http://nflrc.hawaii.edu/prodev/si08oc

Participants and goals of the Filipino Heritage Café

The teachers for the first exchange were Imelda Gasmen and Lilibeth Robotham (University of Hawai'i at Mānoa) and Nenita Pambid Domingo (University of California at Los Angeles). The participating classes, in their second year of study of the language, were primarily intermediate learners, and their level of language ability ranged from 1+ to 2 on the ACTFL scale of oral proficiency. Students could create with the language, but had no firm grasp of cases or the major verb tenses.

For the Fall 2008 exchange, both campuses (UHM and UCLA) had 100% heritage learners. For the purposes of this chapter, a heritage language learner is considered to be any second language learner who lives or who has lived in a Filipino household or the home country and practices Filipino customs and traditions, but does not necessarily speak or read the language before taking university classes. Heritage learners may have been raised or exposed to a bi-cultural household with parents and grandparents speaking a Philippine language, not necessarily the target language in the Café, which is Filipino, but any of the more than 80 languages in the Philippines.

The general motivation of the UHM and UCLA students was to learn the Filipino language to be able to communicate with Filipino family, friends, or romantic relations. They also wanted to recover their cultural roots, learn more about themselves, "reverse the effects of cultural loss," and boost their grade point average (GPA). They were eager to participate in the Café, motivated by a higher grade, since they received points toward their course grade for participating in the exchange. The instructors hypothesized that without the participation points, the activity might not be successful due to students' busy schedules and workload in their other courses, part-time jobs, and demands of the family, not to mention their extra-curricular activities which might be more enticing than sitting in front of a computer. However, in addition to the grade incentive, students at UCLA were, in fact, curious about UHM students who were enrolled in a similar course and had approximately the same level of proficiency in the language.

Despite being heritage learners, the students were linguistically challenged in the Filipino language. They had knowledge and experience of Philippine culture in their family traditions and celebrations, but their acquisition of the language was incomplete and lacked grammatical accuracy and precision. Their vocabulary was also limited to the things around them and to daily interactions and negotiation. Therefore, the following goals were set for the exchange of communication in the Café:

- To improve and enhance intermediate learners' language acquisition and proficiency in reading, writing, comprehension skills, and cultural competence;
- To create a learning environment in cyber space that would expand student awareness of a community of learners, provide a forum to examine Filipino identity and culture, and aid the Filipino-Americans' quest for identity; and
- To enable students to compare and experience Filipino culture vicariously from another perspective and geographical location and to share their insights on Filipino identity and loss of culture.

Mode of exchange and project website

The Café was implemented in late summer 2008, and students at the two universities began to communicate online with each other in the fall, using the BRIX courseware, a web courseware system that is specifically designed for language learning and teaching (Sawatpanit, Suthers, & Fleming, 2003).

The teachers from the participating universities were trained to use the BRIX system and to navigate the site in order to accomplish the aforementioned goals. The language of the exchange was primarily Filipino/Tagalog, the target language, with instructions in English that were translated into Filipino. Code mixing was also welcome, that is, use of the hybrid languages "Taglish" (predominantly Tagalog with mixture of English) or "Engalog" (predominantly English with smattering of Tagalog).

The classes at UHM met in a computer lab and logged on to the Filipino Heritage Café either on Monday, Tuesday, or Wednesday, before the class at UCLA met in a computer lab on Fridays. The Café site was a virtual space where the students at UCLA and UHM left messages for the other class to read and respond to. The exchange was entirely on-line and asynchronous.

The site was password protected. The login page displayed the words "Filipino Heritage Café" and a colored image of the Philippine national flag (see Figure 1). This image served as the logo and appeared on all the pages of the site. This page also stated the technical requirements for using the site.

Figure 1. Filipino Heritage Café login

From the login page, users were taken to the homepage where they could select from a horizontal menu any one of the following links: "Home," "Schedule," "Classmates," "Teachers," "Logout," and "Help" (see Figure 2). On the left was the "Course Menu" with the following links: "Café," "Welcome!," "Questionnaire," the three pre-set topics ("Filipino Family," "Images of Filipinos in the Media," "Celebrations and Traditions)", "Grammar Section," "Tools," "New Postings," "Useful Links," "Language Bank," and "Upload Folio." The Café link opened to a page, which was an open space for participants to write or leave a voice message to which other participants or visitors to the Café could respond. Examples of topics for the Café section of the Fall 2008 exchange were election 2008, one liner "hellos and goodbyes," inquiry, and request to be added to Friendster, Myspace, and Facebook. In the middle of the page was a box for "Notices" where instructors could post guidelines for student postings in the forum and messages about matters pertaining to their particular class.

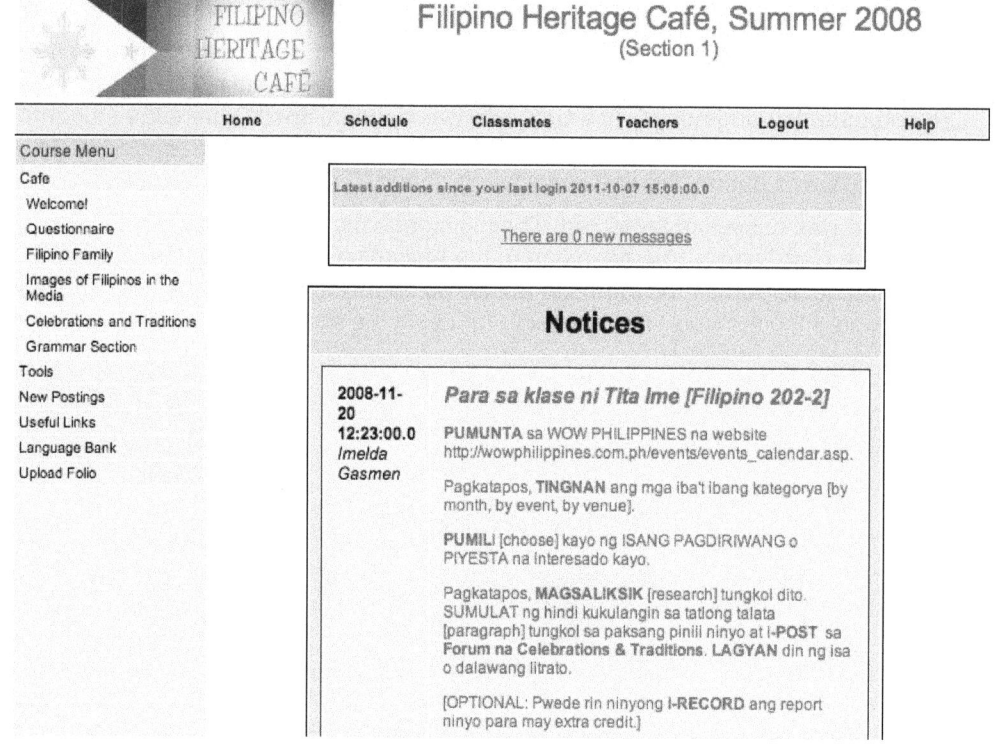

Figure 2. Filipino Heritage Café homepage

Content and sequence of activities

The length of exchange was 8 weeks. Because of the different systems of the universities—UHM is on a 15-week semester system while UCLA is on a 10-week quarter system—the teachers had to coordinate when to begin the exchange and decided on the first week of UCLA's academic year which was the last week of September. Each institution followed its own syllabus and curriculum, intersecting only in the three discussion topics: "Filipino Family," "Filipinos in the Media," and "Celebrations and Traditions" (see Table 1). The teachers moderated, facilitated, and evaluated the exchange, at times participating in the forum in order to encourage student postings. Table 1 outlines the schedule of activities for the inaugural exchange in Fall 2008.

Table 1. Fall 2008 topics and schedule of activities

week	classroom setting		remarks
	online	offline	
1	Orientation. Welcome: Introduction Questionnaire: Word Associations		Sept. 24, 25, 26 (UHM and UCLA)
2	Questionnaire: Sentence Completions	Summarize, analyze, discuss questionnaire results in small groups	Oct. 1, 2, 3
3	Topic 1: Filipino Family Material: Nico Jollibee commercial (YouTube) Watch the video clip and comment based on the prompts.		Oct. 8, 9, 10
4	Summarize similarities and/or differences of student perspectives from each campus about the topic.		Oct. 15, 16, 17
5	Topic 2: Images of Filipinos in the Media Material: Pinoy Ako, Pinoy Tayo (YouTube)		Oct. 22, 23, 24
6	Summarize similarities and/or differences of student perspectives from each campus about the topic.		Oct. 29, 30, 31
7	Topic 3: Celebrations and Traditions Material: [selected by students] Discussion Forum		Nov. 5, 6, 7
8	Summarize similarities and/or differences of student perspectives from each campus about the topic.		Nov. 12, 13, 14

In week 1, students were directed to the Welcome page, which led to the Project Goals (*Mga Layunin ng Proyekto*) and to Introductions (*Pagpapakilala*), where teachers and students introduced themselves with the following instructions in Filipino (without the English translation):

Kumusta?

Sumulat ng dalawang talata (paragraph) para ipakilala ang sarili mo. Sa unang talata, sabihin mo ang pangalan mo, kung may palayaw ka, saan ka ipinanganak at lumaki, saan ka nag-aaral ngayon, anong taon/status mo na sa kolehiyo [sophomore, senior, at iba pa], ano ang medyor mo at ano ang plano mo pagkatapos mong mag-aral sa kolehiyo.

Sa pangalawang talata naman, sabihin mo kung bakit ka nag-aaral ng Filipino. Isulat mo rin kung ano ang mga karanasan (experiences) mo sa pag-aaral ng Filipino sa iyong unibersidad. Idagdag mo na rin kung anu-ano ang mga pinakapaborito mong aktibidad o gawain sa mga klase mo sa Filipino.

Maaari ring magdagdag ng iba pang impormasyon kagaya ng mga interes o mga hilig mo o mga libangan mo.

How are you?

Write two paragraphs introducing yourself. In the first paragraph, indicate your name, if you have a nickname, your place of birth, and where you grew up, where you currently study, your status/year in college (sophomore, senior, etc.), your major, and what your plan is after college.

In the second paragraph, state why you are studying Filipino. Also include your experiences in studying Filipino at your university. Also mention your favorite activities or work in your Filipino class.

You can also include other information like your interests or likes or free time activities.

The next activity was the "Questionnaire: Word Associations" (*Kaugnay na Salita*). As in the Cultura model, the instructors provided a list of 10 Filipino words (e.g., *pamilya* 'family,' *tradisyon* 'tradition'), for which students at both campuses were to write the Filipino words that first came to mind or that they associated with each of the words on the list (see Table 2).

Table 2. Questionnaire: Word Associations

pamilya	family
tradisyon	tradition
identidad	identity
kultura	culture
bayani	hero
pag-ibig	love
parti	party
trabaho	work
immigrant	immigrant
pera	money

In week 2, students filled out the online "Questionnaire: Sentence Completions (*Pagbuo ng Pangungusap*). The instructors had constructed the beginning of seven sentences, and students were asked to complete the thought with at least two possible answers, for example, *Nag-aaral ako ng Filipino kasi ...* 'I am taking Filipino because ...' (see Table 3). During that week, the UCLA students were also asked to summarize, analyze, and discuss the questionnaire results in small, face-to-face groups in class. They then uploaded the results of their analyses to the Café forum.

In weeks 3–8, three different topics were presented and discussed (as shown in Table 1). For Topic 1, "Filipino Family," in week 3, the instructors chose a commercial on YouTube depicting a family, and students watched the video clip *Lolo at Lola Sa Amerika* 'Grandpa and Grandma in America, (see Figure 3). They then each wrote a paragraph about the aspects of the Filipino family that they saw portrayed in the video and noted how what they saw might be related to their own family. All students then read the postings and commented on at least one posting by students at the other campus.

Table 3. Questionnaire: Sentence Completions

1. *Nag-aaral ako ng Filipino kasi* _____.
   I am taking Filipino because _____.
2. *Ang Pilipino ay* _____.
   Being Filipino means _____.
3. *Ang isang mabuting pamilya ay.* _____.
   A good family is _____.
4. *Ang pinakamahalagang itinuro sa akin ng mga magulang ko ay* _____.
   The important lesson my parents taught me is _____.
5. *Pinakapaborito kong pagdiriwang ang* _____.
   My favorite celebration is _____.
6. *Pinakahinahangaan kong Pilipino si* _____.
   The Filipino I admire most is _____.
7. *Pangarap ko sa buhay na* _____.
   My goal in life is _____.

Figure 3. Lola at Lolo sa Amerika[5]

---

[5] http://www.youtube.com/watch?v=D-Xu9oxUOso

In week 4, students at both universities summarized and analyzed the similarities and/or differences in student perspectives from each campus about the topic. They posted their comments and thoughts to the online forum in the Café.

Topic 2, "Images of Filipinos in the Media," was discussed during weeks 5–6. Students first watched YouTube video clips about some famous Filipinos (e.g., see Figure 4[6]) in week 5 and wrote a paragraph about one of the following three options:

1. One person you know from the list and why you think they are "famous."
2. One person who you don't know from the list; find out the reason why he or she was included in the list.
3. The different image(s) of Filipinos depicted in the video.

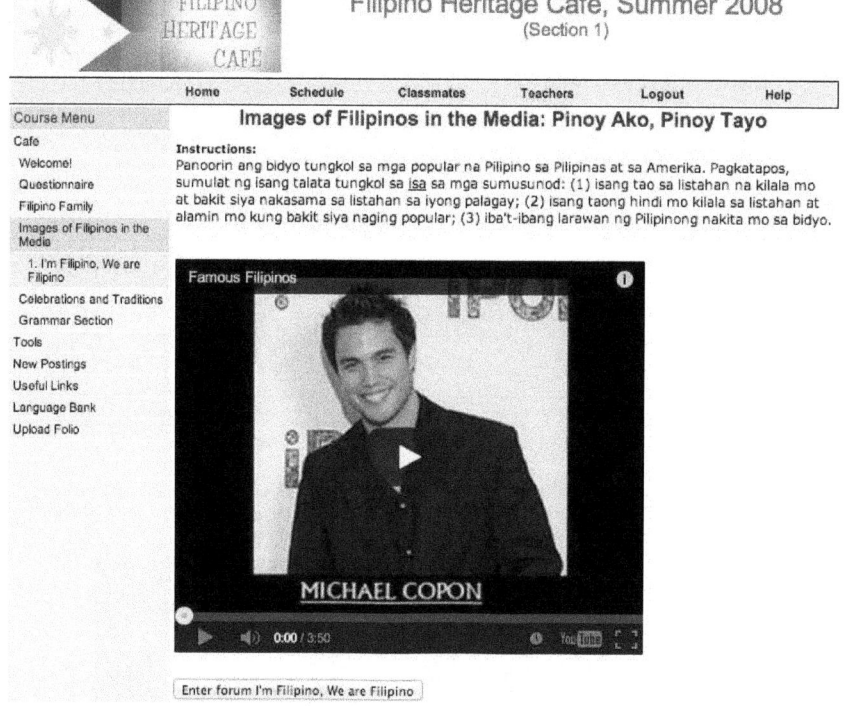

Figure 4. Pinoy Ako, Pinoy Tayo

After both groups of students had posted their paragraphs, students read the postings and made at least one comment on a posting by a student at the other campus. In week 6, they summarized and analyzed similarities and/or differences in student perspectives from each of the respective campuses in face-to-face class discussions.

The third and final topic "Celebrations and Traditions" was discussed during weeks 7–8. Students were asked to search the Internet in week 7 for photos, images, and video clips related to Filipino celebrations. They selected their favorite celebration, uploaded pictures and video clips to the Café, and wrote in the forum, answering the

---

[6] http://www.youtube.com/watch?v=fHA–2jVTPAc

question, "What celebrations and customs were you a part of, and which ones did your family or people around you celebrate?"

In week 8 in small groups or pairs during class time, they discussed, analyzed, and summarized the similarities and/differences in student perspectives from each campus on the topic.

Discussion of results

Student postings

As an overview of student participation in the Fall 2008 exchange, Table 4 provides a tally of student postings (from a total of 35 students) in the different sections of the Filipino Heritage Café.[7]

Table 4. Tally of student postings in Fall 2008

topic	Word Associations and Sentence Completions	Self-Introductions	Filipino Family	Images of Filipinos in the Media	Celebrations & Traditions
no. of postings	159	97	34	47	23

The postings about the Word Associations and Sentence Completions were the most numerous (159), followed by postings on Self-Introductions (97). The unit on "Images of Filipinos in the Media" had 47 postings, followed by the unit on Filipino Family with 34 postings. The unit on "Celebrations and Traditions" had the lowest number of postings (23).

Below is an example of a posting by a UCLA student regarding the word "family" in the Word Associations and the Sentence Completions "The Filipino I admire most is." The posting provides evidence that students synthesized what they had read in the others' postings and hypothesized about why their fellow students wrote what they did.

> *Mayroon mga pareho sa mga sagut ng estudyante taga UCLA at taga UHM. Parang sa lahat ng mga tao, talagang importante ang pamilya nila. Ang mga sagut nila ay "tatay," "ina," "nanay." Parang nakikita sa mga lahat ay importante ang pamilya sa buhay ng mga Pilipino. Pero, mas kilala ang mga estudyante kaysa mga megastars sa Pilipinas. Kilala nila si Rico Yan (RIP) at Vhong Navarro. Hindi naman masikat sila sa Estados Unidos. Ay iwan ko bakit nila nag-kilala sa Rico Yan at Vhong Navarro, pero okay rin iyan. Mas maraming kilala nila ang aktor sa Pilipinas kaysa sa LA. Kasi ang % ng Pilipino doon ay mas malaki kaysa dito.*

> There are similarities in the responses of UCLA students and UHM students. It seems like for all people, their family is really important. Their answers are "father," "mother," "mother" (synonym in Filipino). It appears that family for all is

---

[7] The data were gathered from the Filipino Heritage Café website generated by the "Reporting Tool" under "Assessments," which can be accessed from the "Tools" link on the "Course Menu" located on the left side of the page. In addition, there is a tally of each individual student's replies or postings as well as a tally of the number of new threads started by a student for each unit of the course (i.e., Café, "Filipino Family," "Images of Filipinos in the Media," and "Celebrations and Traditions").

important to the Filipinos' life. But the students know more about the megastars in the Philippines. They know Rico Yan (RIP) [who passed away in 2008] and Vhong Navarro. They are not famous in the United States. Oh, I don't know why they know Rico Yan and Vhong Navarro, but that is also okay. They know more actors from the Philippines than actors from L.A., because the percentage of Filipinos over there is greater than here.

The frequency count and tally of student replies do not reflect the quality or length of postings but can give some indication of the success or failure of the Filipino Heritage Café as a tool for enhancing and facilitating language acquisition. In general, the writing produced faltered grammatically at times, but a sympathetic native speaker could probably understand the drift of the discussion. As a rule, the postings complied with the instruction to write at least a paragraph. In the case of UCLA students, they usually sought help from Google translate, online dictionaries available on the Internet, the teacher, and from peers who could speak the language quite fluently. At first, they were wary and worried about their lack of precision and appropriate vocabulary in the use of the language, but they often received sympathetic responses from participants at the other school about being in the same boat, reassuring them that they were actually doing just fine. Often times, students found comfort in discovering that many of the participants were just as insecure about their own writing as they were.

There are many variables to consider that affect the quality and quantity of student postings. These include gender; status in the university; whether the participant is a 2nd, 3rd, or 4th year undergraduate student or a masters or doctoral student; major; age; and overall proficiency in the language. Native speakers or near-native speakers tended to be the most verbose and articulate, while students who started from 0+ proficiency in their study of the language were less likely to participate frequently in the forum. Another intervening variable was the activities that students had at their university. When a "more important" activity was taking place, the Heritage Café took a back seat. Most intermediate students from UCLA had junior and senior standing and needed 2 years of language as a requirement in their major field of study. Despite the fact that participation in the Heritage Café was part of the students' grade for the course, more than half of the students did not participate in the exercise, especially towards the conclusion of the exchange, for example, the topic "Celebrations and Traditions" had the lowest number of postings.

In summary, the number of postings does not give a clear indication of the success or failure of the heritage Café as an effective pedagogical tool in teaching a second language and culture. But other factors such as students' subjective assessment of the effectiveness of the Café and teachers' evaluations of the actual products produced in the Café are discussed in the next sections.

Students' reflections

UCLA students from the Fall 2008 exchange were asked for their opinions about the exchange. Their responses revealed the inherent strengths and weaknesses of the exchange.

Students thought that the Café engaged them more in the language than traditional classroom activities. It was a novelty to be able to communicate with somebody on the other side of the ocean who was also learning the language. As one student put it,

> What I appreciated most from the forum was the ability to regularly write in Filipino without having to worry too much about correcting the mistakes or providing the "right answer." This allowed me to overcome my fear of just writing Filipino." By the same token, another student noted that, "maybe if we were on a live video feed instead it could have been more fun and instructive. We were only really able to communicate once week and most of us wrote using wrong grammar =(

In the Word Associations activity, students were asked to write about how the words applied to their culture and/or the language from their own points of view, making them experts in their own culture and giving them a multiplicity of voices and knowledge rather than knowledge just from the teacher. One student stated, "It made us dive deeper into the roots of the language as well as the culture that we are all a part of." Another student categorically stated that "the café is definitely good writing practice." Although the students found the interaction between the two classes to be fun and engaging, one student recommended tackling more serious subjects, e.g., Tagalog news, in the online discussions. However, he admitted, "the activity with UHM still helped me to improve my writing and grammar."

The primary language used was Filipino, the target language. Although code mixing was welcome, the students used the Filipino language even in the free space of the Café. One student suggested giving Café participation a higher percentage in the grading schema, and in addition, "The Internet Café can be more effective in language learning if all the students would write regularly in order to always practice thinking and writing in Tagalog."

The students also sharpened their cognitive skills in the discussion of different topics such as popular culture, history, and news and in their comparisons of how the answers of the two groups differed. For example, in the discussion regarding the topic "Filipinos in the Media," students from UCLA called attention to the lack of educators and politicians in the video clip—except for Imelda Marcos, whom they consider infamous and a bad example. A student from UHM countered that Benjamin Cayetano, a Filipino, served as governor of Hawai'i for two terms, indicating the ability to analyze and discuss what another has written.

Through their exchanges in the forum, the students formed their opinions, expressed their feelings, and came to conclusions about Filipino Identity. For example, one student lamented how some famous celebrities who are actually Filipino hide their identity and assume another, more viable ethnicity. Another mused, "Filipinos are classified as singers, sportsmen, and beauty queens. Is Cassie more important than Cory Aquino?" (the first female Philippine president who was featured on the cover of *Time* magazine).

One student pointed out that "the program allowed us to see how much of our understanding of various themes and concepts such as Filipino identity, culture, and beliefs were different based on our location and language." Through comparing and contrasting their responses to the prompts, students were able to form new knowledge from the different contributions of the participants.

Although the forum provided the participants with time to reflect and compose their responses, the students also noted the disadvantages of the asynchronous exchange. They suggested that if a synchronous discussion had been used, the stakes may have been higher, and participants would have had the opportunity to think and respond immediately, rather than waiting a week to get an answer. They also pointed out that in the asynchronous forum exchange, it would have been more convenient if their responses could have been placed directly under the posting of the person to whom they were responding or asking a question, rather than listed in chronological order.

Some near-native speakers and students whose linguistic proficiency was relatively advanced found some of the activities redundant. For example, the grammar clinic was not popular among these students, probably because the teachers were able to adequately discuss the grammar during offline class meetings.

Teachers' observations

Students' comments confirmed what the teachers from University of Hawai'i observed. In a taped interview, Imelda Gasmen stated that she has advocated the use of the online learning community in her languages classes for several years and has noticed that with the use of technology, there is increased participation from students in terms of quantity and quality in language production and writing (NFLRC, 2010a). The students in Hawai'i had different perspectives, and by sharing them with the students from California in the Café, they learned from each other. Moreover, Gasman added, in the Filipino Heritage Café, online asynchronous discussion "generates more substance" since "students have more time to think about and refine what they want to say."

From the point of view of another instructor, Lilibeth Robotham stated,

> I think for them [students] it was fun, it was very different going to the computer lab, different from the usual, from the traditional, from the regular curriculum that we have for intermediate, so I think it was very helpful because they were able to learn from other students as well, not just you know, from me or from the textbook or from the handouts that we have in class." (NFLRC, 2010b)

In the 2008 exchange, the teachers observed that some of the UCLA students were not really communicating with the students at UHM. They were more intent on complying with the requirement of having to post something in the forum. Students from the 2008 Café also pointed out that there were too many students from Hawai'i (23) in comparison to only 12 students from UCLA. But this seems to be a minor issue.

Despite all the limitations that the students themselves pointed out, teachers observed that the students enjoyed the novelty of interacting with students from a campus across the Pacific Ocean. They did discern some subtle cultural differences in the responses from students at UHM and at UCLA and agreed that the Internet Café was a wonderful addition to the course. From a pedagogical standpoint, the online language Café had a built-in analytical framework that allowed students to compare and contrast the postings with varying points of view that forced them to think critically, thereby exercising and enhancing their analytical skills in the process. Language education is not just acquiring the language and becoming linguistically proficient, but is part of the holistic education of the total person. Through the exchange, students were able "to see the world from the eyes of another person," which may promote mutual understanding and therefore be beneficial within a globalized and diverse culture like the United States. Moreover, the ability to discern, analyze, and think critically in order to process the barrage of information coming from YouTube and Twitter, and all the other benefits of the cyber technology revolution, is very important in modern life. These cognitive processes are inherent in the exchange of ideas afforded by the online language Café.

We now return to the goals of the project. The primary goal was second language acquisition, and the secondary goal was for learners to develop an awareness of a community of learners and to jointly define the quest for Filipino identity. Lastly, students were expected to compare and experience Filipino culture from another person's perspective and share their insights with each other.

With regard to the primary goal of improving and enhancing intermediate learners' language proficiency in reading, writing, comprehension skills, and cultural competence, the activities in the Café did enhance language learning to some extent. But they could have been maximized if the Café had been the sole component of the course and not just a supplement to the course. The content and the use of Filipino on a daily basis in a stand-alone intermediate Filipino course would have increased the potential of the Internet Café for language learning. One student astutely put it this way:

> I think that the best way for us to improve our use of the Filipino language on Internet Café is if we use it on a daily basis and talk about topics that are really interesting to us. We would be more likely to learn a language if we are discussing subject matters that are interesting because we are more likely to put in effort into something that we like than something we don't like.

As another student observed,

> Even though we both live in multiethnic societies, Tagalog was literally and figuratively our thread of communication across distances," which highlights both the necessity of language acquisition and the opportunity for community building.

The second objective was to create a learning environment in cyber space that would expand student awareness of a community of learners and provide a forum to examine Filipino identity and culture to fill the need of Filipino-Americans' quest for identity. The fact that different classes in different geographical locations were able to communicate with and get to know one another via the Internet created a virtual community of learners. In the words of a student, "Internet Café is a great way of learning and applying the language while also reaching out to other students who are also trying to master the Filipino language."

Lastly, the final goal was to enable students to compare and experience Filipino culture vicariously from another perspective and geographical location, and to share their insights on Filipino identity and loss of culture. From student postings in the Word Associations and Sentence Completions, one student concluded that, "I don't see a difference between how the students at Hawai'i and here (Los Angeles) view Filipino language and culture. When looking at the Word Associations assignments, we all think similarly about family, life, work, money, etc." Another student added the following comment on Filipino culture and identity:

> From the Internet Café, I can see we all share similar values in that we treasure family and appreciate what we have ... When looking at the Word Associations assignments, we all think similarly about family, life, work, money, etc. .... the Internet Café showed me an interesting perspective of other classes compared

to ours. But at the end of the quarter, I realized that we all share a lot in common in wanting to learn the language and being very fun, easy going people.

One student hypothesized, though, that it is more difficult to assert one's Filipino identity in California:

> Other than some differences in food preferences (i.e., *loco-moco* in Hawai'i), pretty much we are going through the same experiences. Surely though, given the prevalence of Pilipinos in Hawai'i, they probably are not going through the same identity struggle as Pilipino-Americans are here.

From the "artifacts" in the exchange, we can conclude that to some extent the Filipino Heritage Café was able to achieve the goals of the project. As illustrated in the previous discussion, the Café succeeded in improving writing proficiency as well as cultural competence and has also broadly fulfilled the five Cs of the Standards for Foreign Language Learning, namely, Communication, Cultures, Connections, Comparisons, and Communities (ACTFL, 2012).

Lessons learned

The most important positive outcomes of the Filipino Heritage Café were

- Students became aware of other communities of learners, getting to compare themselves with other students and exercise their critical thinking faculties through reading and analysis of Word Associations and postings, and in the process, expand their vocabulary.

- Students were able to demonstrate in their postings language functions such as clarification, agreement, disagreement, synthesis and creation of new knowledge collectively, expression and support of opinions, strategies for obtaining more information, and comparison and contrasting of new ideas and old from different perspectives.

In terms of the technical aspects of the exchange, it is very important that the instructors/facilitators have the necessary training, familiarity with, and knowledge of the BRIX system and its capabilities. Student training in how to navigate the website is also a must before an exchange is started. From a pedagogical perspective, clear and fluid communication among instructors from participating institutions is necessary, and seamless coordination for them to be on the same page is desirable. There is also a need to create clear guidelines for posting and to communicate this to the students and facilitators.

Taking the cues from student comments regarding the Café, there is a need to revise the course curriculum based on the evaluations and reflections in the student responses. In order to accomplish the goal of improved Filipino language proficiency and cultural competency, instructors should make an effort to "go with the flow," which may be quite unsettling for teachers who have been so used to the tried and tested syllabus "etched in stone." From a departmental or curricular perspective, making the Café a stand-alone curriculum would require the support of the participating universities in order for the class to flourish. The Café should not just take place on Fridays or during 2-hour meetings in class but could be the main content or a greater part of the curriculum. This would maximize the benefits that can be derived from the exchange and would allow for full appreciation and reflection on the part of the students, making the class a student-centered classroom without borders. In this way, too, the Heritage Café experience would become a more meaningful and genuine exchange of ideas, where students might realize their limited grammatical abilities and might be encouraged to take more risks in trying to negotiate their intended meaning. As a teacher, I now realize the importance of reflecting on, analyzing, and drawing insight from the student responses.

Quo Vadis Filipino Heritage Café?

Looking ahead, perhaps when the Filipinos and Filipino-Americans have been weaned from the ghost of their colonial past, search for identity, and the angst of cultural loss, the Filipino Heritage Café will be able to move on to other topics, in an emic-etic approach, more encompassing and global in nature. Until then, the search for the lost identity and the campaign for Pilipino studies will continue.

References

ACTFL American Council on the Teaching of Foreign Languages. (2012). *National standards for foreign language education Executive summary* [PDF document]. Retrieved from http://www.actfl.org/publications/all/national-standards-foreign-language-education

Furstenberg, G. (2003). Constructing French-American understanding: The *Cultura* project. *French Politics, Culture, and Society, 21*(2). Retrieved from http://www.questia.com/googleScholar.qst;jsessionid=L1nNhT2CXdxCYtfRkwfP4DG2vJ0FWHGJrGF5QK1mtNLVnw60bW4s!1888687908!−1986555990?docId=5002560565.

Furstenberg, G., Levet, S., English, K., & Maillet, K. (2001). Giving a virtual voice to the silent language of culture: The *Cultura* Project. *Language Learning & Technology, 5*(1), 55–102. Retrieved from http://llt.msu.edu/vol5num1/furstenberg

National Foreign Language Resource Center. (2010a). Online Cafés Audio & Video: Imelda Gasmen. Retrieved from http://nflrc.hawaii.edu/onlinecafes/?page_id=416

National Foreign Language Resource Center (Producer). (2010b). Online Cafés Audio & Video: Lilibeth Robotham. Retrieved from http://nflrc.hawaii.edu/onlinecafes/?page_id=416

Romero, M. C., Santa Romana, J. R., & Santos, L. Y. (2006). *Rizal and the development of national consciousness*. Quezon City, Philippines: Katha Publishing.

Sawatpanit, M., Suthers, D., & Fleming, S. (2003). BRIX—Elements for Language Course Creation. In D. Lassner & C. McNaught (Eds.), *Proceedings of ED-MEDIA 2003: World Conference on Educational Multimedia, Hypermedia & Telecommunications* (pp. 415–422). Norfolk, VA: Association for Advancement of Computing in Education.

U. S. Census Bureau. (2009). *Population: Ancestry, language spoken at home*. Retrieved from http://www.census.gov/compendia/statab/cats/population/ancestry_language_spoken_at_home.html

A High School Japanese and English Intercultural Exchange Project: Design, Implementation, and Evaluation

Yukiko Watanabe
University of California, Berkeley

Yoichi Tsuji
Tezukayama Gakuin Izmigaoka High School

Cindy Wong
Moanalua High School

This chapter describes the implementation and evaluation of an intercultural exchange project between two high schools, Moanalua High School in the United States and Tezukayama Gakuin Izumigaoka High School in Japan. Through online interactive learning activities, the project aimed at (a) providing opportunities for students to learn authentic language use from peer counterparts, and (b) motivating students to learn diverse cultural perspectives of the value systems underlying customs, opinions, and behaviors. The evaluation of the project was based on teacher reflections, online student performance, and student feedback, and examined the factors affecting implementation of the project and the appropriateness of the tasks and materials.

Introduction

Fostering intercultural competence in foreign language (FL) instruction has become an integral part of FL education. In the past, culture and language teaching practices were based on a native-speaker model, where learners were benchmarked against native speaker conventions. However, if language educators view language users as trans-national and cross-cultural language users, classroom instruction should aim at developing learners into *intercultural speakers/mediators* (Byram, 1997, 2008; Kramsch 1998). Byram (2008) asserts that "one of the outcomes of teaching languages (and cultures) should be the ability to see how different cultures relate to each other—in terms of similarities and differences—and to act as mediator between them, or more precisely between people socialized into them" (p. 68).

The FL curriculum can play a crucial role in facilitating and creating intercultural experiences as well as providing opportunities for learners to analyze and reflect on their experiences (Byram, 2008). Byram suggests four educational principles that encourage students to become intercultural mediators as global citizens.

Principle 1: Intercultural experience takes place when people from different social groups with different values, beliefs and behaviors (cultures) meet.

Principle 2: Being "intercultural" involves analysis and reflection about intercultural experiences and acting on that reflection.

Principle 3: Intercultural citizenship experience takes place when people of different social groups and cultures engage in social and political activity.

Principle 4: Intercultural citizenship education involves: causing/facilitating intercultural citizenship experience, and analysis and reflection on it and on the possibility of further social and/or political activity; and creating learning/change in the individual. (pp. 186–187)

In trying to meet the conditions of the first principle, the challenge for the FL environment is the lack of opportunities for students to meet and interact with people from the target language community. Thus, online cultural and language exchange among peer counterparts becomes ideal. With the rise in popularity of computer-mediated language learning, students in FL classrooms can now interact with target language speakers from different social and cultural backgrounds via the World Wide Web (Bauer, de Benedette, Furstenberg, Levet, & Waryn, 2005; Belz, 2005; Levy, 2007). One of the online cultural learning modules currently available for FL instructors is the *Cultura* model, developed by Furstenberg, Levet, and Waryn (1997). The model aims at (a) building intercultural competence through comparative analysis, hypothesis-testing, and discovery tasks; and (b) engaging students in an inter-cultural community beyond classroom boundaries. The *Cultura* model aligns with Byram's (1997, 2008) four principles of intercultural citizenship education as summarized in Table 1.

Table 1. Byram's intercultural citizenship education and *Cultura* model

Byram's (2008, p. 186–187) principles for intercultural citizenship education	*Cultura* model practices
Principle 1: "Intercultural experience takes place when people from different social groups with different values, beliefs and behaviours (cultures) meet."	The online learning platform provides opportunities for students from two cultural groups to interact/meet virtually.
Principle 2: "Being 'intercultural' involves analysis and reflection about intercultural experience and acting on that reflection."	Students compare their reactions with their counterpart's reaction to particular concepts and artifacts. They analyze the underlying beliefs and values manifested in the language, and reflect on their own hidden norms.

Principle 3: "Intercultural citizenship experience takes place when people of different social groups and cultures engage in social and political activity."	A social online community emerges through the discussion forum. The tasks require cooperation and democratic interaction online.
Principle 4: "Intercultural citizenship education involves: causing/facilitating intercultural citizenship experience, and analysis and reflection on it and on the possibility of further social and/or political activity; and creating learning/change in the individual."	The learning tasks in *Cultura* are set up to deliberately unveil cultural views via analysis and reflection, which lead to the development of a more global perspective.

Cultura not only provides space and opportunities for students to interact with others from different socio-cultural contexts, but also promotes the expansion of learners' global perspectives via interactive, analytical, evaluative, and reflective tasks. The online learning platform allows students and their cultural counterparts to interact with different socio-cultural groups and socialize them into otherness (i.e., their counterparts' cultural values, beliefs, and behavioral norms; Principle 1). *Cultura*'s online comparative and analytical tasks require students to analyze underlying beliefs and values manifested in the language, and reflect on their own cultural practices (Principle 2). Further, social interactions in the online learning community require democratic principles of tolerance, openness, responsiveness, and cooperation (Principle 3). As explained in Byram's (2008) Principle 4, material content and tasks in *Cultura* are deliberately designed to reveal (potentially) conflicting views, which facilitate learners' attitudinal, cognitive, and behavioral change. Thus, *Cultura* encourages learners from different socio-cultural groups to become conscious of the explicit and hidden norms of the culture to which they belong as well as to their counterparts' culture, and presumably to anticipate conflicts that may arise as a result of socio-cultural preconceptions.

Ultimately, because the *Cultura* model closely aligns with Byram's principles for intercultural citizenry, and because the technology brings together two socio-cultural groups across national boundaries, the *Cultura* model became the basis for the current online cultural exchange project (hence forth Online Café project) between Moanalua High School (Moanalua) in the United States and Tezukayama Gakuin Izmigaoka High School (Tezukayama) in Japan.[1] Additionally, since two of the authors of this chapter previously collaborated on a technology-enhanced language instruction project, they had sustained interest in creating virtual cultural exchange opportunities for their students.

An initial project goal of the Online Café project was to test the viability and feasibility of the *Cultura* model in a high school environment. As a potential guide to future collaborative online cultural exchange projects in high schools, the following sections describe in detail the project implementation, issues encountered, and lessons learned from the project.

Program context

The Japanese Online Café project was implemented in five intact classes: Two were Japanese language courses at Moanalua and the other three were 2nd year English courses at Tezukayama.

---

[1] The second and third authors of this chapter are instructors from Moanalua and Tezukayama, and the first author engaged in the project as a collaborator. We all participated in the 2008 Summer Institute on Online Café hosted by the NFLRC to familiarize ourselves with the design and principles of the Cultura model.

School contexts

Moanalua High School is one of the largest public high schools in Hawai'i. Students come from a range of socio-economic and ethnic backgrounds, many from military families. Approximately 90 students were enrolled in Japanese language courses. There were four Japanese instructors teaching levels one to four.

Tezukayama High School has a six-year continual secondary education program and a three-year high school program. However, project participants were from the three-year high school program, which had two tracks: a Science/Math Track and an International Track. The total number of high school students in the three-year program was approximately 90 at the time of the project. All students were required to take English as part of their curriculum, though the number of required credits differed depending on the track to which students belonged.

Participants

Both Moanalua and Tezukayama students were in the 10th grade and their ages ranged between 16 and 17. The students' language proficiency level, their motivation, and their purposes for learning the target language in each program are described below.

Moanalua participants

Participating cohorts of students at Moanalua included 68 students from two intact Japanese Level Two courses. Some Moanalua students were heritage language learners of Japanese, who were placed into the Level Two course. Their Japanese proficiency levels varied from beginner to low-intermediate. At the beginning of the project, the Moanalua students had completed one year of language study at the high school level. Most students were able to read and write *hiragana* and *katakana* with exposure to about 50 high-frequency *kanji* throughout the project year. Their language functions were limited to (a) introducing themselves, family, friends, and school; (b) asking and answering questions to identify items in their surroundings; (c) inquiring about family members and getting basic information such as age, occupation, likes and dislikes, hobbies, and daily activities; and (d) expressing their preferences. Throughout the project year, they were exposed to more complex grammatical structures that allowed them to comment on their environment, give their opinions, and do basic commercial transactions.

At the time of the exchange, students participated in a community project that exposed them to local Japanese cultural events, such as celebrations, lectures, presentations and activities that perpetuate Japanese culture in Hawai'i. In the course, the students compared the values and activities of the local Japanese communities to their own.

Participating students had moderate motivation, mostly to earn passing grades to fulfill a requirement for a high school diploma; a few were very interested in Japanese comics and animation. Most students claimed to want to learn Japanese to communicate with family and friends. Thus, peer-moderated online interaction with Japanese high school students was considered to be intrinsically valuable for the students.

Tezukayama participants

Tezukayama students who participated in the project had at least four years of English language instruction since grade 7. A majority of students in the program were motivated to learn English to pass university entrance exams, since English is one of the major exam subjects.

The students in the current project were from three intact English classes. Class A students (*N*=44) belonged to the International Track, and were more interested in communicative English than the other two classes. Several female students in Class A had been taking English conversation courses at private language schools for a few years before they entered Tezukayama. Classes B and C (*N*s=30) belonged to the Science/Math Track. In general, these students regarded English as just a compulsory subject. Science/Math Track students were less motivated to learn English, and progressed less in English proficiency than those in the International Track. They spent more time studying science and math than English. Hence, they were less able to direct their attention to communicative English and related extra-curricular language learning activities.

Class A received 8 hours of English instruction every week, while Classes B and C received 6 hours; all three classes were taught by Japanese teachers of English. In addition, Class A had 2 hours of English instruction from an American teacher.

Project goals and student learning outcomes

The instructional goals of the Japanese Online Café project were to (a) increase students' cultural knowledge and language proficiency, (b) provide an opportunity for students to exchange perspectives, and (c) motivate students to further explore the target culture and language learning. In order to facilitate these goals, the instructors set culture and language learning outcomes to guide the Online Café content. Note that the two groups of students, Japanese students learning English and American students learning Japanese, were at different target language proficiency levels. The Tezukayama students had at least four years of English instruction, while the Moanalua students had completed one year of Japanese. Therefore, specific language learning outcomes for the project were kept abstract and more specific language targets were addressed in the intact courses. Table 2 describes the student learning outcomes aimed at in the project.

Table 2. Overall student learning outcomes of the Japanese online café project

type	learning outcomes
cultural learning outcomes	By the end of the project, students will be able to... • identify and describe cultural differences and similarities between host and target cultures • build willingness/openness to share and express cultural knowledge and practices of their participating community (e.g., school, home, neighborhood). • understand the target and their own cultures • understand and identify local adaptation of the target culture • explain popular culture, cultural values, and common behaviors
language learning outcomes	By the end of the project, students will be able to... • understand daily expressions of the target language in real-world settings • appropriately use daily expressions in their second language (L2) • communicate in L2 with partners in the target country • describe and explain their own culture in L2 and read about the target culture in L2

Design and implementation

Design of the modules

Tasks in the Online Café modules followed the *Cultura* model. In order to create an online learning community, students posted a short self-introduction and a photo prior to working in the main module. The main learning module consisted of three main parts: questionnaire tasks, analysis, and self-reflection. First, students responded to the questionnaire prompts and then critically analyzed the underlying cultural and social values behind each group's responses. Based on this analysis, students then generated their own cultural hypotheses and reflected on their a priori cultural assumptions. Comprising the questionnaire tasks originally were word association, sentence completion, and situation reaction. However, due to the complexity of the situation reaction task, it was ultimately excluded from the module.

Word association task

In the word association task (see Figure 1), the students provided two to three words that they thought were semantically related to a stimulus word. Students wrote responses in their first language (L1). The Tezukayama students mainly wrote in *hiragana* and were instructed not to use too many Chinese characters, so that the Moanalua students could read the entry. Responses from each school were compiled and sorted alphabetically in a Microsoft Excel sheet in order to count the number of occurrences of each word-token. Unique words were listed from high to low frequency along with the frequency count information, so that students could compare the word lists generated from each school side by side (see Table 3).

> Write 2 or 3 words that come to mind when you hear the word given. Moanalua High Students, please respond in English. Tezukayama students, please respond in your own section.

#1 family
example:
Please provide at least 2-3 English words that come to mind when you hear the word above.

Figure 1. Word association task prompt

Table 3. Response comparison for the word association task (target word: family)

Moanalua		Tezukayama	
frequency	associated words	frequency	associated words
35	love あい	4	あたたかい *warm
14	caring	2	優しい sweet
10	parents りょうしん	2	やさしい kind
10	mother	2	たのしい enjoy
10	father	2	うるさい nag

9	home	2	friendly
7	warmth	1	大切 *important
7	together-ness	1	頼れる *reliable
7	support	1	血がつながってる *blood relationship
7	happiness	1	社会の第一歩 *A first step to become a member of the society
6	loving	1	母父兄弟姉妹 *parents and siblings
...	(continued)	...	(continued)

note: Japanese translations with an asterisk (*) were provided by the author. Otherwise, students provided the translations.

Using the word lists, students were asked to discuss their findings in a small group online discussion forum (15 students per group). In order to guide their word list analysis, we provided the following questions:

Individual list analysis

- Which words are used most frequently?
- Which words, if any, did you find surprising to see on the list? Why?
- Can you categorize or group any words together?
- What do you think these words say about how people think or feel?
- What do these words represent in terms of cultural values or perspectives?

Comparative analysis

- How are the word lists similar?

  Are there words from both lists that are the same?

  Why do you think they are the same?

  Are they really the same? Do they mean the same thing?

  What do these similarities represent in terms of values or perspectives?

- How are the word lists different?

  Are there words that appear only on one list and not the other?

  Why do you think these words appear only on one side? What do they mean?

  What does it represent in terms of values or perspectives?

  What did you learn from the word lists about the cultures we are dealing with?

Sentence completion task

The sentence completion task (see Figure 2) prompted students to explain personal views of a concept or personal experiences (e.g., "The ideal family is..."; "I show respect to family by..."). Responses from each school were simply compiled and shown side-by-side as a list. Unfortunately, due to time constraints, there were only a few responses to the sentence completion task, which prevented any effective response comparisons.

> Please provide at least 2-3 English sentences following the following prompt. Please write one sentence per line.

#1 The ideal family is...

  example:
  Please provide at least 2-3 English sentences.

Figure 2. Sentence completion task

Topics for the units

We had a set of five units with different topics (see Table 4). These topics were chosen based on commonly discussed everyday themes that are easy for students to communicate about in their target language. The five themes were family/home, school, community, communication technology, and future plans. These themes were also chosen partly to match the existing curriculum. Table 4 displays the prompts for the word association and sentence completion tasks for each unit.

Table 4. Themes and topics

unit	theme	prompts
1	home/family	Word association: family members, roles, chores, family communication, respect Sentence completion: The ideal family is...; My family expects me...; Family chores are...; Communication in my family is...; I show respect to my family by...
2	school	Word association: environment, timetable, calendar, rules, extra/co-curricular activities, events Sentence completion: My school is...; Ideal school schedules should be...; School calendars should allow for...; School rules are...; The students who do extra curricular activities are...; Our school activities and events are...
3	community	Word association: precaution, events, location, dialect, curfew, activities Sentence completion: Violent crime in my community/neighborhood is...; Cultural celebrations and events in my community are...; Visiting students must go to/do...; Outsiders who eavesdrop on our conversations would...; Limits imposed on teens/children are...; Friends spend their time together doing...
4	technology	Word association: communication, maturity, cellular phones, restrictions, interactions, time Sentence completion: The best communication tools are...; Children carrying cellular phones are...; Cellular phones are used for...; Restrictions on the use of cellular phones are...; Cellular phone use has affected human interaction by...; Time is well spent by doing...
5	future plans	Word association: goals, expectations, marriage, part-time jobs, overseas jobs, income Sentence completion: My dream career would be...; My parents' career expectations of me are...; Marriage is...; Part-time jobs are for...; Working in a foreign country would be...; My first real paycheck will...

Languages of the exchange

Students used English and Japanese on both ends of the exchange. In order to facilitate L2 learning, the instructors encouraged students to post in the target language. As a result, students wrote in their target language to the extent they could, with some occasional code-switching into their L1, or wrote their online entries with a complete translation. For example, Excerpts 1 and 2 are self-introduction entries made by a Moanalua student and the Tezukauyama student's response.

Excerpt 1. Code switching between English and Japanese

> Oh!!You like かんこく
> I will go to かんこく by school trip
> My favorite korean singer is BOA♪
> かのじょはとてもうたがじょうずです
> And,today, a korean artist,
> とうほうしんき is very popular in japan
> Do you know them??
> Who is your favorite korean singer??
> Do you interested in Japan ??
> Please reply soon

Excerpt 2. Complete sentence translation

> I like sports too
> わたしもスポーツがだいすきです。
> Especially I like dancing and swimming
> とくにわたしはダンスとすいえいがすきです
> When I was 6 years old, I started to dancing
> わたしは6さいのときに、ダンスをはじめました
> And I really like PARTY too
> そして、わたしはパーティもだいすきです
> But most Japanese don't hold a party (((ΦXΦ)))
> しかしおおくのにほんじんはパーティーをしません
> So I joined a party only once.
> だかtらわたしはいちどしかパーティーにさんかしたことがありません
> How about you ???
> あなたはどうですか？？？
> How many times do you hold parties a month?
> 1かげつになんかいパーティーをひらきますか？
> I looking forward to seeing your reply.

Integration of modules into existing curriculum

The Online Café modules were integrated into the curriculum in different ways at the two high schools. The Moanalua students were given the activity as a regular assignment. They performed each task over a weekend, and reviewed Japanese students' responses in class. As part of the course requirement, the instructor asked students to integrate what they learned from the online module into their final course project. Frequency of entries were not a part of the grade, and emphasis was put on how students were able to take their online communication and learning as evidence and work it into their finals.

The Online Café at Tezukayama was implemented as a supplementary activity in an English composition course, which was strictly textbook-based. Setting up a personal profile was done in class, but students were individually responsible for accessing and participating online. Though the instructor regularly encouraged them to participate, students became less engaged in the online discussion forums as the semester progressed. Participation was graded by the number of postings in the Online Café, though the impact on the final course grade was minimal.

Lessons learned

From the one-semester pilot implementation of the Online Cafe, we would like to reflect on the issues we encountered so that similar programs can anticipate issues and better prepare appropriate online learning environments. In this informal project evaluation, we focused on unexpected factors that affected project implementation and the appropriateness of the tasks and materials. The evaluative judgments and suggestions are based on teacher reflections, online student performance, and student feedback.

Factors affecting implementation

Various factors affected the planned implementation of the project, but among them, the largest factors were infrastructure and student motivation.

Infrastructure

Unanticipated technological issues at the beginning of the project resulted in spending the first month only on self-introduction. Technological policies and requirements need to be dealt with prior to launching the project, otherwise resolving such issues during the semester can take away students' and instructors' time to focus on the online learning and instruction.

Additionally, the difference in school calendars between the two counterparts was a challenge in setting up an Online Café program. We initially intended to implement five units of Online Café modules from August to February; however, intense exchange was only possible between August and December. In Japanese high schools, the third semester (January to March) is generally intensive for teachers and students, as the semester is short and schools need to administer entrance exams. Therefore, we were only able to implement two out of five units. Programs need to develop the necessary infrastructure beforehand so that the scope and implementation of the project can be adapted to the reality of the program constraints (e.g., technology, school calendar).

When it came to engaging in the tasks, students had difficulty tracing the interactions in the lengthy discussion forums and needed to track multiple postings by others. These difficulties were partly due to the technological limitations of the forum and also due to the unmanageable group size in the forum. Comments to a question and responses for a particular entry were all stacked up in chronological order under one thread, rather than responses to a particular comment being displayed as a sub-level. Although we foresaw these issues from the beginning and limited the number of students participating in each forum, an average of 20 students contributing to one forum was overwhelming. One of the discussion forums had over 250 threads, and locating who responded to which message became time consuming for the students, thus hindering interaction.

Student motivation

Key to maintaining the pace of learning in an Online Café is student engagement and ongoing dialogue in the online discussion. In the self-introduction unit, both Tezukayama and Moanalua students were highly engaged in online discussions, as indicated by the 285 postings. They were willing to share their cultural and personal experiences with each other to form a sense of community. However, when it came to more structured discussions (i.e., questionnaire and analysis tasks), students were less interactive in the forum. Since the Tezukayama students posted less, the Moanalua students were not able to keep the dialogue going. Moreover, the increase of their workload in other courses and the fall break for the Moanalua students also contributed to the dwindling interest in the communication. From the end-of-term student feedback, some students commented that their main interest was to socialize, make friends, and find common interests, rather than work on structured questionnaire exercises that required critical perspectives.

Tasks and materials

Task appropriateness

We determined from this experience that the text-based tasks need to be level-appropriate. Since *Cultura* originated at the Massachusetts Institute of Technology, the task-appropriateness was targeted at the university level. We have found that high school students had a hard time observing cross-cultural differences and uncovering hidden values and views when they compared and analyzed the posted messages. Many posted "not different" when asked to post an analytic summary for word association and sentence completion tasks. During in-class discussions at Moanalua, students had a great difficulty recognizing the reasons for the differences or the significance of the similarities. They were ready to agree with suggestions from the instructor about the cultural implications and impact, but did not come to any conclusions on their own. In grade 10, students may not have the critical lens to fully attend to the nuances of the responses and conduct a textual analysis. They found only surface-level similarities and differences and were not able to make deeper analyses of the semantic networks. Text-based comparative analysis tasks require much more scaffolded instruction in class with examples, practice, and guidance.

Language required for the tasks

Because high school students are not so familiar with academic prose in the target language (i.e., Cognitive Academic Language Proficiency; Cummins, 1984), comprehending extensive prose of cultural comparison, evaluation, and hypothesis-testing in the target language will require extensive scaffolded instruction in class. For example, students from Moanalua posted extensively in English with the instructor as the imagined audience (instead of the Tezukayama students) for the video clips of school life that the Tezukayama instructor had posted in the discussion forum. Some of the postings were over 450 words in English, written in an essay style. The English entries were too difficult for the Tezukayama students to understand, and for some of the longer postings, the Japanese instructor had to provide translations. Therefore, we recommend that for beginning and low-intermediate language learners, instructors provide language support when requiring writing or reading extensive cultural analysis and reflection in the target language.

Multimedia materials

Compared to the text-based tasks, the audio-visual materials seemed to appeal more to the high school students. In order to gain students' interest, we included video clips in the second unit. The video clips posted by the Japanese instructor were scenes from school life and the community, such as footage of students preparing for the school festival and a local cultural festival. These videos were received favorably and triggered extensive comments posted by the Moanalua students. In contrast to the textual analysis in the word association and sentence completion tasks, when audio-visual material was posted, students were able to identify similarities and differences much more easily. Watching the videos, most students were able to identify behavioral characteristics, and take the first steps toward reflecting on their own behaviors in school and in the local community (see Excerpts 3 and 4).

Excerpt 3

> I learned that the students are all close to the teacher and to each other. They do many activities together and they were willing to stay later after school to watch the firework together… I saw that all Japanese people are very organized. They like to have people always matching, like in school the students have to wear uniforms and the people in the festival were all wearing the same uniform.

Excerpt 4

> The first thing I noticed is that everyone was in a uniform. I also noticed that in the preperation for the school fesival, many students were participatiing. At our school we usually can only find a few people who will help out. In the video about the Kishiwada festival there are are also lots of people participating. The communities seem to be very close to each other with their culture and beliefs. At home I barely even talk to my neighbors.

Conclusion

Despite the above-mentioned issues, from the students' perspective, the Moanalua students commented that the Online Café was one of the activities they enjoyed the most in the course. For those students who continued to interact online until the end of the project, the connections and friendships they formed online were the highlight of the project. Students' interest in learning Japanese piqued from their interaction with the Tezukayama students that an instructor alone could not have sparked.

For the Tezukayama students, cultural learning happened immediately when they were surprised to see a variety of ethnic backgrounds reflected in Moanalua students' names. Students were also able to see themselves as members of a language learning community; as a result of their excitement at seeing each other's use of second language, mixed with their first language in the postings (some commented "very cool" and "cute").

Looking forward, we can conclude that with some modifications to the tasks, material types, and commitment from both participating schools, this Online Café project could be expanded to supplement any program, even at the high school level. The curriculum could be adjusted to include the project as an integral part of the course grade and to ensure more in-class instructional time for cultural learning.

References

Bauer, B., de Benedette, L., Furstenberg, G., Levet, S., & Waryn, S. (2005). Computer-mediated intercultural foreign language education: The *Cultura* Project. In J. A. Belz & S. L. Thorne (Eds.), *Internet-mediated intercultural foreign language education* (pp. 31–62). Boston, MA: Heinle & Heinle.

Belz, J. (2005). Intercultural questioning, discovery and tension in Internet-mediated language learning partnerships. *Language and Intercultural Communication, 5*(1), 3–39.

Byram, M. (1997). *Teaching and assessing intercultural communicative competence.* Clevedon, England: Multilingual Matters.

Byram, M. (2008). *From foreign language education to education for intercultural citizenship: Essays and reflection.* Clevedon, England: Multilingual Matters.

Cummins, J. (1984). *Bilingual education and special education: Issues in assessment and pedagogy.* San Diego, CA: College Hill.

Furstenberg, G., Levet, S., Waryn, S. (1997). *The* Cultura *exchanges site.* Retrieved from http://cultura.mit.edu

Kramsch, C. (1998). The privilege of the intercultural speaker. In M. Byram & M. Fleming (Eds.), *Language learning in intercultural perspective: Approaches through drama and ethnography* (pp. 16–31). New York, NY: Cambridge University Press.

Levy, M. (2007). Culture, culture learning and new technologies: Towards a pedagogical framework. *Language Learning & Technology, 11*(2), 104–127. Retrieved from http://llt.msu.edu/vol11num2/levy/

Appendix A: Parameters for word association task

Goals

1. Students will understand how words reflect cultural values and perspectives.
2. Students will increase vocabulary knowledge.
3. Students will compare and analyze responses from Japan and Hawai'i.

目標

1. 言葉が文化的価値観やみ方を反映することを理解する。
2. 語彙に関する知識を増す
3. 日本とハワイのレスポンスを比較・分析する。

Comparison

1. Complete the word association survey individually.
2. Do not discuss words prior to doing the survey.
3. Input your first impressions and thoughts, don't over analyze as there are no correct answers.
4. Use appropriate spelling and forms.
5. Analyze the results of the completed word association lists created by students in Hawai'i.

a. What words are repeated?
b. What words appear only once?
c. What concepts or values do these words represent?

6. Analyze the results of the completed word association lists created by students in Japan.
   a. Define the words; make a glossary or word list.
   b. What words are repeated?
   c. What words appear only once?
   d. What concepts or values do these words represent?

7. Compare the lists.

8. What words appear on both lists?

9. What words only appear on one side?

10. What does this say about the perspectives and values of the cultures?

パラメータ

1. 連想言葉を一人一人行う。

2. 実施の前に指定された言葉について話し合わないこと。

3. 最初に頭に浮かんだことを書く。正解というものはないので、深く分析せずに書き込むこと。

4. スペルや書き方に注意。

5. 日本の生徒が書き込んだ連想言葉のリストを分析すること。
   a. 同じ言葉が書き込まれていないか、何回書き込まれているか。
   b. 一回しか書き込まれていない言葉は何か。
   c. 言葉の背後にある価値観や考え方は何か。

6. 日本の生徒が書き込んだ連想言葉のリストを分析すること
   a. 言葉の定義をし、用語解説集を作成すること
   b. 同じ言葉が書き込まれていないか、何回書き込まれているか。
   c. 一回しか書き込まれていない言葉は何か。
   d. 言葉の背後にある価値観や考え方は何か。

7. リストの比較をする

8. 日米両方のリストにあがっている言葉は何か。

9. 日米の一方にしかあがっていない言葉は何か。

10. 以上のことから、日米の文化の価値観や考え方の相違点・類似点が現れていないか。

Discussion entry on the results

Instructions

1. Do your word list in English.

2. Use accurate resources in finding the definitions of the Japanese words.

3. Analysis may be done in English, although you should do as much as you can in Japanese.

4. Use proper grammar, forms and vocabulary as you are modeling language for the Japanese students.

指示 (以下の指示に従って作業を進めてください)
1. あなたが上げた言葉は英語（日本語）のリストに上がっているか。
2. 日本語（英語）の定義を正確に調べられる辞書類を見つけること
3. 分析は日本語でもかまわないが、できるだけ、英語で書くようにすること。
4. 日本語を書く場合は、アメリカの生徒の手本となるように、正しい日本語を書くこと。

Appendix B: Parameters for the sentence completion task

Goals

1. Students will understand how the cultural values and perspectives of the Japanese and Hawai'i students are reflected in the language.
2. Students will increase vocabulary knowledge and comprehension.
3. Students will use the responses to initiate and participate in in-depth discussions to compare and analyze perspectives from Japan and Hawai'i.

目標

1. 日米の生徒が作成した文章の中に日米の価値観や視点の違いや類似点がどのように反映されているか理解する。
2. 語彙を増やし語彙の理解を進める
3. 日米双方の生徒のレスポンスが日米の視点の比較・分析をうながし、より深い議論に至る。

Parameters

1. Complete the sentence completion survey individually.
2. Do not discuss phrases prior to doing the survey.
3. Input your first impressions and thoughts, don't over analyze as there are no correct answers.
4. Use appropriate spelling and forms.
5. Use the data provided by the results to discuss the key points in the forum.
6. Analyze the importance of the concepts introduced.
7. Discuss the impact of the word choices and meanings.
8. Quote or paraphrase to support your perspectives.

パラメータ

1. 文章作成調査を生徒一人一人で行う
2. 実施の前に指定された言葉について話し合わないこと。
3. 最初に頭に浮かんだことを書く。正解というものはないので、深く分析せずに書き込むこと。
4. スペルや書き方に注意。
5. 結果から生まれたデータをフォーラムの中心テーマを議論するために使うこと。
6. 中心テーマを議論する中で生まれてきた概念の重要度を分析すること。

7. 言葉の選択や言葉の意味がもつインパクトについて論じること。
8. 自分の視点を支持する言葉を引用したり、パラフレーズして書くこと。

Instructions

1. Complete the sentences in proper English only.
2. Use accurate resources in finding the definitions of the Japanese words and sentences.
3. Analysis during the forums may be done in English, although you should do as much as you can in Japanese.
4. Use proper grammar, forms and vocabulary as you are modeling language for the Japanese students.

指示 (以下の指示に従って作業を進めてください)

1. 正しい日本語で文章を作成してください (英語訳をつけること)。
2. 日本語 (英語) の定義を正確に調べられる辞書類を見つけること
3. 分析は日本語でもかまわないが、できるだけ、英語で書くようにすること。
4. 日本語を書く場合は、アメリカの生徒の手本となるように、正しい日本語を書くこと。

Appendix C: Parameters for the forum

Goals

1. Gain insights into Japanese, Hawaiian, American, and students' own cultures identifying, describing, and analyzing data provided by the students in Japan and Hawai'i.
2. Improve language competency in comprehension and production of Japanese.
3. Encourage cohesion and cooperation among students in multiple groups.

目標

1. 日米の生徒が提供するデータの特徴を見極め、表現し、分析する中で日米の文化に対する理解を深める。
2. 英語の運用能力を高めること。
3. 複数グループ間での活動をまとまって協力体制がとれるように努力すること。

Parameters

1. Stay on topic.
2. Answers, responses, observations within each thread should be on task and related to the topic at hand.
3. Social inquiries beyond the topic should be done in the appropriate threads.
4. Answer truthfully and with integrity.
5. Use appropriate word choice (vocabulary), spelling, forms, grammar and proper language.
6. Stay away from slang (unless it is explained).

7. No expletives, profanity, improper topics.
8. ESL students should do their best to improve English language competency.
9. Do not use texting language or informal language in the forum.
10. Write/speak as much as you can in Japanese and add in the rest of your thoughts and ideas in English.

パラメータ

1. トピックから外れないこと
2. それぞれのスレッドの中に書き込む返事、レスポンス、意見は課題に添ったもので課題に関連していること。
3. トピックから外れた質問をする場合は、該当するスレッドの中で行うこと。
4. まじめに誠実に返事・回答を書くこと。
5. 適切な語彙・言葉使いをし、スペル、形式、文法に気をつけて書くこと。
6. スラングは使わないこと（必要な場合は注釈をつけること）。
7. ひわいな言葉、口汚い言葉、不適切なトピックは避けること。
8. 英語力を伸ばすべく、努力すること。
9. フォーラムの中では、携帯電話などで使用する略語や絵文字は避けること。
10. できるだけ英語で話し書くとともに、自分の考えを明確にあらわすために日本語で付け加えること。。

Instructions

1. Read the questions carefully.
2. Read the other responses before adding your own thoughts.
3. Respond to the questions, stay on task.
4. Quote, refer, paraphrase others as you continue to add to the discussion.
5. Agree or disagree with other posts.
6. Comment on the entries of others to show your understanding of the flow of the conversation.
7. Ask follow up questions to clarify meaning and understand the underlying connotations of the discussion.
8. Summarize the thread and describe the key elements/understandings.

指示（以下の指示に従って作業を進めてください）

1. 質問を注意して読むこと。
2. 自分の考えを書き込む前に他の人々のレスポンスを読むようにすること。
3. 質問に答えるように、また、その際には、テーマから外れないこと
4. ディスカッションに書き込む際には他の人の書き込みに言及や引用をしたり、パラフレーズすること。（自分の言いたいことだけ書き込むことのないよう、他の人の書き込みを参照することを心がけること）
5. 他の人の書き込みに対して賛成・反対のレスポンスを返すこと。

6. 議論の流れを理解しながら他人の書き込みにコメントを返すこと。
7. 議論の背後に流れている考え方を把握するため追加質問をすること。
8. スレッドを要約しキーとなる要素や視点を書くこと。

About the Contributors

Dorothy M. Chun is a professor of Applied Linguistics and Education at the University of California, Santa Barbara. Her research areas include L2 phonology and intonation, L2 reading and vocabulary acquisition, computer-assisted language learning (CALL), and telecollaboration for intercultural learning. She has conducted studies on cognitive process in learning with multimedia and has authored courseware for language and culture acquisition. Since 2000, she has been the editor-in-chief of the online journal *Language Learning and Technology*. The founding director of the PhD Emphasis in Applied Linguistics at UCSB, she has also served on the national advisory boards of the National Foreign Language Resource Center at the University of Hawai'i and the Center for Language Education and Research at Michigan State University.

Nenita Pambid Domingo obtained her PhD in Philippine Studies from the University of the Philippines. She teaches all levels of Filipino language, literature, and culture at the University of California, Los Angeles. She wrote *Anting-Anting o kung bakit nagtatago sa loob ng bato si Bathala (Amulet or Why the Tagalog God Bathala is hiding inside the stone*; University of the Philippines Press, 2000) and co-authored the book and the workbook *Tara, Mag-Tagalog Tayo! (Come On, Let's Speak Tagalog!*; TUTTLE Publishing, 2012). She believes that to learn a language is "to use it or lose it."

Kathryn English is a maître de conférences at the Université de Paris II (Panthéon Assas) and the Ecole Polytechnique. She holds a PhD in Sciences du Langage and has designed, co-authored, and participated in cross-cultural, computer-mediated language teaching projects based in the USA, France, Finland, and Taiwan. She has worked as a conference interpreter for the European Union, television and radio, and the French National Assembly. She also coaches the university debating teams.

Gilberte Furstenberg, Senior Lecturer Emerita, Massachusetts Institute of Technology, was born and educated in France where she received her Agrégation. After teaching English at the University of Paris-Nanterre, she moved to the United States where she became a correspondent for the French news magazine *L'Express*. Her next career move brought her to the Foreign Languages and Literatures Department at Massachusetts Institute of Technology where she taught French language and culture for 30 years and developed innovative multimedia and web-based materials for fostering students' active, experiential linguistic and cultural learning.

She is the principal author of *A la Rencontre de Philippe*, a pioneering interactive fiction, and *Dans un quartier de Paris*, an interactive multimedia documentary, which have both won national and international awards. In 1977, she created *Cultura* with Shoggy Waryn and Sabine Levet, thanks to funding from the National Endowment for the Humanities.

Song Jiang is an assistant professor in the Department of East Asian Languages and Literatures at the University of Hawai'i at Mānoa. His primary areas of interest lie in Chinese theoretical and historical linguistics, cognitive linguistics, second language acquisition, language teaching pedagogy, instructional materials development, and integration of technology into language teaching. He has been involved in a number of online course development and research projects. He is currently on the editorial board of the *Journal of Technology and Chinese Language Teaching* and serves as the review editor.

Sabine Levet is a senior lecturer in French in the Department of Foreign Languages and Literatures at MIT. She is one of the original authors of *Cultura*. She has written articles and chapters in books about the development of tools for cross-cultural understanding and has given talks and workshops on intercultural communication, the teaching of culture, and the integration of technology into the foreign language curriculum. She collaborated with Gilberte Furstenberg on *A la Rencontre de Philippe*, published by CLE International, and *Dans un quartier de Paris*, published by Yale University Press, and is the author of the *Tramway et Vélib'* Project.

Meei-Ling Liaw is a professor in the Department of English at National Taichung University of Education. Her research focuses on using computer technology to facilitate EFL teaching and learning, intercultural learning, and teacher education. Her publications have appeared in professional journals including *System, Foreign Language Annals, Computer-Assisted Language Learning, ReCALL,* and *Language Learning and Technology*. She has served on the editorial board of *Language Learning and Technology* since 2008.

Stephen L. Tschudi, Specialist in Technology for Language Education at the National Foreign Language Resource Center, has taught Chinese language at the University of Hawai'i for the past 25 years. He is past recipient of an Excellence in Teaching Award from the Hawai'i Association of Language Teachers and past board member of the Chinese Language Teachers Association. He has designed and delivered teacher training courses and workshops focusing on effective strategies for teaching languages on interactive television and on various aspects of online teaching and learning, and has designed numerous online courses in Chinese language.

Haidan Wang is an assistant professor in the Department of East Asian Languages and Literatures at the University of Hawai'i at Mānoa (UHM). She played a leading role in the establishment and expansion of the business Chinese program at UHM, and has been serving as the program coordinator since 2007. Her research interests include cognitive linguistics, Chinese language pedagogy, program development and assessment, curriculum design, and teaching Chinese for specific purposes. She has been involved in projects including integrating pragmatics into Chinese teaching, developing hybrid language courses, designing online instructional materials, and constructing a blended learning community for language and cultural acquisition.

Yukiko Watanabe received her PhD in Second Language Studies from the University of Hawai'i at Mānoa in 2013 and is currently a senior consultant (assessment and evaluation specialist) in the Center for Teaching and Learning at the University of California, Berkeley. She is a program evaluator, educational researcher, and teacher educator with background in program evaluation and assessment, classroom research, curriculum and instructional design, language teaching, and applied linguistics.

Cindy S. Wong, high school teacher and World Language Learning Center coordinator at Moanalua High School, has taught Japanese for over 25 years. She is a past recipient of the Hawai'i Association of Language Teacher's (HALT) Teacher of the Year award and has served on the Hawai'i Association of Teachers of Japanese and HALT boards. She also a regular presenter at the HALT and Hawai'i Association of Teachers of Japanese symposiums and conferences, and has presented at the Southwest Conference on Language Teaching and at American Council on the Teaching of Foreign Languages. She incorporates a wide range of technology to enhance teaching strategies and presentation formats.

National Foreign Language Resource Center
University of Hawai'i at Mānoa

ordering information at nflrc.hawaii.edu

Pragmatics & Interaction
Gabriele Kasper, series editor

Pragmatics & Interaction ("P&I"), a refereed series sponsored by the University of Hawai'i National Foreign Language Resource Center, publishes research on topics in pragmatics and discourse as social interaction from a wide variety of theoretical and methodological perspectives. P&I welcomes particularly studies on languages spoken in the Asia-Pacific region.

PRAGMATICS OF VIETNAMESE AS NATIVE AND TARGET LANGUAGE
CARSTEN ROEVER & HANH THI NGUYEN (EDITORS), 2013

The volume offers a wealth of new information about the forms of several speech acts and their social distribution in Vietnamese as L1 and L2, complemented by a chapter on address forms and listener responses. As the first of its kind, the book makes a valuable contribution to the research literature on pragmatics, sociolinguistics, and language and social interaction in an under-researched and less commonly taught Asian language.

282pp., ISBN 978–0–9835816–2–8 $30.

L2 LEARNING AS SOCIAL PRACTICE: CONVERSATION-ANALYTIC PERSPECTIVES
GABRIELE PALLOTTI & JOHANNES WAGNER (EDITORS), 2011

This volume collects empirical studies applying Conversation Analysis to situations where second, third, and other additional languages are used. A number of different aspects are considered, including how linguistic systems develop over time through social interaction, how participants 'do' language learning and teaching in classroom and everyday settings, how they select languages and manage identities in multilingual contexts, and how the linguistic-interactional divide can be bridged with studies combining Conversation Analysis and Functional Linguistics. This variety of issues and approaches clearly shows the fruitfulness of a socio-interactional perspective on second language learning.

380pp., ISBN 978–0–9800459–7–0 $30.

TALK-IN-INTERACTION: MULTILINGUAL PERSPECTIVES
HANH THI NGUYEN & GABRIELE KASPER (EDITORS), 2009

This volume offers original studies of interaction in a range of languages and language varieties, including Chinese, English, Japanese, Korean, Spanish, Swahili, Thai, and Vietnamese; monolingual and bilingual interactions; and activities designed for second or foreign language learning. Conducted from the perspectives of conversation analysis and membership categorization analysis, the chapters examine ordinary conversation and institutional activities in face-to-face, telephone, and computer-mediated environments.

420pp., ISBN 978–09800459–1–8 $30.

Pragmatics & Language Learning
Gabriele Kasper, series editor

Pragmatics & Language Learning ("PLL"), a refereed series sponsored by the National Foreign Language Resource Center, publishes selected papers from the International Pragmatics & Language Learning conference under the editorship of the conference hosts and the series editor. Check the NFLRC website for upcoming PLL conferences and PLL volumes.

PRAGMATICS AND LANGUAGE LEARNING VOLUME 13
TIM GREER, DONNA TATSUKI, & CARSTEN ROEVER (EDITORS), 2013

Pragmatics & Language Learning Volume 13 examines the organization of second language and multilingual speakers' talk and pragmatic knowledge across a range of naturalistic and experimental activities. Based on data collected among ESL and EFL learners from a variety of backgrounds, the contributions explore the nexus of pragmatic knowledge, interaction, and L2 learning outside and inside of educational settings.

292pp., ISBN 978–0–9835816–4–2 $30.

PRAGMATICS AND LANGUAGE LEARNING VOLUME 12
GABRIELE KASPER, HANH THI NGUYEN, DINA R. YOSHIMI, & JIM K. YOSHIOKA (EDITORS), 2010

This volume examines the organization of second language and multilingual speakers' talk and pragmatic knowledge across a range of naturalistic and experimental activities. Based on data collected on Danish, English, Hawai'i Creole, Indonesian, and Japanese as target languages, the contributions explore the nexus of pragmatic knowledge, interaction, and L2 learning outside and inside of educational settings.

364pp., ISBN 978–09800459–6–3 $30.

PRAGMATICS AND LANGUAGE LEARNING VOLUME 11
KATHLEEN BARDOVI-HARLIG, CÉSAR FÉLIX-BRASDEFER, & ALWIYA S. OMAR (EDITORS), 2006

This volume features cutting-edge theoretical and empirical research on pragmatics and language learning among a wide variety of learners in diverse learning contexts from a variety of language backgrounds and target languages (English, German, Japanese, Kiswahili, Persian, and Spanish). This collection of papers from researchers around the world includes critical appraisals on the role of formulas in interlanguage pragmatics, and speech-act research from a conversation analytic perspective. Empirical studies examine learner data using innovative methods of analysis and investigate issues in pragmatic development and the instruction of pragmatics.

430pp., ISBN 978–0–8248–3137–0 $30.

NFLRC Monographs

Monographs of the National Foreign Language Resource Center present the findings of recent work in applied linguistics that is of relevance to language teaching and learning (with a focus on the less commonly taught languages of Asia and the Pacific) and are of particular interest to foreign language educators, applied linguists, and researchers. Prior to 2006, these monographs were published as "SLTCC Technical Reports."

NOTICING AND SECOND LANGUAGE ACQUISITION: STUDIES IN HONOR OF RICHARD SCHMIDT
Joara Martin Bergsleithner, Sylvia Nagem Frota, & Jim Kei Yoshioka (Editors), 2013

This volume celebrates the life and groundbreaking work of Richard Schmidt, the developer of the influential Noticing Hypothesis in the field of second language acquisition. The 19 chapters encompass a compelling collection of cuttingedge research studies exploring such constructs as noticing, attention, and awareness from multiple perspectives, which expand, fine tune, sometimes support, and sometimes challenge Schmidt's seminal ideas and take research on noticing in exciting new directions.

374pp., ISBN 978–0–9835816–6–6 $25.

NEW PERSPECTIVES ON JAPANESE LANGUAGE LEARNING, LINGUISTICS, AND CULTURE
Kimi Kondo-Brown, Yoshiko Saito-Abbott, Shingo Satsutani, Michio Tsutsui, & Ann Wehmeyer (Editors), 2013

This volume is a collection of selected refereed papers presented at the Association of Teachers of Japanese Annual Spring Conference held at the University of Hawai'i at Mānoa in March of 2011. It not only covers several important topics on teaching and learning spoken and written Japanese and culture in and beyond classroom settings but also includes research investigating certain linguistics items from new perspectives.

208pp., ISBN 978–0–9835816–3–5 $25.

DEVELOPING, USING, AND ANALYZING RUBRICS IN LANGUAGE ASSESSMENT WITH CASE STUDIES IN ASIAN AND PACIFIC LANGUAGES
James Dean Brown (Editor), 2012

Rubrics are essential tools for all language teachers in this age of communicative and task-based teaching and assessment—tools that allow us to efficiently communicate to our students what we are looking for in the productive language abilities of speaking and writing and then effectively assess those abilities when the time comes for grading students, giving them feedback, placing them into new courses, and so forth. This book provides a wide array of ideas, suggestions, and examples (mostly from Māori, Hawaiian, and Japanese language assessment projects) to help language educators effectively develop, use, revise, analyze, and report on rubric-based assessments.

212pp., ISBN 978–0–9835816–1–1 $25.

RESEARCH AMONG LEARNERS OF CHINESE AS A FOREIGN LANGUAGE
Michael E. Everson & Helen H. Shen (Editors), 2010

Cutting-edge in its approach and international in its authorship, this fourth monograph in a series sponsored by the Chinese Language Teachers Association features eight research studies that explore a variety of themes, topics, and perspectives important to a variety of stakeholders in the Chinese language learning community. Employing a wide range of research methodologies, the volume provides data from actual Chinese language learners and will be of value to both theoreticians and practitioners alike. *[in English & Chinese]*

180pp., ISBN 978-0-9800459-4-9 $20.

MANCHU: A TEXTBOOK FOR READING DOCUMENTS (SECOND EDITION)
Gertraude Roth Li, 2010

This book offers students a tool to gain a basic grounding in the Manchu language. The reading selections provided in this volume represent various types of documents, ranging from examples of the very earliest Manchu writing (17th century) to samples of contemporary Sibe (Xibo), a language that may be considered a modern version of Manchu. Since Manchu courses are only rarely taught at universities anywhere, this second edition includes audio recordings to assist students with the pronunciation of the texts.

418pp., ISBN 978-0-9800459-5-6 $36.

TOWARD USEFUL PROGRAM EVALUATION IN COLLEGE FOREIGN LANGUAGE EDUCATION
John M. Norris, John McE. Davis, Castle Sinicrope, & Yukiko Watanabe (Editors), 2009

This volume reports on innovative, useful evaluation work conducted within U.S. college foreign language programs. An introductory chapter scopes out the territory, reporting key findings from research into the concerns, impetuses, and uses for evaluation that FL educators identify. Seven chapters then highlight examples of evaluations conducted in diverse language programs and institutional contexts. Each case is reported by program-internal educators, who walk readers through critical steps, from identifying evaluation uses, users, and questions, to designing methods, interpreting findings, and taking actions. A concluding chapter reflects on the emerging roles for FL program evaluation and articulates an agenda for integrating evaluation into language education practice.

240pp., ISBN 978-0-9800459-3-2 $30.

SECOND LANGUAGE TEACHING AND LEARNING IN THE NET GENERATION
Raquel Oxford & Jeffrey Oxford (Editors), 2009

Today's young people—the Net Generation—have grown up with technology all around them. However, teachers cannot assume that students' familiarity with technology in general transfers successfully to pedagogical settings. This volume examines various technologies and offers concrete advice on how each can be successfully implemented in the second language curriculum.

240pp., ISBN 978-0-9800459-2-5 $30.

CASE STUDIES IN FOREIGN LANGUAGE PLACEMENT: PRACTICES AND POSSIBILITIES
Thom Hudson & Martyn Clark (Editors), 2008

Although most language programs make placement decisions on the basis of placement tests, there is surprisingly little published about different contexts and systems of placement testing. The present volume contains case studies of placement programs in foreign language programs at the tertiary level across the United States. The different programs span the spectrum from large programs servicing hundreds of students annually to small language programs with very few students. The contributions to this volume address such issues as how the size of the program, presence or absence of heritage learners, and population changes affect language placement decisions.

201pp., ISBN 0–9800459–0–8 $20.

CHINESE AS A HERITAGE LANGUAGE: FOSTERING ROOTED WORLD CITIZENRY
AGNES WEIYUN HE & YUN XIAO (EDITORS), 2008

Thirty-two scholars examine the sociocultural, cognitive-linguistic, and educational-institutional trajectories along which Chinese as a Heritage Language may be acquired, maintained, and developed. They draw upon developmental psychology, functional linguistics, linguistic and cultural anthropology, discourse analysis, orthography analysis, reading research, second language acquisition, and bilingualism. This volume aims to lay a foundation for theories, models, and master scripts to be discussed, debated, and developed, and to stimulate research and enhance teaching both within and beyond Chinese language education.

280pp., ISBN 978–0–8248–3286–5 $20.

PERSPECTIVES ON TEACHING CONNECTED SPEECH TO SECOND LANGUAGE SPEAKERS
JAMES DEAN BROWN & KIMI KONDO-BROWN (EDITORS), 2006

This book is a collection of fourteen articles on connected speech of interest to teachers, researchers, and materials developers in both ESL/EFL (ten chapters focus on connected speech in English) and Japanese (four chapters focus on Japanese connected speech). The fourteen chapters are divided up into five sections:

- What do we know so far about teaching connected speech?
- Does connected speech instruction work?
- How should connected speech be taught in English?
- How should connected speech be taught in Japanese?
- How should connected speech be tested?

290pp., ISBN 978–0–8248–3136–3 $20.

CORPUS LINGUISTICS FOR KOREAN LANGUAGE LEARNING AND TEACHING
ROBERT BLEY-VROMAN & HYUNSOOK KO (EDITORS), 2006

Dramatic advances in personal-computer technology have given language teachers access to vast quantities of machine-readable text, which can be analyzed with a view toward improving the basis of language instruction. Corpus linguistics provides analytic techniques and practical tools for studying language in use. This volume provides both an introductory framework for the use of corpus linguistics for language teaching and examples of its application for Korean teaching and learning. The collected papers cover topics in Korean syntax, lexicon, and discourse, and second language acquisition research, always with a focus on application in the classroom. An overview of Korean corpus linguistics tools and available Korean corpora are also included.

265pp., ISBN 0–8248–3062–8 $25.

NEW TECHNOLOGIES AND LANGUAGE LEARNING: CASES IN THE LESS COMMONLY TAUGHT LANGUAGES
CAROL ANNE SPREEN (EDITOR), 2002

In recent years, the National Security Education Program (NSEP) has supported an increasing number of programs for teaching languages using different technological media. This compilation of case study initiatives funded through the NSEP Institutional Grants Program presents a range of technology-based options for language programming that will help universities make more informed decisions about teaching less commonly taught languages. The eight chapters describe how different types of technologies are used to support language programs (i.e., web, ITV, and audio- or video-based materials), discuss identifiable trends in e-language learning, and explore how technology addresses issues of equity, diversity, and opportunity. This book offers many lessons learned and decisions made as technology changes and learning needs become more complex.

188pp., ISBN 0–8248–2634–5 $25.

AN INVESTIGATION OF SECOND LANGUAGE TASK-BASED PERFORMANCE ASSESSMENTS
James Dean Brown, Thom Hudson, John M. Norris, & William Bonk, 2002

This volume describes the creation of performance assessment instruments and their validation (based on work started in a previous monograph). It begins by explaining the test and rating scale development processes and the administration of the resulting three seven-task tests to 90 university-level EFL and ESL students. The results are examined in terms of (a) the effects of test revision; (b) comparisons among the task-dependent, task-independent, and self-rating scales; and (c) reliability and validity issues.

240pp., ISBN 0–8248–2633–7 $25.

MOTIVATION AND SECOND LANGUAGE ACQUISITION
Zoltán Dörnyei & Richard Schmidt (Editors), 2001

This volume—the second in this series concerned with motivation and foreign language learning—includes papers presented in a state-of-the-art colloquium on L2 motivation at the American Association for Applied Linguistics (Vancouver, 2000) and a number of specially commissioned studies. The 20 chapters, written by some of the best known researchers in the field, cover a wide range of theoretical and research methodological issues, and also offer empirical results (both qualitative and quantitative) concerning the learning of many different languages (Arabic, Chinese, English, Filipino, French, German, Hindi, Italian, Japanese, Russian, and Spanish) in a broad range of learning contexts (Bahrain, Brazil, Canada, Egypt, Finland, Hungary, Ireland, Israel, Japan, Spain, and the U.S.).

520pp., ISBN 0–8248–2458–X $30.

A FOCUS ON LANGUAGE TEST DEVELOPMENT: EXPANDING THE LANGUAGE PROFICIENCY CONSTRUCT ACROSS A VARIETY OF TESTS
Thom Hudson & James Dean Brown (Editors), 2001

This volume presents eight research studies that introduce a variety of novel, nontraditional forms of second and foreign language assessment. To the extent possible, the studies also show the entire test development process, warts and all. These language testing projects not only demonstrate many of the types of problems that test developers run into in the real world but also afford the reader unique insights into the language test development process.

230pp., ISBN 0–8248–2351–6 $20.

STUDIES ON KOREAN IN COMMUNITY SCHOOLS
Dong-Jae Lee, Sookeun Cho, Miseon Lee, Minsun Song, & William O'Grady (Editors), 2000

The papers in this volume focus on language teaching and learning in Korean community schools. Drawing on innovative experimental work and research in linguistics, education, and psychology, the contributors address issues of importance to teachers, administrators, and parents. Topics covered include childhood bilingualism, Korean grammar, language acquisition, children's literature, and language teaching methodology. [in Korean]

256pp., ISBN 0-8248-2352-4 $20.

A COMMUNICATIVE FRAMEWORK FOR INTRODUCTORY JAPANESE LANGUAGE CURRICULA
WASHINGTON STATE JAPANESE LANGUAGE CURRICULUM GUIDELINES COMMITTEE, 2000

In recent years, the number of schools offering Japanese nationwide has increased dramatically. Because of the tremendous popularity of the Japanese language and the shortage of teachers, quite a few untrained, nonnative and native teachers are in the classrooms and are expected to teach several levels of Japanese. These guidelines are intended to assist individual teachers and professional associations throughout the United States in designing Japanese language curricula. They are meant to serve as a framework from which language teaching can be expanded and are intended to allow teachers to enhance and strengthen the quality of Japanese language instruction.

168pp., ISBN 0-8248-2350-8 $20.

FOREIGN LANGUAGE TEACHING AND MINORITY LANGUAGE EDUCATION
KATHRYN A. DAVIS (EDITOR), 1999

This volume seeks to examine the potential for building relationships among foreign language, bilingual, and ESL programs towards fostering bilingualism. Part I of the volume examines the sociopolitical contexts for language partnerships, including:

- obstacles to developing bilingualism;
- implications of acculturation, identity, and language issues for linguistic minorities; and
- the potential for developing partnerships across primary, secondary, and tertiary institutions.

Part II of the volume provides research findings on the Foreign Language Partnership Project, designed to capitalize on the resources of immigrant students to enhance foreign language learning.

152pp., ISBN 0-8248-2067-3 $20.

DESIGNING SECOND LANGUAGE PERFORMANCE ASSESSMENTS
JOHN M. NORRIS, JAMES DEAN BROWN, THOM HUDSON, & JIM YOSHIOKA, 1998, 2000

This technical report focuses on the decision-making potential provided by second language performance assessments. The authors first situate performance assessment within a broader discussion of alternatives in language assessment and in educational assessment in general. They then discuss issues in performance assessment design, implementation, reliability, and validity. Finally, they present a prototype framework for second language performance assessment based on the integration of theoretical underpinnings and research findings from the task-based language teaching literature, the language testing literature, and the educational measurement literature. The authors outline test and item specifications, and they present numerous examples of prototypical language tasks. They also propose a research agenda focusing on the operationalization of second language performance assessments.

248pp., ISBN 0-8248-2109-2 $20.

SECOND LANGUAGE DEVELOPMENT IN WRITING: MEASURES OF FLUENCY, ACCURACY, AND COMPLEXITY
Kate Wolfe-Quintero, Shunji Inagaki, & Hae-Young Kim, 1998, 2002

In this book, the authors analyze and compare the ways that fluency, accuracy, grammatical complexity, and lexical complexity have been measured in studies of language development in second language writing. More than 100 developmental measures are examined, with detailed comparisons of the results across the studies that have used each measure. The authors discuss the theoretical foundations for each type of developmental measure, and they consider the relationship between developmental measures and various types of proficiency measures. They also examine criteria for determining which developmental measures are the most successful and suggest which measures are the most promising for continuing work on language development.

208pp., ISBN 0-8248-2069-X $20.

THE DEVELOPMENT OF A LEXICAL TONE PHONOLOGY IN AMERICAN ADULT LEARNERS OF STANDARD MANDARIN CHINESE
Sylvia Henel Sun, 1998

The study reported is based on an assessment of three decades of research on the SLA of Mandarin tone. It investigates whether differences in learners' tone perception and production are related to differences in the effects of certain linguistic, task, and learner factors. The learners of focus are American students of Mandarin in Beijing, China. Their performances on two perception and three production tasks are analyzed through a host of variables and methods of quantification.

328pp., ISBN 0-8248-2068-1 $20.

NEW TRENDS AND ISSUES IN TEACHING JAPANESE LANGUAGE AND CULTURE
Haruko M. Cook, Kyoko Hijirida, & Mildred Tahara (Editors), 1997

In recent years, Japanese has become the fourth most commonly taught foreign language at the college level in the United States. As the number of students who study Japanese has increased, the teaching of Japanese as a foreign language has been established as an important academic field of study. This technical report includes nine contributions to the advancement of this field, encompassing the following five important issues:

- Literature and literature teaching
- Technology in the language classroom
- Orthography
- Testing
- Grammatical versus pragmatic approaches to language teaching

164pp., ISBN 0-8248-2067-3 $20.

SIX MEASURES OF JSL PRAGMATICS
Sayoko Okada Yamashita, 1996

This book investigates differences among tests that can be used to measure the cross-cultural pragmatic ability of English-speaking learners of Japanese. Building on the work of Hudson, Detmer, and Brown (Technical Reports #2 and #7 in this series), the author modified six test types that she used to gather data from North American learners of Japanese. She found numerous problems with the multiple-choice discourse completion test but reported that the other five tests all proved highly reliable and reasonably valid. Practical issues involved in creating and using such language tests are discussed from a variety of perspectives.

213pp., ISBN 0-8248-1914-4 $15.

LANGUAGE LEARNING STRATEGIES AROUND THE WORLD: CROSS-CULTURAL PERSPECTIVES
Rebecca L. Oxford (Editor), 1996, 1997, 2002

Language learning strategies are the specific steps students take to improve their progress in learning a second or foreign language. Optimizing learning strategies improves language performance. This groundbreaking book presents new information about cultural influences on the use of language learning strategies. It also shows innovative ways to assess students' strategy use and remarkable techniques for helping students improve their choice of strategies, with the goal of peak language learning.

166pp., ISBN 0–8248–1910–1 $20.

TELECOLLABORATION IN FOREIGN LANGUAGE LEARNING: PROCEEDINGS OF THE HAWAI'I SYMPOSIUM
Mark Warschauer (Editor), 1996

The Symposium on Local & Global Electronic Networking in Foreign Language Learning & Research, part of the National Foreign Language Resource Center's 1995 Summer Institute on Technology & the Human Factor in Foreign Language Education, included presentations of papers and hands-on workshops conducted by Symposium participants to facilitate the sharing of resources, ideas, and information about all aspects of electronic networking for foreign language teaching and research, including electronic discussion and conferencing, international cultural exchanges, real-time communication and simulations, research and resource retrieval via the Internet, and research using networks. This collection presents a sampling of those presentations.

252pp., ISBN 0–8248–1867–9 $20.

LANGUAGE LEARNING MOTIVATION: PATHWAYS TO THE NEW CENTURY
Rebecca L. Oxford (Editor), 1996

This volume chronicles a revolution in our thinking about what makes students want to learn languages and what causes them to persist in that difficult and rewarding adventure. Topics in this book include the internal structures of and external connections with foreign language motivation; exploring adult language learning motivation, self-efficacy, and anxiety; comparing the motivations and learning strategies of students of Japanese and Spanish; and enhancing the theory of language learning motivation from many psychological and social perspectives.

218pp., ISBN 0–8248–1849–0 $20.

LINGUISTICS & LANGUAGE TEACHING: PROCEEDINGS OF THE SIXTH JOINT LSH-HATESL CONFERENCE
Cynthia Reves, Caroline Steele, & Cathy S. P. Wong (Editors), 1996

Technical Report #10 contains 18 articles revolving around the following three topics:
- Linguistic issues—These six papers discuss various linguistic issues: ideophones, syllabic nasals, linguistic areas, computation, tonal melody classification, and wh-words.
- Sociolinguistics—Sociolinguistic phenomena in Swahili, signing, Hawaiian, and Japanese are discussed in four of the papers.
- Language teaching and learning—These eight papers cover prosodic modification, note taking, planning in oral production, oral testing, language policy, L2 essay organization, access to dative alternation rules, and child noun phrase structure development.

364pp., ISBN 0–8248–1851–2 $20.

ATTENTION & AWARENESS IN FOREIGN LANGUAGE LEARNING
Richard Schmidt (Editor), 1995

Issues related to the role of attention and awareness in learning lie at the heart of many theoretical and practical controversies in the foreign language field. This collection of papers presents research into the learning of Spanish, Japanese, Finnish, Hawaiian, and English as a second language (with additional comments and examples from French, German, and miniature artificial languages) that bear on these crucial questions for foreign language pedagogy.

394pp., ISBN 0–8248–1794–X $20.

VIRTUAL CONNECTIONS: ONLINE ACTIVITIES AND PROJECTS FOR NETWORKING LANGUAGE LEARNERS
Mark Warschauer (Editor), 1995, 1996

Computer networking has created dramatic new possibilities for connecting language learners in a single classroom or across the globe. This collection of activities and projects makes use of email, the Internet, computer conferencing, and other forms of computer-mediated communication for the foreign and second language classroom at any level of instruction. Teachers from around the world submitted the activities compiled in this volume—activities that they have used successfully in their own classrooms.

417pp., ISBN 0–8248–1793–1 $30.

DEVELOPING PROTOTYPIC MEASURES OF CROSS-CULTURAL PRAGMATICS
Thom Hudson, Emily Detmer, & J. D. Brown, 1995

Although the study of cross-cultural pragmatics has gained importance in applied linguistics, there are no standard forms of assessment that might make research comparable across studies and languages. The present volume describes the process through which six forms of cross-cultural assessment were developed for second language learners of English. The models may be used for second language learners of other languages. The six forms of assessment involve two forms each of indirect discourse completion tests, oral language production, and self-assessment. The procedures involve the assessment of requests, apologies, and refusals.

198pp., ISBN 0–8248–1763–X $15.

THE ROLE OF PHONOLOGICAL CODING IN READING KANJI
Sachiko Matsunaga, 1995

In this technical report, the author reports the results of a study that she conducted on phonological coding in reading kanji using an eye-movement monitor, and draws some pedagogical implications. In addition, she reviews current literature on the different schools of thought regarding instruction in reading kanji and its role in the teaching of nonalphabetic written languages like Japanese.

64pp., ISBN 0–8248–1734–6 $10.

PRAGMATICS OF CHINESE AS NATIVE AND TARGET LANGUAGE
Gabriele Kasper (Editor), 1995

This technical report includes six contributions to the study of the pragmatics of Mandarin Chinese:

- A report of an interview study conducted with nonnative speakers of Chinese; and
- Five data-based studies on the performance of different speech acts by native speakers of Mandarin—requesting, refusing, complaining, giving bad news, disagreeing, and complimenting.

312pp., ISBN 0–8248–1733–8 $20.

A BIBLIOGRAPHY OF PEDAGOGY AND RESEARCH IN INTERPRETATION AND TRANSLATION
Etilvia Arjona, 1993

This technical report includes four types of bibliographic information on translation and interpretation studies:

- Research efforts across disciplinary boundaries—cognitive psychology, neurolinguistics, psycholinguistics, sociolinguistics, computational linguistics, measurement, aptitude testing, language policy, decision-making, theses, and dissertations;
- Training information covering program design, curriculum studies, instruction, and school administration;
- Instructional information detailing course syllabi, methodology, models, available textbooks; and
- Testing information about aptitude, selection, and diagnostic tests.

115pp., ISBN 0–8248–1572–6 $10.

PRAGMATICS OF JAPANESE AS NATIVE AND TARGET LANGUAGE
Gabriele Kasper (Editor), 1992, 1996

This technical report includes three contributions to the study of the pragmatics of Japanese:

- A bibliography on speech-act performance, discourse management, and other pragmatic and sociolinguistic features of Japanese;
- A study on introspective methods in examining Japanese learners' performance of refusals; and
- A longitudinal investigation of the acquisition of the particle *ne* by nonnative speakers of Japanese.

125pp., ISBN 0–8248–1462–2 $10.

A FRAMEWORK FOR TESTING CROSS-CULTURAL PRAGMATICS
Thom Hudson, Emily Detmer, & J. D. Brown, 1992

This technical report presents a framework for developing methods that assess cross-cultural pragmatic ability. Although the framework has been designed for Japanese and American cross-cultural contrasts, it can serve as a generic approach that can be applied to other language contrasts. The focus is on the variables of social distance, relative power, and the degree of imposition within the speech acts of requests, refusals, and apologies. Evaluation of performance is based on recognition of the speech act, amount of speech, forms or formulae used, directness, formality, and politeness.

51pp., ISBN 0–8248–1463–0 $10.

RESEARCH METHODS IN INTERLANGUAGE PRAGMATICS
Gabriele Kasper & Merete Dahl, 1991

This technical report reviews the methods of data collection employed in 39 studies of interlanguage pragmatics, defined narrowly as the investigation of nonnative speakers' comprehension and production of speech acts, and the acquisition of L2-related speech-act knowledge. Data collection instruments are distinguished according to the degree to which they constrain informants' responses, and whether they tap speech-act perception/comprehension or production. A main focus of discussion is the validity of different types of data, in particular their adequacy to approximate authentic performance of linguistic action.

51pp., ISBN 0–8248–1419–3 $10.